Also from Westphalia Press
westphaliapress.org

BEASTS, MEN AND GODS

Beasts, Men and Gods:
Russia, Mongolia, Tibet and the Living Buddha
All Rights Reserved © 2018 by Policy Studies Organization

Westphalia Press
An imprint of Policy Studies Organization
1527 New Hampshire Ave. NW
Washington, D.C. 20036
info@ipsonet.org

ISBN-13: 9781633916029
ISBN-10: 1633916022

Cover design by Jeffrey Barnes:
jbarnesbook.design

Daniel Gutierrez-Sandoval, Executive Director
PSO and Westphalia Press

Updated material and comments on this edition
can be found at the Westphalia Press website:
www.westphaliapress.org

BEASTS, MEN AND GODS

BY

FERDINAND OSSENDOWSKI
Officier d'Académie Française

NEW YORK
E. P. DUTTON & COMPANY
681 FIFTH AVENUE

First Printing	. .	*Aug., 1922*
Second Printing	.	*Sept., 1922*
Third Printing	. .	*Oct., 1922*
Fourth Printing	. .	*Nov., 1922*
Fifth Printing	. .	*Dec., 1922*
Sixth Printing	. .	*Dec., 1922*
Seventh Printing	.	*Dec., 1922*
Eighth Printing	. .	*Jan., 1923*
Ninth Printing	.	*Jan., 1923*
Tenth Printing	.	*Feb., 1923*

EXPLANATORY NOTE

WHEN one of the leading publicists in America, Dr. Albert Shaw of the *Review of Reviews*, after reading the manuscript of Part I of this volume, characterized the author as "The Robinson Crusoe of the Twentieth Century," he touched the feature of the narrative which is at once most attractive and most dangerous; for the succession of trying and thrilling experiences recorded seems in places too highly colored to be real or, sometimes, even possible in this day and generation. I desire, therefore, to assure the reader at the outset that Dr. Ossendowski is a man of long and diverse experience as a scientist and writer with a training for careful observation which should put the stamp of accuracy and reliability on his chronicle. Only the extraordinary events of these extraordinary times could have thrown one with so many talents back into the surroundings of the "Cave Man" and thus given to us this unusual account of personal adventure, of great human mysteries and of the political and religious motives which are energizing the "Heart of Asia."

My share in the work has been to induce Dr. Ossendowski to write his story at this time and to assist him in rendering his experiences into English.

LEWIS STANTON PALEN.

CONTENTS

PART I. DRAWING LOTS WITH DEATH

PART II. THE LAND OF DEMONS

vii

CONTENTS

BEASTS, MEN AND GODS

There are times, men and events about which History alone can record the final judgments; contemporaries and individual observers must only write what they have seen and heard. The very truth demands it.

TITUS LIVIUS.

Part I

DRAWING LOTS WITH DEATH

BEASTS, MEN AND GODS

Part I
DRAWING LOTS WITH DEATH

CHAPTER I

INTO THE FORESTS

IN the beginning of the year 1920 I happened to be
living in the Siberian town of Krasnoyarsk, situated
on the shores of the River Yenisei, that noble stream
which is cradled in the sun-bathed mountains of Mongolia to pour its warming life into the Arctic Ocean and
to whose mouth Nansen has twice come to open the
shortest road for commerce from Europe to the heart
of Asia. There in the depths of the still Siberian winter
I was suddenly caught up in the whirling storm of mad
revolution raging all over Russia, sowing in this peaceful and rich land vengeance, hate, bloodshed and crimes
that go unpunished by the law. No one could tell the
hour of his fate. The people lived from day to day
and left their homes not knowing whether they should

return to them or whether they should be dragged from the streets and thrown into the dungeons of that travesty of courts, the Revolutionary Committee, more terrible and more bloody than those of the Mediaeval Inquisition. We who were strangers in this distraught land were not saved from its persecutions and I personally lived through them.

One morning, when I had gone out to see a friend, I suddenly received the news that twenty Red soldiers had surrounded my house to arrest me and that I must escape. I quickly put on one of my friend's old hunting suits, took some money and hurried away on foot along the back ways of the town till I struck the open road, where I engaged a peasant, who in four hours had driven me twenty miles from the town and set me down in the midst of a deeply forested region. On the way I bought a rifle, three hundred cartridges, an ax, a knife, a sheepskin overcoat, tea, salt, dry bread and a kettle. I penetrated into the heart of the wood to an abandoned half-burned hut. From this day I became a genuine trapper but I never dreamed that I should follow this rôle as long as I did. The next morning I went hunting and had the good fortune to kill two heathcock. I found deer tracks in plenty and felt sure that I should not want for food. However, my sojourn in this place was not for long. Five days later when I returned from hunting I noticed smoke curling up out of the chimney of my hut. I stealthily crept along closer to the cabin and discovered two saddled horses with soldiers' rifles slung to the saddles. Two disarmed men were not dangerous for me with a weapon, so I quickly rushed across the open and entered the hut. From the bench two soldiers started up in fright. They were Bolsheviki. On their big Astrakhan caps I made out the red stars of Bolshevism and on their blouses the dirty red bands. We greeted each other and sat down. The soldiers had already prepared tea and so we drank this ever welcome hot beverage and chatted, suspiciously eyeing one another the while. To disarm this suspicion on their part, I told them that I was a hunter from a distant place and was living there because I found it good country for sables. They announced to me that they were soldiers of a detachment sent from a town into the woods to pursue all suspicious people.

"Do you understand, 'Comrade,' " said one of them to me, "we are looking for counter-revolutionists to shoot them?"

I knew it without his explanations. All my forces were directed to assuring them by my conduct that I was a simple peasant hunter and that I had nothing in common with the counter-revolutionists. I was thinking also all the time of where I should go after the departure of my unwelcome guests. It grew dark. In the darkness their faces were even less attractive. They took out bottles of *vodka* and drank and the alcohol began to act very noticeably. They talked loudly and constantly interrupted each other, boasting how many bourgeoisie they had killed in Krasnoyarsk and how many Cossacks they had slid under the ice in the river. Afterwards they began to quarrel but soon they were tired and prepared to sleep. All of a sudden and without any warning the door of the hut swung wide open and the steam of the heated room rolled out in a great cloud, out of which seemed to rise like a genie, as the steam settled, the figure of a tall, gaunt peasant impressively crowned with the high Astrakhan cap and wrapped in the great sheepskin overcoat that added to the massiveness of his figure. He stood with his rifle ready to fire. Under his girdle lay the sharp ax without which the Siberian peasant cannot exist. Eyes, quick and glimmering like those of a wild beast, fixed themselves alternately on each of us. In a moment he took off his cap, made the sign of the cross on his breast and asked of us: "Who is the master here?"

I answered him.

"May I stop the night?"

"Yes," I replied, "places enough for all. Take a cup of tea. It is still hot."

The stranger, running his eyes constantly over all of us and over everything about the room, began to take off his skin coat after putting his rifle in the corner. He was dressed in an old leather blouse with trousers of the same material tucked in high felt boots. His face was quite young, fine and tinged with something akin to mockery. His white, sharp teeth glimmered as his eyes penetrated everything they rested upon. I noticed the locks of grey in his shaggy head. Lines of bitterness circled his mouth. They showed his life had been very stormy and full of danger. He took a seat beside his rifle and laid his ax on the floor below.

"What? Is it your wife?" asked one of the drunken soldiers, pointing to the ax.

The tall peasant looked calmly at him from the quiet eyes under their heavy brows and as calmly answered:

"One meets a different folk these days and with an ax it is much safer."

He began to drink tea very greedily, while his eyes looked at me many times with sharp inquiry in them and ran often round the whole cabin in search of the answer to his doubts. Very slowly and with a guarded drawl he answered all the questions of the soldiers between gulps of the hot tea, then he turned his glass upside down as evidence of having finished, placed on the top of it the small lump of sugar left and remarked to the soldiers:

"I am going out to look after my horse and will unsaddle your horses for you also."

"All right," exclaimed the half-sleeping young soldier, "bring in our rifles as well."

The soldiers were lying on the benches and thus left for us only the floor. The stranger soon came back, brought the rifles and set them in the dark corner. He dropped the saddle pads on the floor, sat down on them and began to take off his boots. The soldiers and my guest soon were snoring but I did not sleep for thinking of what next to do. Finally as dawn was breaking, I dozed off only to awake in the broad daylight and find my stranger gone. I went outside the hut and discovered him saddling a fine bay stallion.

"Are you going away?" I asked.

"Yes, but I want to go together with these —— 'comrades,'" he whispered, "and afterwards I shall come back."

I did not ask him anything further and told him only that I would wait for him. He took off the bags that had been hanging on his saddle, put them away out of sight in the burned corner of the cabin, looked over the stirrups and bridle and, as he finished saddling, smiled and said:

"I am ready. I'm going to awake my 'comrades.'"

Half an hour after the morning drink of tea, my three guests took their leave. I remained out of doors and was engaged in splitting wood for my stove. Suddenly, from a distance, rifle shots rang through the woods, first one, then a second. Afterwards all was still. From the place near the shots a frightened covey of blackcock broke and came over me. At the top of a high pine a jay cried out. I listened for a long time to see if anyone was approaching my hut but everything was still.

On the lower Yenisei it grows dark very early. I built a fire in my stove and began to cook my soup, constantly listening for every noise that came from beyond the cabin walls. Certainly I understood at all times very clearly that death was ever beside me and might claim me by means of either man, beast, cold, accident or disease. I knew that nobody was near me to assist and that all my help was in the hands of God, in the power of my hands and feet, in the accuracy of my aim and in my presence of mind. However, I listened in vain. I did not notice the return of my stranger. Like yesterday he appeared all at once on the threshold. Through the steam I made out his laughing eyes and his fine face. He stepped into the hut and dropped with a good deal of noise three rifles into the corner.

"Two horses, two rifles, two saddles, two boxes of dry bread, half a brick of tea, a small bag of salt, fifty cartridges, two overcoats, two pairs of boots," laughingly he counted out. "In truth today I had a very successful hunt."

In astonishment I looked at him.

"What are you surprised at?" he laughed. *"Komu nujny eti tovarischi?* Who's got any use for these fellows? Let us have tea and go to sleep. Tomorrow I will guide you to another safer place and then go on."

CHAPTER II

THE SECRET OF MY FELLOW TRAVELER

AT the dawn of day we started forth, leaving my first place of refuge. Into the bags we packed our personal estate and fastened them on one of the saddles.

"We must go four or five hundred *versts*," very calmly announced my fellow traveler, who called himself "Ivan," a name that meant nothing to my mind or heart in this land where every second man bore the same.

"We shall travel then for a very long time," I remarked regretfully.

"Not more than one week, perhaps even less," he answered.

That night we spent in the woods under the wide spreading branches of the fir trees. It was my first night in the forest under the open sky. How many like this I was destined to spend in the year and a half of my wanderings! During the day there was very sharp cold. Under the hoofs of the horses the frozen snow crunched and the balls that formed and broke from their hoofs rolled away over the crust with a sound like crackling glass. The heathcock flew from the trees very idly, hares loped slowly down the beds of summer streams. At night the wind began to sigh and whistle as it bent the tops of the trees over our heads; while below it was still and calm. We stopped in a deep ravine bordered by heavy trees, where we found fallen firs, cut them into logs for the fire and, after having boiled our tea, dined.

Ivan dragged in two tree trunks, squared them on one side with his ax, laid one on the other with the squared faces together and then drove in a big wedge at the butt ends which separated them three or four inches. Then we placed live coals in this opening and watched the fire run rapidly the whole length of the squared faces *vis-à-vis*.

"Now there will be a fire in the morning," he announced. "This is the '*naida*' of the gold prospectors. We prospectors wandering in the woods summer and winter always sleep beside this '*naida*.' Fine! You shall see for yourself," he continued.

He cut fir branches and made a sloping roof out of them, resting it on two uprights toward the *naida*. Above our roof of boughs and our *naida* spread the branches of protecting fir. More branches were brought and spread on the snow under the roof, on these were placed the saddle cloths and together they made a seat for Ivan to rest on and to take off his outer garments down to his blouse. Soon I noticed his forehead was wet with perspiration and that he was wiping it and his neck on his sleeves.

"Now it is good and warm!" he exclaimed.

In a short time I was also forced to take off my overcoat and soon lay down to sleep without any covering at all, while through the branches of the fir trees and our roof glimmered the cold bright stars and just beyond the *naida* raged a stinging cold, from which we were cosily defended. After this night I was no longer frightened by the cold. Frozen during the days on horse-back, I was thoroughly warmed through by the genial *naida* at night and rested from my heavy overcoat, sitting only in my blouse under the roofs of pine and fir and sipping the ever welcome tea.

During our daily treks Ivan related to me the stories of his wanderings through the mountains and woods of Transbaikalia in the search for gold. These stories were very lively, full of attractive adventure, danger and struggle. Ivan was a type of these prospectors who have discovered in Russia, and perhaps in other countries, the richest gold mines, while they themselves remain beggars. He evaded telling me why he left Transbaikalia to come to the Yenisei. I understood from his manner that he wished to keep his own counsel and so did not press him. However, the blanket of secrecy covering this part of his mysterious life was one day quite fortuitously lifted a bit. We were already at the objective point of our trip. The whole day we had traveled with difficulty through a thick growth of willow, approaching the shore of the big right branch of the Yenisei, the Mana. Everywhere we saw runways packed hard by the feet of the hares living in this bush. These small white denizens of the wood ran to and fro in front of us. Another time we saw the red tail of a fox hiding behind a rock, watching us and the unsuspecting hares at the same time.

Ivan had been silent for a long while. Then he spoke up and told me that not far from there was a small branch of the Mana, at the mouth of which was a hut.

"What do you say? Shall we push on there or spend the night by the *naida?*"

I suggested going to the hut, because I wanted to wash and because it would be agreeable to spend the night under a genuine roof again. Ivan knitted his brows but acceded.

It was growing dark when we approached a hut surrounded by the dense wood and wild raspberry bushes. It contained one small room with two microscopic windows and a gigantic Russian stove. Against the building were the remains of a shed and a cellar. We fired the stove and prepared our modest dinner. Ivan drank from the bottle inherited from the soldiers and in a short time was very eloquent, with brilliant eyes and with hands that coursed frequently and rapidly through his long locks. He began relating to me the story of one of his adventures, but suddenly stopped and, with fear in his eyes, squinted into a dark corner.

"Is it a rat?" he asked.

"I did not see anything," I replied.

He again became silent and reflected with knitted brow. Often we were silent through long hours and consequently I was not astonished. Ivan leaned over near to me and began to whisper.

"I want to tell you an old story. I had a friend in Transbaikalia. He was a banished convict. His name was Gavronsky. Through many woods and over many mountains we traveled in search of gold and we had an agreement to divide all we got into even shares. But Gavronsky suddenly went out to the 'Taiga' on the Yenisei and disappeared. After five years we heard that he had found a very rich gold mine and had become a rich man; then later that he and his wife with

him had been murdered. . . . " Ivan was still for a
moment and then continued:

"This is their old hut.   Here he lived with his wife
and somewhere on this river he took out his gold.   But
he told nobody where.   All the peasants around here
know that he had a lot of money in the bank and that
he had been selling gold to the Government.   Here they
were murdered."

Ivan stepped to the stove, took out a flaming stick
and, bending over, lighted a spot on the floor.

"Do you see these spots on the floor and on the wall?
It is their blood, the blood of Gavronsky.   They died
but they did not disclose the whereabouts of the gold.
It was taken out of a deep hole which they had drifted
into the bank of the river and was hidden in the cellar
under the shed.   But Gavronsky gave nothing away.
. . . *And Lord how I tortured them!*   I burned them
with fire; I bent back their fingers; I gouged out their
eyes; but Gavronsky died in silence."

He thought for a moment, then quickly said to me:

"I have heard all this from the peasants."   He threw
the log into the stove and flopped down on the bench.
"It's time to sleep," he snapped out, and was still.

I listened for a long time to his breathing and his
whispering to himself, as he turned from one side to
the other and smoked his pipe.

In the morning we left this scene of so much suffering and crime and on the seventh day of our journey
we came to the dense cedar wood growing on the foothills of a long chain of mountains.

"From here," Ivan explained to me, "it is eighty *versts*
to the next peasant settlement.   The people come to these

woods to gather cedar nuts but only in the autumn. Before then you will not meet anyone. Also you will find many birds and beasts and a plentiful supply of nuts, so that it will be possible for you to live here. Do you see this river? When you want to find the peasants, follow along this stream and it will guide you to them."

Ivan helped me build my mud hut. But it was not the genuine mud hut. It was one formed by the tearing out of the roots of a great cedar, that had probably fallen in some wild storm, which made for me the deep hole as the room for my house and flanked this on one side with a wall of mud held fast among the upturned roots. Overhanging ones formed also the framework into which we interlaced the poles and branches to make a roof, finished off with stones for stability and snow for warmth. The front of the hut was ever open but was constantly protected by the guardian *naida*. In that snow-covered den I spent two months like summer without seeing any other human being and without touch with the outer world where such important events were transpiring. In that grave under the roots of the fallen tree I lived before the face of nature with my trials and my anxiety about my family as my constant companions, and in the hard struggle for my life. Ivan went off the second day, leaving for me a bag of dry bread and a little sugar. I never saw him again.

CHAPTER III

THE STRUGGLE FOR LIFE

THEN I was alone. Around me only the wood of eternally green cedars covered with snow, the bare bushes, the frozen river and, as far as I could see out through the branches and the trunks of the trees, only the great ocean of cedars and snow. Siberian *taiga!* How long shall I be forced to live here? Will the Bolsheviki find me here or not? Will my friends know where I am? What is happening to my family? These questions were constantly as burning fires in my brain. Soon I understood why Ivan guided me so long. We passed many secluded places on the journey, far away from all people, where Ivan could have safely left me but he always said that he would take me to a place where it would be easier to live. And it was so. The charm of my lone refuge was in the cedar wood and in the mountains covered with these forests which stretched to every horizon. The cedar is a splendid, powerful tree with wide-spreading branches, an eternally green tent, attracting to its shelter every living being. Among the cedars was always effervescent life. There the squirrels were continually kicking up a row, jumping from tree to tree; the nut-jobbers cried shrilly; a flock of bullfinches with carmine breasts swept through the trees like a flame; or a small army of goldfinches broke in and filled the amphitheatre of trees with their whistling; a hare scooted from one tree trunk to another and behind him stole up the hardly visible shadow of a white ermine, crawling on the snow, and I watched for a long time the black spot which I knew to be the tip of his tail; carefully treading the hard crusted snow approached a noble deer; at last there visited me from the top of the mountain the king of the Siberian forest, the brown bear. All this distracted me and carried away the black thoughts from my brain, encouraging me to persevere. It was good for me also, though difficult, to climb to the top of my mountain, which reached up out of the forest and from which I could look away to the range of red on the horizon. It was the red cliff on the farther bank of the Yenisei. There lay the country, the towns, the enemies and the friends; and there was even the point which I located as the place of my family. It was the reason why Ivan had guided me here. And as the days in this solitude slipped by I began to miss sorely this companion who, though the murderer of Gavronsky, had taken care of me like a father, always saddling my horse for me, cutting the wood and doing everything to make me comfortable. He had spent many winters alone with nothing except his thoughts, face to face with nature —I should say, before the face of God. He had tried the horrors of solitude and had acquired facility in bearing them. I thought sometimes, if I had to meet my end in this place, that I would spend my last strength to drag myself to the top of the mountain to die there, looking away over the infinite sea of mountains and forest toward the point where my loved ones were.

However, the same life gave me much matter for

reflection and yet more occupation for the physical side. It was a continuous struggle for existence, hard and severe. The hardest work was the preparation of the big logs for the *naida*. The fallen trunks of the trees were covered with snow and frozen to the ground. I was forced to dig them out and afterwards, with the help of a long stick as a lever, to move them from their place. For facilitating this work I chose the mountain for my supplies, where, although difficult to climb, it was easy to roll the logs down. Soon I made a splendid discovery. I found near my den a great quantity of larch, this beautiful yet sad forest giant, fallen during a big storm. The trunks were covered with snow but remained attached to their stumps, where they had broken off. When I cut into these stumps with the ax, the head buried itself and could with difficulty be drawn and, investigating the reason, I found them filled with pitch. Chips of this wood needed only a spark to set them aflame and ever afterward I always had a stock of them to light up quickly for warming my hands on returning from the hunt or for boiling my tea.

The greater part of my days was occupied with the hunt. I came to understand that I must distribute my work over every day, for it distracted me from my sad and depressing thoughts. Generally, after my morning tea, I went into the forest to seek heathcock or blackcock. After killing one or two I began to prepare my dinner, which never had an extensive menu. It was constantly game soup with a handful of dried bread and afterwards endless cups of tea, this essential beverage of the woods. Once, during my search for birds, I heard a rustle in the dense shrubs and, carefully peering

about, I discovered the points of a deer's horns. I
crawled along toward the spot but the watchful animal
heard my approach. With a great noise he rushed from
the bush and I saw him very clearly, after he had run
about three hundred steps, stop on the slope of the
mountain. It was a splendid animal with dark grey
coat, with almost a black spine and as large as a small
cow. I laid my rifle across a branch and fired. The
animal made a great leap, ran several steps and fell.
With all my strength I ran to him but he got up again
and half jumped, half dragged himself up the mountain.
The second shot stopped him. I had won a warm carpet
for my den and a large stock of meat. The horns I
fastened up among the branches of my wall, where they
made a fine hat rack.

I cannot forget one very interesting but wild picture,
which was staged for me several kilometres from my
den. There was a small swamp covered with grass and
cranberries scattered through it, where the blackcock and
sand partridges usually came to feed on the berries. I
approached noiselessly behind the bushes and saw a whole
flock of blackcock scratching in the snow and picking
out the berries. While I was surveying this scene, suddenly one of the blackcock jumped up and the rest of
the frightened flock immediately flew away. To my
astonishment the first bird began going straight up in
a spiral flight and afterwards dropped directly down
dead. When I approached there sprang from the body
of the slain cock a rapacious ermine that hid under the
trunk of a fallen tree. The bird's neck was badly torn.
I then understood that the ermine had charged the cock,
fastened itself on his neck and had been carried by the

bird into the air, as he sucked the blood from its throat, and had been the cause of the heavy fall back to the earth. Thanks to his aeronautic ability I saved one cartridge.

So I lived fighting for the morrow and more and more poisoned by hard and bitter thoughts. The days and weeks passed and soon I felt the breath of warmer winds. On the open places the snow began to thaw. In spots the little rivulets of water appeared. Another day I saw a fly or a spider awakened after the hard winter. The spring was coming. I realized that in spring it was impossible to go out from the forest. Every river overflowed its banks; the swamps became impassable; all the runways of the animals turned into beds for streams of running water. I understood that until summer I was condemned to a continuation of my solitude. Spring very quickly came into her rights and soon my mountain was free from snow and was covered only with stones, the trunks of birch and aspen trees and the high cones of ant hills; the river in places broke its covering of ice and was coursing full with foam and bubbles.

CHAPTER IV

A FISHERMAN

ONE day during the hunt, I approached the bank of the river and noticed many very large fish with red backs, as though filled with blood. They were swimming on the surface enjoying the rays of the sun. When the river was entirely free from ice, these fish appeared in enormous quantities. Soon I realized that they were working up-stream for the spawning season in the smaller rivers. I thought to use a plundering method of catching, forbidden by the law of all countries; but all the lawyers and legislators should be lenient to one who lives in a den under the roots of a fallen tree and dares to break their rational laws.

Gathering many thin birch and aspen trees I built in the bed of the stream a weir which the fish could not pass and soon I found them trying to jump over it. Near the bank I left a hole in my barrier about eighteen inches below the surface and fastened on the up-stream side a high basket plaited from soft willow twigs, into which the fish came as they passed the hole. Then I stood cruelly by and hit them on the head with a strong stick. All my catch were over thirty pounds, some more than eighty. This variety of fish is called the *taimen,* is of the trout family and is the best in the Yenisei.

After two weeks the fish had passed and my basket gave me no more treasure, so I began anew the hunt.

CHAPTER V

A DANGEROUS NEIGHBOR

THE hunt became more and more profitable and enjoyable, as spring animated everything. In the mornmg at the break of day the forest was full of voices, strange and undiscernible to the inhabitant of the town. There the heathcock clucked and sang his song of love, as he sat on the top branches of the cedar and admired the grey hen scratching in the fallen leaves below. It was very easy to approach this full-feathered Caruso and with a shot to bring him down from his more poetic to his more utilitarian duties. His going out was an euthanasia, for he was in love and heard nothing. Out in the clearing the blackcocks with their wide-spread spotted tails were fighting, while the hens strutting near, craning and chattering, probably some gossip about their fighting swains, watched and were delighted with them. From the distance flowed in a stern and deep roar, yet full of tenderness and love, the mating call of the deer; while from the crags above came down the short and broken voice of the mountain buck. Among the bushes frolicked the hares and often near them a red fox lay flattened to the ground watching his chance. I never heard any wolves and they are usually not found in the Siberian regions covered with mountains and forest.

But there was another beast, who was my neighbor,

and one of us had to go away. One day, coming back from the hunt with a big heathcock, I suddenly noticed among the trees a black, moving mass. I stopped and, looking very attentively, saw a bear, digging away at an ant-hill. Smelling me, he snorted violently, and very quickly shuffled away, astonishing me with the speed of his clumsy gait. The following morning, while still lying under my overcoat, I was attracted by a noise behind my den. I peered out very carefully and discovered the bear. He stood on his hind legs and was noisily sniffing, investigating the question as to what living creature had adopted the custom of the bears of housing during the winter under the trunks of fallen trees. I shouted and struck my kettle with the ax. My early visitor made off with all his energy; but his visit did not please me. It was very early in the spring that this occurred and the bear should not yet have left his hibernating place. He was the so-called "ant-eater," an abnormal type of bear lacking in all the etiquette of the first families of the bear clan.

I knew that the "ant-eaters" were very irritable and audacious and quickly I prepared myself for both the defence and the charge. My preparations were short. I rubbed off the ends of five of my cartridges, thus making dum-dums out of them, a sufficiently intelligible argument for so unwelcome a guest. Putting on my coat I went to the place where I had first met the bear and where there were many ant-hills. I made a detour of the whole mountain, looked in all the ravines but nowhere found my caller. Disappointed and tired, I was approaching my shelter quite off my guard when I suddenly discovered the king of the forest himself just com-

ing out of my lowly dwelling and sniffing all around
the entrance to it. I shot. The bullet pierced his side.
He roared with pain and anger and stood up on his hind
legs. As the second bullet broke one of these, he squatted
down but immediately, dragging the leg and endeavor-
ing to stand upright, moved to attack me. Only the third
bullet in his breast stopped him. He weighed about
two hundred to two hundred fifty pounds, as near as
I could guess, and was very tasty. He appeared at his
best in cutlets but only a little less wonderful in the
Hamburg steaks which I rolled and roasted on hot
stones, watching them swell out into great balls that were
as light as the finest soufflé omelettes we used to have
at the "Medved" in Petrograd. On this welcome addi-
tion to my larder I lived from then until the ground
dried out and the stream ran down enough so that I
could travel down along the river to the country whither
Ivan had directed me.

Ever traveling with the greatest precautions I made
the journey down along the river on foot, carrying from
my winter quarters all my household furniture and goods,
wrapped up in the deerskin bag which I formed by tying
the legs together in an awkward knot; and thus laden
fording the small streams and wading through the
swamps that lay across my path. After fifty odd miles
of this I came to the country called Sifkova, where I
found the cabin of a peasant named Tropoff, located
closest to the forest that came to be my natural environ-
ment. With him I lived for a time.

*   *   *   *   *

Now in these unimaginable surroundings of safety and

peace, summing up the total of my experience in the Siberian *taiga,* I make the following deductions. In every healthy spiritual individual of our times, occasions of necessity resurrect the traits of primitive man, hunter and warrior, and help him in the struggle with nature. It is the prerogative of the man with the trained mind and spirit over the untrained, who does not possess sufficient science and will power to carry him through. But the price that the cultured man must pay is that for him there exists nothing more awful than absolute solitude and the knowledge of complete isolation from human society and the life of moral and aesthetic culture. One step, one moment of weakness and dark madness will seize a man and carry him to inevitable destruction. I spent awful days of struggle with the cold and hunger but I passed more terrible days in the struggle of the will to kill weakening destructive thoughts. The memories of these days freeze my heart and mind and even now, as I revive them so clearly by writing of my experiences, they throw me back into a state of fear and apprehension. Moreover, I am compelled to observe that the people in highly civilized states give too little regard to the training that is useful to man in primitive conditions, in conditions incident to the struggle against nature for existence. It is the single normal way to develop a new generation of strong, healthy, iron men, with at the same time sensitive souls.

Nature destroys the weak but helps the strong, awakening in the soul emotions which remain dormant under the urban conditions of modern life.

CHAPTER VI

A RIVER IN TRAVAIL

MY presence in the Sifkova country was not for long but I used it in full measure. First, I sent a man in whom I had confidence and whom I considered trustworthy to my friends in the town that I had left and received from them linen, boots, money and a small case of first aid materials and essential medicines, and, what was most important, a passport in another name, since I was dead for the Bolsheviki. Secondly, in these more or less favorable conditions I reflected upon the plan for my future actions. Soon in Sifkova the people heard that the Bolshevik commissar would come for the requisition of cattle for the Red Army. It was dangerous to remain longer. I waited only until the Yenisei should lose its massive lock of ice, which kept it sealed long after the small rivulets had opened and the trees had taken on their spring foliage. For one thousand roubles I engaged a fisherman who agreed to take me fifty-five miles up the river to an abandoned gold mine as soon as the river, which had then only opened in places, should be entirely clear of ice. At last one morning I heard a deafening roar like a tremendous cannonade and ran out to find the river had lifted its great bulk of ice and then given way to break it up. I rushed on down to the bank, where I witnessed an awe-inspiring but magnificent scene. The river had brought down the great volume of ice that had been dislodged in the south and was carrying it northward under the thick layer which still covered parts of the stream until finally its weight had broken the winter dam to the north and released the whole grand mass in one last rush for the Arctic. The Yenisei, "Father Yenisei," "Hero Yenisei," is one of the longest rivers in Asia, deep and magnificent, especially through the middle range of its course, where it is flanked and held in cañon-like by great towering ranges. The huge stream had brought down whole miles of ice fields, breaking them up on the rapids and on isolated rocks, twisting them with angry swirls, throwing up sections of the black winter roads, carrying down the tepees built for the use of passing caravans which in the winter always go from Minnusinsk to Krasnoyarsk on the frozen river. From time to time the stream stopped in its flow, the roar began and the great fields of ice were squeezed and piled upward, sometimes as high as thirty feet, damming up the water behind, so that it rapidly rose and ran out over the low places, casting on the shore great masses of ice. Then the power of the reinforced waters conquered the towering dam of ice and carried it downward with a sound like breaking glass. At the bends in the river and round the great rocks developed terrifying chaos. Huge blocks of ice jammed and jostled until some were thrown clear into the air, crashing against others already there, or were hurled against the curving cliffs and banks, tearing out boulders, earth and trees high up the sides. All along the low embankments this giant of nature flung upward with a suddenness that leaves man but a pigmy in force a great wall of ice fifteen to twenty feet high, which the peasants call *"Zaberega"* and through which they cannot get to the river without cutting out a road. One incredible feat I saw the giant perform, when a block many feet thick and many yards square was hurled through the air and dropped to crush saplings and little trees more than a half hundred feet from the bank.

Watching this glorious withdrawal of the ice, I was filled with terror and revolt at seeing the awful spoils which the Yenisei bore away in this annual retreat. These were the bodies of the executed counter-revolutionaries—officers, soldiers and Cossacks of the former army of the Superior Governor of all anti-Bolshevik Russia, Admiral Kolchak. They were the results of the bloody work of the "Cheka" at Minnusinsk. Hundreds of these bodies with heads and hands cut off, with mutilated faces and bodies half burned, with broken skulls, floated and mingled with the blocks of ice, looking for their graves; or, turning in the furious whirlpools among the jagged blocks, they were ground and torn to pieces into shapeless masses, which the river, nauseated with its task, vomited out upon the islands and projecting sand bars. I passed the whole length of the middle Yenisei and constantly came across these putrifying and terrifying reminders of the work of the Bolsheviki. In one place at a turn of the river I saw a great heap of horses, which had been cast up by the ice and current, in number not less than three hundred. A *verst* below there I was sickened beyond endurance by the discovery of a grove of willows along the bank which had raked from the polluted stream and held in their finger-like drooping branches human bodies in all shapes and attitudes with a semblance of naturalness which made an everlasting picture on my distraught mind. Of this pitiful gruesome company I counted seventy.

At last the mountain of ice passed by, followed by the muddy freshets that carried down the trunks of fallen trees, logs and bodies, bodies, bodies. The fisherman and his son put me and my luggage into their dugout made from an aspen tree and poled upstream along the bank. Poling in a swift current is very hard work. At the sharp curves we were compelled to row, struggling against the force of the stream and even in places hugging the cliffs and making headway only by clutching the rocks with our hands and dragging along slowly. Sometimes it took us a long while to do five or six metres through these rapid holes. In two days we reached the goal of our journey. I spent several days in this gold mine, where the watchman and his family were living. As they were short of food, they had nothing to spare for me and consequently my rifle again served to nourish me, as well as contributing something to my hosts. One day there appeared here a trained agriculturalist. I did not hide because during my winter in the woods I had raised a heavy beard, so that probably my own mother could not have recognized me. However, our guest was very shrewd and at once deciphered me. I did not fear him because I saw that he was not a Bolshevik and later had confirmation of this. We found common acquaintances and a common viewpoint on current events. He lived close to the gold mine in a small village where he superintended public works. We determined to escape together from Russia. For a long time I had puzzled over this matter and now my plan was ready. Knowing the position in Siberia and its geography, I decided that the best way to safety was through Urianhai, the northern part of Mongolia on the head waters of the Yenisei, then through Mongolia and out to the Far East and the Pacific. Before the overthrow of the Kolchak Government I had received a commission to investigate Urianhai and Western Mongolia and then, with great accuracy, I studied all the maps and literature I could get on this question. To accomplish this audacious plan I had the great incentive of my own safety.

CHAPTER VII

THROUGH SOVIET SIBERIA

AFTER several days we started through the forest on the left bank of the Yenisei toward the south, avoid‑ing the villages as much as possible in fear of leaving ome trail by which we might be followed. Whenever we did have to go into them, we had a good reception at the hands of the peasants, who did not penetrate our disguise; and we saw that they hated the Bolsheviki, who had destroyed many of their villages. In one place we were told that a detachment of Red troops had been sent out from Minnusinsk to chase the Whites. We were forced to work far back from the shore of the Yenisei and to hide in the woods and mountains. Here we re-mained nearly a fortnight, because all this time the Red soldiers were traversing the country and capturing in the woods half-dressed unarmed officers who were in hiding from the atrocious vengeance of the Bolsheviki. After-wards by accident we passed a meadow where we found the bodies of twenty-eight officers hung to the trees, with their faces and bodies mutilated. There we determined never to allow ourselves to come alive into the hands of the Bolsheviki. To prevent this we had our weapons and a supply of cyanide of potassium.

Passing across one branch of the Yenisei, once we saw a narrow, miry pass, the entrance to which was strewn with the bodies of men and horses. A little farther along we found a broken sleigh with rifled boxes and papers scattered about. Near them were also torn garments and bodies. Who were these pitiful ones? What tragedy was staged in this wild wood? We tried to guess this enigma and we began to investigate the documents and papers. These were official papers addressed to the Staff of General Pepelaieff. Probably one part of the Staff during the retreat of Kolchak's army went through this wood, striving to hide from the enemy approaching from all sides; but here they were caught by the Reds and killed. Not far from here we found the body of a poor unfortunate woman, whose condition proved clearly what had happened before relief came through the beneficent bullet. The body lay beside a shelter of branches, strewn with bottles and conserve tins, telling the tale of the bantering feast that had preceded the destruction of this life.

The further we went to the south, the more pronouncedly hospitable the people became toward us and the more hostile to the Bolsheviki. At last we emerged from the forests and entered the spacious vastness of the Minnusinsk steppes, crossed by the high red mountain range called the "Kizill-Kaiya" and dotted here and there with salt lakes. It is a country of tombs, thousands of large and small dolmens, the tombs of the earliest proprietors of this land: pyramids of stone ten metres high, the marks set by Jenghiz Khan along his road of conquest and afterwards by the cripple Tamerlane-Temur. Thousands of these dolmens and stone pyramids stretch in endless rows to the north. In these plains the Tartars now live. They were robbed by the Bolsheviki and therefore hated them ardently. We openly told them that we were escaping. They gave us food for nothing and supplied us with guides, telling us with whom we might stop and where to hide in case of danger.

After several days we looked down from the high bank of the Yenisei upon the first steamer, the "Oriol," from Krasnoyarsk to Minnusinsk, laden with Red soldiers. Soon we came to the mouth of the river Tuba, which we were to follow straight east to the Sayan mountains, where Urianhai begins. We thought the stage along the Tuba and its branch, the Amyl, the most dangerous part of our course, because the valleys of these two rivers had a dense population which had contributed large numbers of soldiers to the celebrated Communist Partisans, Schetinkin and Krafcheno.

A Tartar ferried us and our horses over to the right bank of the Yenisei and afterwards sent us some Cossacks at daybreak who guided us to the mouth of the Tuba, where we spent the whole day in rest, gratifying ourselves with a feast of wild black currants and cherries.

CHAPTER VIII

THREE DAYS ON THE EDGE OF A PRECIPICE

ARMED with our false passports, we moved along up the valley of the Tuba. Every ten or fifteen *versts* we came across large villages of from one to six hundred houses, where all administration was in the hands of Soviets and where spies scrutinized all passers-by. We could not avoid these villages for two reasons. First, our attempts to avoid them when we were constantly meeting the peasants in the country would have aroused suspicion and would have caused any Soviet to arrest us and send us to the "Cheka" in Minnusinsk, where we should have sung our last song. Secondly, in his documents my fellow traveler was granted permission to use the government post relays for forwarding him on his journey. Therefore, we were forced to visit the village Soviets and change our horses. Our own mounts we had given to the Tartar and Cossack who helped us at the mouth of the Tuba, and the Cossack brought us in his wagon to the first village, where we received the post horses. All except a small minority of the peasants were against the Bolsheviki and voluntarily assisted us. I paid them for their help by treating their sick and my fellow traveler gave them practical advice in the management of their agriculture. Those who helped us chiefly were the old dissenters and the Cossacks.

34

Sometimes we came across villages entirely Communistic but very soon we learned to distinguish them. When we entered a village with our horse bells tinkling and found the peasants who happened to be sitting in front of their houses ready to get up with a frown and a grumble that here were more new devils coming, we knew that this was a village opposed to the Communists and that here we could stop in safety. But, if the peasants approached and greeted us with pleasure, calling us "Comrades," we knew at once that we were among the enemy and took great precautions. Such villages were inhabited by people who were not the Siberian liberty-loving peasants but by emigrants from the Ukraine, idle and drunk, living in poor dirty huts, though their village were surrounded with the black and fertile soil of the steppes. Very dangerous and pleasant moments we spent in the large village of Karatuz. It is rather a town. In the year 1912 two colleges were opened here and the population reached 15,000 people. It is the capital of the South Yenisei Cossacks. But by now it is very difficult to recognize this town. The peasant emigrants and Red army murdered all the Cossack population and destroyed and burned most of the houses; and it is at present the center of Bolshevism and Communism in the eastern part of the Minnusinsk district. In the building of the Soviet, where we came to exchange our horses, there was being held a meeting of the "Cheka." We were immediately surrounded and questioned about our documents. We were not any too calm about the impression which might be made by our papers and attempted to avoid this examination. My fellow traveler afterwards often said to me:

"It is great good fortune that among the Bolsheviki the good-for-nothing shoemaker of yesterday is the Governor of today and scientists sweep the streets or clean the stables of the Red cavalry. I can talk with the Bolsheviki because they do not know the difference between 'disinfection' and 'diphtheria,' 'anthracite' and 'appendicitis' and can talk them round in all things, even up to persuading them not to put a bullet into me."

And so we talked the members of the "Cheka" round to everything that we wanted. We presented to them a bright scheme for the future development of their district, when we would build the roads and bridges which would allow them to export the wood from Urianhai, iron and gold from the Sayan Mountains, cattle and furs from Mongolia. What a triumph of creative work for the Soviet Government! Our ode occupied about an hour and afterwards the members of the "Cheka," forgetting about our documents, personally changed our horses, placed our luggage on the wagon and wished us success. It was the last ordeal within the borders of Russia.

When we had crossed the valley of the river Amyl, Happiness smiled on us. Near the ferry we met a member of the militia from Karatuz. He had on his wagon several rifles and automatic pistols, mostly Mausers, for outfitting an expedition through Urianhai in quest of some Cossack officers who had been greatly troubling the Bolsheviki. We stood upon our guard. We could very easily have met this expedition and we were not quite assured that the soldiers would be so appreciative of our high-sounding phrases as were the members of the "Cheka." Carefully questioning the militiaman, we ferreted out the route their expedition was to take. In the next village we stayed in the same house with him. I had to open my luggage and suddenly I noticed his admiring glance fixed upon my bag.

"What pleases you so much?" I asked.

He whispered: "Trousers . . . Trousers."

I had received from my townsmen quite new trousers of black thick cloth for riding. Those trousers attracted the rapt attention of the militiaman.

"If you have no other trousers. . . . " I remarked, reflecting upon my plan of attack against my new friend.

"No," he explained with sadness, "the Soviet does not furnish trousers. They tell me they also go without trousers. And my trousers are absolutely worn out. Look at them."

With these words he threw back the corner of his overcoat and I was astonished how he could keep himself inside these trousers, for they had such large holes that they were more of a net than trousers, a net through which a small shark could have slipped.

"Sell me," he whispered, with a question in his voice.

"I cannot, for I need them myself," I answered decisively.

He reflected for a few minutes and afterward, approaching me, said: "Let us go out doors and talk. Here it is inconvenient."

We went outside. "Now, what about it?" he began. "You are going into Urianhai. There the Soviet bank-notes have no value and you will not be able to buy anything, where there are plenty of sables, fox-skins, ermine and gold dust to be purchased, which they very willingly exchange for rifles and cartridges. You have each of you a rifle and I will give you one more rifle with a hundred cartridges if you give me the trousers."

"We do not need weapons. We are protected by our documents," I answered, as though I did not understand.

"But no," he interrupted, "you can change that rifle there into furs and gold. I shall give you that rifle outright."

"Ah, that's it, is it? But it's very little for those trousers. Nowhere in Russia can you now find trousers. All Russia goes without trousers and for your rifle I should receive a sable and what use to me is one skin?"

Word by word I attained to my desire. The militiaman got my trousers and I received a rifle with one hundred cartridges and two automatic pistols with forty cartridges each. We were armed now so that we could defend ourselves. Moreover, I persuaded the happy possessor of my trousers to give us a permit to carry the weapons. Then the law and force were both on our side.

In a distant village we bought three horses, two for riding and one for packing, engaged a guide, purchased dried bread, meat, salt and butter and, after resting twenty-four hours, began our trip up the Amyl toward the Sayan Mountains on the border of Urianhai. There we hoped not to meet Bolsheviki, either sly or silly. In three days from the mouth of the Tuba we passed the last Russian village near the Mongolian-Urianhai border, three days of constant contact with a lawless population, of continuous danger and of the ever present possibility of fortuitous death. Only iron will power, presence of mind and dogged tenacity brought us through all the dangers and saved us from rolling back down our precipice of adventure, at whose foot lay so many others who had failed to make this same climb to freedom which we had just accomplished. Perhaps they lacked the persistence or the presence of mind, perhaps they had not the poetic ability to sing odes about "roads, bridges and gold mines" or perhaps they simply had no spare trousers.

CHAPTER IX

TO THE SAYANS AND SAFETY

DENSE virgin wood surrounded us. In the high, already yellow grass the trail wound hardly noticeable in among bushes and trees just beginning to drop their many colored leaves. It is the old, already forgotten Amyl pass road. Twenty-five years ago it carried the provision machinery and workers for the numerous, now abandoned, gold mines of the Amyl valley. The road now wound along the wide and rapid Amyl, then penetrated into the deep forest, guiding us round the swampy ground filled with those dangerous Siberian quagmires, through the dense bushes, across mountains and wide meadows. Our guide probably did not surmise our real intention and sometimes, apprehensively looking down at the ground, would say:

"Three riders on horses with shoes on have passed here. Perhaps they were soldiers."

His anxiety was terminated when he discovered that the tracks led off to one side and then returned to the trail.

"They did not proceed farther," he remarked, slyly smiling.

"That's too bad," we answered. "It would have been more lively to travel in company."

But the peasant only stroked his beard and laughed. Evidently he was not taken in by our statement. We passed on the way a gold mine that had been formerly planned and equipped on splendid lines but was now abandoned and the buildings all destroyed. The Bolsheviki had taken away the machinery, supplies and also some parts of the buildings. Nearby stood a dark and gloomy church with windows broken, the crucifix torn off and the tower burned, a pitifully typical emblem of the Russia of today. The starving family of the watchman lived at the mine in continuing danger and privation. They told us that in this forest region were wandering about a band of Reds who were robbing anything that remained on the property of the gold mine, were working the pay dirt in the richest part of the mine and, with a little gold washed, were going to drink and gamble it away in some distant villages where the peasants were making the forbidden *vodka* out of berries and potatoes and selling it for its weight in gold. A meeting with this band meant death. After three days we crossed the northern ridge of the Sayan chain, passed the border river Algiak and, after this day, were abroad in the territory of Urianhai.

This wonderful land, rich in most diverse forms of natural wealth, is inhabited by a branch of the Mongols, which is now only sixty thousand and which is gradually dying off, speaking a language quite different from any of the other dialects of this folk and holding as their life ideal the tenet of "Eternal Peace." Urianhai long ago became the scene of administrative attempts by Russians, Mongols and Chinese, all of whom claimed sovereignty over the region whose unfortunate inhabitants, the Soyots, had to pay tribute to all three of these overlords. It was due to this that the land was not an entirely safe refuge for us. We had heard already from our militiaman about the expedition preparing to go into Urianhai and from the peasants we learned that the villages along the Little Yenisei and farther south had formed Red detachments, who were robbing and killing everyone who fell into their hands. Recently they had killed sixty-two officers attempting to pass Urianhai into Mongolia; robbed and killed a caravan of Chinese merchants; and killed some German war prisoners who escaped from the Soviet paradise. On the fourth day we reached a swampy valley where, among open forests, stood a single Russian house. Here we took leave of our guide, who hastened away to get back before the snows should block his road over the Sayans. The master of the establishment agreed to guide us to the Seybi River for ten thousand roubles in Soviet notes. Our horses were tired and we were forced to give them a rest, so we decided to spend twenty-four hours here.

We were drinking tea when the daughter of our host cried:

"The Soyots are coming!" Into the room with their rifles and pointed hats came suddenly four of them.

"Mendé," they grunted to us and then, without ceremony, began examining us critically. Not a button or a seam in our entire outfit escaped their penetrating gaze. Afterwards one of them, who appeared to be the local "Merin" or governor, began to investigate our political views. Listening to our criticisms of the Bolsheviki, he was evidently pleased and began talking freely.

"You are good people. You do not like Bolsheviki. We will help you."

I thanked him and presented him with the thick silk cord which I was wearing as a girdle. Before night they left us saying that they would return in the morning. It grew dark. We went to the meadow to look after our exhausted horses grazing there and came back to the house. We were gaily chatting with the hospitable host when suddenly we heard horses' hoofs in the court and raucous voices, followed by the immediate entry of five Red soldiers armed with rifles and swords. Something unpleasant and cold rolled up into my throat and my heart hammered. We knew the Reds as our enemies. These men had the red stars on their Astrakhan caps and red triangles on their sleeves. They were members of the detachment that was out to look for Cossack officers. Scowling at us they took off their overcoats and sat down. We first opened the conversation, explaining the purpose of our journey in exploring for bridges, roads and gold mines. From them we then learned that their commander would arrive in a little while with seven more men and that they would take our host at once as a guide to the Seybi River, where they thought the Cossack officers must be hidden. Immediately I remarked that our affairs were moving fortunately and that we must travel along together. One of the soldiers replied that that would depend upon the "Comrade-officer."

During our conversation the Soyot Governor entered. Very attentively he studied again the new arrivals and then asked: "Why did you take from the Soyots the good horses and leave bad ones?"

The soldiers laughed at him.

"Remember that you are in a foreign country!" answered the Soyot, with a threat in his voice.

"God and the Devil!" cried one of the soldiers.

But the Soyot very calmly took a seat at the table and accepted the cup of tea the hostess was preparing for him. The conversation ceased. The Soyot finished the tea, smoked his long pipe and, standing up, said:

"If tomorrow morning the horses are not back at the owner's, we shall come and take them." And with these words he turned and went out.

I noticed an expression of apprehension on the faces of the soldiers. Shortly one was sent out as a messenger while the others sat silent with bowed heads. Late in the night the officer arrived with his other seven men. As he received the report about the Soyot, he knitted his brows and said:

"It's a bad mess. We must travel through the swamp where a Soyot will be behind every mound watching us."

He seemed really very anxious and his trouble fortunately prevented him from paying much attention to us. I began to calm him and promised on the morrow to arrange this matter with the Soyots. The officer was a coarse brute and a silly man, desiring strongly to be promoted for the capture of the Cossack officers, and feared that the Soyot could prevent him from reaching the Seybi.

At daybreak we started together with the Red detachment. When we had made about fifteen kilometers, we discovered behind the bushes two riders. They were Soyots. On their backs were their flint rifles.

"Wait for me!" I said to the officer. "I shall go for a parley with them."

I went forward with all the speed of my horse. One of the horsemen was the Soyot Governor, who said to me:

"Remain behind the detachment and help us."

"All right," I answered, "but let us talk a little, in order that they may think we are parleying."

After a moment I shook the hand of the Soyot and returned to the soldiers.

"All right," I exclaimed, "we can continue our journey. No hindrance will come from the Soyots."

We moved forward and, when we were crossing a large meadow, we espied at a long distance two Soyots riding at full gallop right up the side of a mountain. Step by step I accomplished the necessary manœuvre to bring me and my fellow traveler somewhat behind the detachment. Behind our backs remained only one soldier, very brutish in appearance and apparently very hostile to us. I had time to whisper to my companion only one word: "Mauser," and saw that he very carefully unbuttoned the saddle bag and drew out a little the handle of his pistol.

Soon I understood why these soldiers, excellent woodsmen as they were, would not attempt to go to the Seybi without a guide. All the country between the Algiak and the Seybi is formed by high and narrow mountain ridges separated by deep swampy valleys. It is a cursed and dangerous place. At first our horses mired to the knees, lunging about and catching their feet in the roots of bushes in the quagmires, then falling and pinning us under their sides, breaking parts of their saddles and bridles. Then we would go in up to the riders' knees. My horse went down once with his whole breast and head under the red fluid mud and we just saved it and no more. Afterwards the officer's horse fell with him so that he bruised his head on a stone. My companion injured one knee against a tree. Some of the men also fell and were injured. The horses breathed heavily. Somewhere dimly and gloomily a crow cawed. Later the road became worse still. The trail followed through the same miry swamp but everywhere the road was blocked with fallen tree trunks. The horses, jumping over the trunks, would land in an unexpectedly deep hole and flounder. We and all the soldiers were covered with blood and mud and were in great fear of exhausting our mounts. For a long distance we had to get down and lead them. At last we entered a broad meadow covered with bushes and bordered with rocks. Not only horses but riders also began to sink to their middle in a quagmire with apparently no bottom. The whole surface of the meadow was but a thin layer of turf, covering a lake with black putrefying water. When we finally learned to open our column and proceed at big intervals, we found we could keep on this surface that undulated like rubber ice and swayed the bushes up and down. In places the earth buckled up and broke.

Suddenly, three shots sounded. They were hardly more than the report of a Flobert rifle; but they were genuine shots, because the officer and two soldiers fell to the ground. The other soldiers grabbed their rifles and, with fear, looked about for the enemy. Four more were soon unseated and suddenly I noticed our rearguard brute raise his rifle and aim right at me. However, my

Mauser outstrode his rifle and I was allowed to continue my story.

"Begin!" I cried to my friend and we took part in the shooting. Soon the meadow began to swarm with Soyots, stripping the fallen, dividing the spoils and re-capturing their horses. In some forms of warfare it is never safe to leave any of the enemy to renew hostilities later with overwhelming forces.

After an hour of very difficult road we began to ascend the mountain and soon arrived on a high plateau covered with trees.

"After all, Soyots are not a too peaceful people," I remarked, approaching the Governor.

He looked at me very sharply and replied:

"It was not Soyots who did the killing."

He was right. It was the Abakan Tartars in Soyot clothes who killed the Bolsheviki. These Tartars were running their herds of cattle and horses down out of Russia through Urianhai to Mongolia. They had as their guide and negotiator a Kalmuck Lamaite. The following morning we were approaching a small settlement of Russian colonists and noticed some horsemen looking out from the woods. One of our young and brave Tartars galloped off at full speed toward these men in the wood but soon wheeled and returned with a reassuring smile.

"All right," he exclaimed, laughing, "keep right on."

We continued our travel on a good broad road along a high wooden fence surrounding a meadow filled with a fine herd of wapiti or *izubr,* which the Russian colonists breed for the horns that are so valuable in the velvet for sale to Tibetan and Chinese medicine dealers. These horns, when boiled and dried, are called *panti* and are sold to the Chinese at very high prices.

We were received with great fear by the settlers.

"Thank God!" exclaimed the hostess, "we thought . . . " and she broke off, looking at her husband.

CHAPTER X

THE BATTLE ON THE SEYBI

CONSTANT dangers develop one's watchfulness and keenness of perception. We did not take off our clothes nor unsaddle our horses, tired as we were. I put my Mauser inside my coat and began to look about and scrutinize the people. The first thing I discovered was the butt end of a rifle under the pile of pillows always found on the peasants' large beds. Later I noticed the employees of our host constantly coming into the room for orders from him. They did not look like simple peasants, although they had long beards and were dressed very dirtily. They examined me with very attentive eyes and did not leave me and my friend alone with the host. We could not, however, make out anything. But then the Soyot Governor came in and, noticing our strained relations, began explaining in the Soyot language to the host all about us.

"I beg your pardon," the colonist said, "but you know yourself that now for one honest man we have ten thousand murderers and robbers."

With this we began chatting more freely. It appeared that our host knew that a band of Bolsheviki would attack him in the search for the band of Cossack officers who were living in his house on and off. He had heard also about the "total loss" of one detachment. However, it did not entirely calm the old man to have our news, for he had heard of the large detachment of Reds that was coming from the border of the Usinsky District in pursuit of the Tartars who were escaping with their cattle south to Mongolia.

"From one minute to another we are awaiting them with fear," said our host to me. "My Soyot has come in and announced that the Reds are already crossing the Seybi and the Tartars are prepared for the fight."

We immediately went out to look over our saddles and packs and then took the horses and hid them in the bushes not far off. We made ready our rifles and pistols and took posts in the enclosure to wait for our common enemy. An hour of trying impatience passed, when one of the workmen came running in from the wood and whispered:

"They are crossing our swamp. . . . The fight is on."

In fact, like an answer to his words, came through the woods the sound of a single rifle-shot, followed closely by the increasing rat-tat-tat of the mingled guns. Nearer to the house the sounds gradually came. Soon we heard the beating of the horses' hoofs and the brutish cries of the soldiers. In a moment three of them burst into the house, from off the road where they were being raked now by the Tartars from both directions, cursing violently. One of them shot at our host. He stumbled along and fell on his knee, as his hand reached out toward the rifle under his pillows.

"Who are *you?*" brutally blurted out one of the soldiers, turning to us and raising his rifle. We answered with Mausers and successfully, for only one soldier in the rear by the door escaped, and that merely to fall into the hands of a workman in the courtyard who strangled him. The fight had begun. The soldiers called on their comrades for help. The Reds were strung along in the ditch at the side of the road, three hundred paces from the house, returning the fire of the surrounding Tartars. Several soldiers ran to the house to help their comrades but this time we heard the regular volley of the workmen of our host. They fired as though in a manœuvre calmly and accurately. Five Red soldiers lay on the road, while the rest now kept to their ditch. Before long we discovered that they began crouching and crawling out toward the end of the ditch nearest the wood where they had left their horses. The sounds of shots became more and more distant and soon we saw fifty or sixty Tartars pursuing the Reds across the meadow.

Two days we rested here on the Seybi. The workmen of our host, eight in number, turned out to be officers hiding from the Bolsheviks. They asked permission to go on with us, to which we agreed.

When my friend and I continued our trip we had a guard of eight armed officers and three horses with packs. We crossed a beautiful valley between the Rivers Seybi and Ut. Everywhere we saw splendid grazing lands with numerous herds upon them, but in two or three houses along the road we did not find anyone living. All had hidden away in fear after hearing the sounds of the fight with the Reds. The following day we went up over the high chain of mountains called Daban and, traversing a great area of burned timber where our trail lay among the fallen trees, we began to descend into a valley hidden from us by the intervening foothills. There

behind these hills flowed the Little Yenisei, the last large
river before reaching Mongolia proper. About ten kilometers from the river we spied a column of smoke rising up out of the wood. Two of the officers slipped
away to make an investigation. For a long time they
did not return and we, fearful lest something had happened, moved off carefully in the direction of the smoke,
all ready for a fight if necessary. We finally came near
enough to hear the voices of many people and among
them the loud laugh of one of our scouts. In the middle
of a meadow we made out a large tent with two tepees
of branches and around these a crowd of fifty or sixty
men. When we broke out of the forest all of them
rushed forward with a joyful welcome for us. It
appeared that it was a large camp of Russian officers
and soldiers who, after their escape from Siberia, had
lived in the houses of the Russian colonists and rich
peasants in Urianhai.

"What are you doing here?" we asked with surprise.

"Oh, ho, you know nothing at all about what has been
going on?" replied a fairly old man who called himself
Colonel Ostrovsky. "In Urianhai an order has been
issued from the Military Commissioner to mobilize all
men over twenty-eight years of age and everywhere
toward the town of Belotzarsk are moving detachments
of these Partisans. They are robbing the colonists and
peasants and killing everyone that falls into their hands.
We are hiding here from them."

The whole camp counted only sixteen rifles and three
bombs, belonging to a Tartar who was traveling with
his Kalmuck guide to his herds in Western Mongolia.
We explained the aim of our journey and our intention

to pass through Mongolia to the nearest port on the Pacific. The officers asked me to bring them out with us. I agreed. Our reconnaisance proved to us that there were no Partisans near the house of the peasant who was to ferry us over the Little Yenisei. We moved off at once in order to pass as quickly as possible this dangerous zone of the Yenisei and to sink ourselves into the forest beyond. It snowed but immediately thawed. Before evening a cold north wind sprang up, bringing with it a small blizzard. Late in the night our party reached the river. Our colonist welcomed us and offered at once to ferry us over and swim the horses, although there was ice still floating which had come down from the head-waters of the stream. During this conversation there was present one of the peasant's workmen, red-haired and squint-eyed. He kept moving around all the time and suddenly disappeared. Our host noticed it and, with fear in his voice, said:

"He has run to the village and will guide the Partisans here. We must cross immediately."

Then began the most terrible night of my whole journey. We proposed to the colonist that he take only our food and ammunition in the boat, while we would swim our horses across, in order to save the time of the many trips. The width of the Yenisei in this place is about three hundred metres. The stream is very rapid and the shore breaks away abruptly to the full depth of the stream. The night was absolutely dark with not a star in the sky. The wind in whistling swirls drove the snow and sleet sharply against our faces. Before us flowed the stream of black, rapid water, carrying down thin, jagged blocks of ice, twisting and grinding in the whirls and eddies. For a long time my horse refused to take the plunge down the steep bank, snorted and braced himself. With all my strength I lashed him with my whip across his neck until, with a pitiful groan, he threw himself into the cold stream. We both went all the way under and I hardly kept my seat in the saddle. Soon I was some metres from the shore with my horse stretching his head and neck far forward in his efforts and snorting and blowing incessantly. I felt the every motion of his feet churning the water and the quivering of his whole body under me in this trial. At last we reached the middle of the river, where the current became exceedingly rapid and began to carry us down with it. Out of the ominous darkness I heard the houtings of my companions and the dull cries of fear and suffering from the horses. I was chest deep in the icy water. Sometimes the floating blocks struck me; sometimes the waves broke up over my head and face. I had no time to look about or to feel the cold. The animal wish to live took possession of me; I became filled with the thought that, if my horse's strength failed in his struggle with the stream, I must perish. All my attention was turned to his efforts and to his quivering fear. Suddenly he groaned loudly and I noticed he was sinking. The water evidently was over his nostrils, because the intervals of his frightened snorts through the nostrils became longer. A big block of ice struck his head and turned him so that he was swimming right downstream. With difficulty I reined him around toward the shore but felt now that his force was gone. His head several times disappeared under the swirling surface. I had no choice. I slipped from the saddle and, holding this by

my left hand, swam with my right beside my mount,
encouraging him with my shouts. For a time he floated
with lips apart and his teeth set firm. In his widely
opened eyes was indescribable fear. As soon as I was
out of the saddle, he had at once risen in the water and
swam more calmly and rapidly. At last under the hoofs
of my exhausted animal I heard the stones. One after
another my companions came up on the shore. The well-
trained horses had brought all their burdens over. Much
farther down our colonist landed with the supplies.
Without a moment's loss we packed our things on the
horses and continued our journey. The wind was growing stronger and colder. At the dawn of day the cold
was intense. Our soaked clothes froze and became hard
as leather; our teeth chattered; and in our eyes showed
the red fires of fever: but we traveled on to put as much
space as we could between ourselves and the Partisans.
Passing about fifteen kilometres through the forest we
emerged into an open valley, from which we could see
the opposite bank of the Yenisei. It was about eight
o'clock. Along the road on the other shore wound the
black serpent-like line of riders and wagons which we
made out to be a column of Red soldiers with their transport. We dismounted and hid in the bushes in order
to avoid attracting their attention.

All the day with the thermometer at zero and below
we continued our journey, only at night reaching the
mountains covered with larch forests, where we made
big fires, dried our clothes and warmed ourselves thoroughly. The hungry horses did not leave the fires but
stood right behind us with drooped heads and slept. Very
early in the morning several Soyots came to our camp.

"Ulan? (Red?)" asked one of them.

"No! No!" exclaimed all our company.

"Tzagan? (White?)" followed the new question.

"Yes, yes," said the Tartar, "all are Whites."

"Mendé! Mendé!" they grunted and, after starting their cups of tea, began to relate very interesting and important news. It appeared that the Red Partisans, moving from the mountains Tannu Ola, occupied with their outposts all the border of Mongolia to stop and seize the peasants and Soyots driving out their cattle. To pass the Tannu Ola now would be impossible. I saw only one way—to turn sharp to the southeast, pass the swampy valley of the Buret Hei and reach the south shore of Lake Kosogol, which is already in the territory of Mongolia proper. It was very unpleasant news. To the first Mongol post in Samgaltai was not more than sixty miles from our camp, while to Kosogol by the shortest line not less than two hundred seventy-five. The horses my friend and I were riding, after having traveled more than six hundred miles over hard roads and without proper food or rest, could scarcely make such an additional distance. But, reflecting upon the situation and studying my new fellow travelers, I determined not to attempt to pass the Tannu Ola. They were nervous, morally weary men, badly dressed and armed and most of them were without weapons. I knew that during a fight there is no danger so great as that of disarmed men. They are easily caught by panic, lose their heads and infect all the others. Therefore, I consulted with my friends and decided to go to Kosogol. Our company agreed to follow us. After luncheon, consisting of soup with big lumps of meat, dry bread and

tea, we moved out. About two o'clock the mountains began to rise up before us. They were the northeast out-spurs of the Tannu Ola, behind which lay the Valley of Buret Hei.

CHAPTER XI

THE BARRIER OF RED PARTISANS

IN a valley between two sharp ridges we discovered a herd of yaks and cattle being rapidly driven off to the north by ten mounted Soyots. Approaching us warily they finally revealed that Noyon (Prince) of Todji had ordered them to drive the herds along the Buret Hei into Mongolia, apprehending the pillaging of the Red Partisans. They proceeded but were informed by some Soyot hunters that this part of the Tannu Ola was occupied by the Partisans from the village of Vladimirovka. Consequently they were forced to return. We inquired from them the whereabouts of these outposts and how many Partisians were holding the mountain pass over into Mongolia. We sent out the Tartar and the Kalmuck for a reconnaissance while all of us prepared for the further advance by wrapping the feet of our horses in our shirts and by muzzling their noses with straps and bits of rope so that they could not neigh. It was dark when our investigators returned and reported to us that about thirty Partisans had a camp some ten kilometers from us, occupying the *yurtas* of the Soyots. At the pass were two outposts, one of two soldiers and the other of three. From the outposts to the camp was a little over a mile. Our trail lay between the two outposts. From the top of the mountain one could plainly see the two posts and could shoot them all. When we had come near to the top of this mountain, I left our party and, taking with me my friend, the Tartar, the Kalmuck and two of the young officers, advanced. From the mountain I saw about five hundred yards ahead two fires. At each of the fires sat a soldier with his rifle and the others slept. I did not want to fight with the Partisans but we had to do away with these outposts and that without firing or we never should get through the pass. I did not believe the Partisans could afterwards track us because the whole trail was thickly marked with the spoors of horses and cattle.

"I shall take for my share these two," whispered my friend, pointing to the left outpost.

The rest of us were to take care of the second post. I crept along through the bushes behind my friend in order to help him in case of need; but I am bound to admit that I was not at all worried about him. He was about seven feet tall and so strong that, when a horse used to refuse sometimes to take the bit, he would wrap his arm around its neck, kick its forefeet out from under it and throw it so that he could easily bridle it on the ground. When only a hundred paces remained, I stood behind the bushes and watched. I could see very distinctly the fire and the dozing sentinel. He sat with his rifle on his knees. His companion, asleep beside him, did not move. Their white felt boots were plainly visible to me. For a long time I did not remark my friend. At the fire all was quiet. Suddenly from the other outpost floated over a few dim shouts and all was still. Our sentinel slowly raised his head. But just at this moment the huge body of my friend rose up and blanketed the fire from me and in a twinkling the feet of the sentinel flashed through the air, as my companion had seized him by the throat and swung him clear into the bushes, where both figures disappeared. In a second he re-appeared, flourished the rifle of the Partisan over his head and I heard the dull blow which was followed by an absolute calm. He came back toward me and, confusedly smiling, said:

"It is done. God and the Devil! When I was a boy, my mother wanted to make a priest out of me. When I grew up, I became a trained agronome in order . . . to strangle the people and smash their skulls. Revolution is a very stupid thing!"

And with anger and disgust he spit and began to smoke his pipe.

At the other outpost also all was finished. During this night we reached the top of the Ta au Ola and descended again into a valley covered with dense bushes and twined with a whole network of small rivers and streams. It was the headwaters of the Buret Hei. About one o'clock we stopped and began to feed our horses, as the grass just there was very good. Here we thought ourselves in safety. We saw many calming indications. On the mountains were seen the grazing herds of reindeers and yaks and approaching Soyots confirmed our supposition. Here behind the Tannu Ola the Soyots had not seen the Red soldiers. We presented to these Soyots a brick of tea and saw them depart happy and sure that we were *"Tzagan,"* a "good people."

While our horses rested and grazed on the well-pre-served grass, we sat by the fire and deliberated upon our further progress. There developed a sharp controversy between two sections of our company, one led by a

Colonel who with four officers were so impressed by the absence of Reds south of the Tannu Ola that they determined to work westward to Kobdo and then on to the camp on the Emil River where the Chinese authorities had interned six thousand of the forces of General Bakitch, which had come over into Mongolian territory. My friend and I with sixteen of the officers chose to carry through our old plan to strike for the shores of Lake Kosogol and thence out to the Far East. As neither side could persuade the other to abandon its ideas, our company was divided and the next day at noon we took leave of one another. It turned out that our own wing of eighteen had many fights and difficulties on the way, which cost us the lives of six of our comrades, but that the remainder of us came through to the goal of our journey so closely knit by the ties of devotion which fighting and struggling for our very lives entailed that we have ever preserved for one another the warmest feelings of friendship. The other group under Colonel Jukoff perished. He met a big detachment of Red cavalry and was defeated by them in two fights. Only two officers escaped. They related to me this sad news and the details of the fights when we met four months later in Urga.

Our band of eighteen riders with five packhorses moved up the valley of the Buret Hei. We floundered in the swamps, passed innumerable miry streams, were frozen by the cold winds and were soaked through by the snow and sleet; but we persisted indefatigably toward the south end of Kosogol. As a guide our Tartar led us confidently over these trails well marked by the feet of many cattle being run out of Urianhai to Mongolia.

CHAPTER XII

IN THE COUNTRY OF ETERNAL PEACE

THE inhabitants of Urianhai, the Soyots, are proud of being the genuine Buddhists and of retaining the pure doctrine of holy Rama and the deep wisdom of Sakkia-Mouni. They are the eternal enemies of war and of the shedding of blood. Away back in the thirteenth century they preferred to move out from their native land and take refuge in the north rather than fight or become a part of the empire of the bloody conqueror Jenghiz Khan, who wanted to add to his forces these wonderful horsemen and skilled archers. Three times in their history they have thus trekked northward to avoid struggle and now no one can say that on the hands of the Soyots there has ever been seen human blood. With their love of peace they struggled against the evils of war. Even the severe Chinese administrators could not apply here in this country of peace the full measure of their implacable laws. In the same manner the Soyots conducted themselves when the Russian people, mad with blood and crime, brought this infection into their land. They avoided persistently meetings and encounters with the Red troops and Partisans, trekking off with their families and cattle southward into the distant principalities of Kemchik and Soldjak. The eastern branch of this stream of emigration passed through the valley of the Buret Hei, where we constantly outstrode groups of them with their cattle and herds.

We traveled quickly along the winding trail of the Buret Hei and in two days began to make the elevations of the mountain pass between the valleys of the Buret Hei and Kharga. The trail was not only very steep but was also littered with fallen larch trees and frequently intercepted, incredible as it may seem, with swampy places where the horses mired badly. Then again we picked our dangerous road over cobbles and small stones that rolled away under our horses' feet and bumped off over the precipice nearby. Our horses fatigued easily in passing this moraine that had been strewn by ancient glaciers along the mountain sides. Sometimes the trail led right along the edge of the precipices where the horses started great slides of stones and sand. I remember one whole mountain covered with these moving sands. We had to leave our saddles and, taking the bridles in our hands, to trot for a mile or more over these sliding beds, sometimes sinking in up to our knees and going down the mountain side with them toward the precipices below. One imprudent move at times would have sent us over the brink. This destiny met one of our horses. Belly down in the moving trap, he could not work free to change his direction and so slipped on down with a mass of it until he rolled over the precipice and was lost to us forever. We heard only the crackling of breaking trees along his road to death. Then with great difficulty we worked down to salvage the saddle and bags. Further along we had to abandon one of our pack horses which had come all the way from the northern border of Urianhai with us. We first unburdened it but this did not help; no more did our shouting and threats. He only stood with his head down and looked so exhausted that we realized he had reached the further bourne of his land of toil. Some Soyots with us examined him, felt of his muscles on the fore and hind legs, took his head in their hands and moved it from side to side, examined his head carefully after that and then said:

"That horse will not go further. His brain is dried out." So we had to leave him.

That evening we came to a beautiful change in scene when we topped a rise and found ourselves on a broad plateau covered with larch. On it we discovered the *yurtas* of some Soyot hunters, covered with bark instead of the usual felt. Out of these ten men with rifles rushed toward us as we approached. They informed us that the Prince of Soldjak did not allow anyone to pass this way, as he feared the coming of murderers and robbers into his dominions.

"Go back to the place from which you came," they advised us with fear in their eyes.

I did not answer but I stopped the beginnings of a quarrel between an old Soyot and one of my officers. I pointed to the small stream in the valley ahead of us and asked him its name.

"Oyna," replied the Soyot. "It is the border of the principality and the passage of it is forbidden."

"All right," I said, "but you will allow us to warm and rest ourselves a little."

"Yes, yes!" exclaimed the hospitable Soyots, and led us into their tepees.

On our way there I took the opportunity to hand to the old Soyot a cigarette and to another a box of matches. We were all walking along together save one Soyot who limped slowly in the rear and was holding his hand up over his nose.

"Is he ill?" I asked.

"Yes," sadly answered the old Soyot. "That is my son. He has been losing blood from the nose for two days and is now quite weak."

I stopped and called the young man to me.

"Unbutton your outer coat," I ordered, "bare your neck and chest and turn your face up as far as you can." I pressed the jugular vein on both sides of his head for some minutes and said to him:

"The blood will not flow from your nose any more. Go into your tepee and lie down for some time."

The "mysterious" action of my fingers created on the Soyots a strong impression. The old Soyot with fear and reverence whispered:

"Ta Lama, Ta Lama! (Great Doctor)."

In the *yurta* we were given tea while the old Soyot sat thinking deeply about something. Afterwards he took counsel with his companions and finally announced:

"The wife of our Prince is sick in her eyes and I think the Prince will be very glad if I lead the 'Ta Lama' to him. He will not punish me, for he ordered that no 'bad people' should be allowed to pass; but that should not stop the 'good people' from coming to us."

"Do as you think best," I replied rather indifferently. "As a matter of fact, I know how to treat eye diseases but I would go back if you say so."

"No, no!" the old man exclaimed with fear. "I shall guide you myself."

Sitting by the fire, he lighted his pipe with a flint,

wiped the mouthpiece on his sleeve and offered it to me in true native hospitality. I was *"comme il faut"* and smoked. Afterwards he offered his pipe to each one of our company and received from each a cigarette, a little tobacco or some matches. It was the seal on our friendship. Soon in our *yurta* many persons piled up around us, men, women, children and dogs. It was impossible to move. From among them emerged a Lama with shaved face and close cropped hair, dressed in the flowing red garment of his caste. His clothes and his expression were very different from the common mass of dirty Soyots with their queues and felt caps finished off with squirrel tails on the top. The Lama was very kindly disposed towards us but looked ever greedily at our gold rings and watches. I decided to exploit this avidity of the Servant of Buddha. Supplying him with tea and dried bread, I made known to him that I was in need of horses.

"I have a horse. Will you buy it from me?" he asked. "But I do not accept Russian bank notes. Let us exchange something."

For a long time I bargained with him and at last for my gold wedding ring, a raincoat and a leather saddle bag I received a fine Soyot horse—to replace one of the pack animals we had lost—and a young goat. We spent the night here and were feasted with fat mutton. In the morning we moved off under the guidance of the old Soyot along the trail that followed the valley of the Oyna, free from both mountains and swamps. But we knew that the mounts of my friend and myself, together with three others, were too worn down to make Kosogol and determined to try to buy others in Soldjak. Soon we began to meet little groups of Soyot *yurtas* with their cattle and horses round about. Finally we approached the shifting capital of the Prince. Our guide rode on ahead for the parley with him after assuring us that the Prince would be glad to welcome the Ta Lama, though at the time I remarked great anxiety and fear in his features as he spoke. Before long we emerged on to a large plain well covered with small bushes. Down by the shore of the river we made out big *yurtas* with yellow and blue flags floating over them and easily guessed that this was the seat of government. Soon our guide returned to us. His face was wreathed with smiles. He flourished his hands and cried:

"Noyon (the Prince) asks you to come! He is very glad!"

From a warrior I was forced to change myself into a diplomat. As we approached the *yurta* of the Prince, we were met by two officials, wearing the peaked Mongol caps with peacock feathers *rampants* behind. With low obeisances they begged the foreign "Noyon" to enter the *yurta*. My friend the Tartar and I entered. In the rich *yurta* draped with expensive silk we discovered a feeble, wizen-faced little old man with shaven face and cropped hair, wearing also a high pointed beaver cap with red silk apex topped off with a dark red button with the long peacock feathers streaming out behind. On his nose were big Chinese spectacles. He was sitting on a low divan, nervously clicking the beads of his rosary. This was Ta Lama, Prince of Soldjak and High Priest of the Buddhist Temple. He welcomed us very cordially and invited us to sit down before the fire burning in the copper brazier. His surprisingly beautiful Princess served us with tea and Chinese confections and cakes. We smoked our pipes, though the Prince as a Lama did not indulge, fulfilling, however, his duty as a host by raising to his lips the pipes we offered him and handing us in return the green nephrite bottle of snuff. Thus with the etiquette accomplished we awaited the words of the Prince. He inquired whether our travels had been felicitous and what were our further plans. I talked with him quite frankly and requested his hospitality for the rest of our company and for the horses. He agreed immediately and ordered four *yurtas* set up for us.

"I hear that the foreign Noyon," the Prince said, "is a good doctor."

"Yes, I know some diseases and have with me some medicines," I answered, "but I am not a doctor. I am a scientist in other branches."

But the Prince did not understand this. In his simple directness a man who knows how to treat disease is a doctor.

"My wife has had constant trouble for two months with her eyes," he announced. "Help her."

I asked the Princess to show me her eyes and I found the typical conjunctivitis from the continual smoke of the *yurta* and the general uncleanliness. The Tartar brought me my medicine case. I washed her eyes with boric acid and dropped a little cocaine and a feeble solution of sulphurate of zinc into them.

"I beg you to cure me," pleaded the Princess. "Do not go away until you have cured me. We shall give you sheep, milk and flour for all your company. I weep now very often because I had very nice eyes and my husband used to tell me they shone like the stars and now they are red. I cannot bear it, I cannot!"

She very capriciously stamped her foot and, coquettishly smiling at me, asked:

"Do you want to cure me? Yes?"

The character and manners of lovely woman are the same everywhere: on bright Broadway, along the stately Thames, on the vivacious boulevards of gay Paris and in the silk-draped *yurta* of the Soyot Princess behind the larch covered Tannu Ola.

"I shall certainly try," assuringly answered the new oculist.

We spent here ten days, surrounded by the kindness and friendship of the whole family of the Prince. The eyes of the Princess, which eight years ago had seduced the already old Prince Lama, were now recovered. She was beside herself with joy and seldom left her looking-glass.

The Prince gave me five fairly good horses, ten sheep and a bag of flour, which was immediately transformed into dry bread. My friend presented him with a Romanoff five-hundred-rouble note with a picture of Peter the Great upon it, while I gave to him a small nugget of gold which I had picked up in the bed of a stream. The Prince ordered one of the Soyots to guide us to the Kosogol. The whole family of the Prince conducted us to the monastery ten kilometres from the "capital." We did not visit the monastery but we stopped at the *"Dugun,"* a Chinese trading establishment. The Chinese merchants looked at us in a very hostile manner though they simultaneously offered us all sorts of goods, thinking especially to catch us with their round bottles

(*lanhon*) of *maygolo* or sweet brandy made from ani-
seed. As we had neither lump silver nor Chinese dollars,
we could only look with longing at these attractive bottles,
till the Prince came to the rescue and ordered the Chinese
to put five of them in our saddle bags.

CHAPTER XIII

MYSTERIES, MIRACLES AND A NEW FIGHT¡

IN the evening of the same day we arrived at the Sacred Lake of Teri Noor, a sheet of water eight kilometres across, muddy and yellow, with low unattractive shores studded with large holes. In the middle of the lake lay what was left of a disappearing island. On this were a few trees and some old ruins. Our guide explained to us that two centuries ago the lake did not exist and that a very strong Chinese fortress stood here on the plain. A Chinese chief in command of the fortress gave offence to an old Lama who cursed the place and prophesied that it would all be destroyed. The very next day the water began rushing up from the ground, destroyed the fortress and engulfed all the Chinese soldiers. Even to this day when storms rage over the lake the waters cast up on the shores the bones of men and horses who perished in it. This Teri Noor increases its size every year, approaching nearer and nearer to the mountains. Skirting the eastern shore of the lake, we began to climb a snow-capped ridge. The road was easy at first but the guide warned us that the most difficult bit was there ahead. We reached this point two days later and found there a steep mountain side thickly set with forest and covered with snow. Beyond it lay the lines of eternal snow—ridges studded with dark rocks

set in great banks of the white mantle that gleamed
bright under the clear sunshine. These were the eastern
and highest branches of the Tannu Ola system. We
spent the night beneath this wood and began the passage
of it in the morning. At noon the guide began leading
us by zigzags in and out but everywhere our trail was
blocked by deep ravines, great jams of fallen trees and
walls of rock caught in their mad tobogganings from
the mountain top. We struggled for several hours, wore
out our horses and, all of a sudden, turned up at the
place where we had made our last halt. It was very
evident our Soyot had lost his way; and on his face I
noticed marked fear.

"The old devils of the cursed forest will not allow
us to pass," he whispered with trembling lips. "It is a
very ominous sign. We must return to Kharga to the
Noyon."

But I threatened him and he took the lead again evidently without hope or effort to find the way. Fortunately, one of our party, an Urianhai hunter, noticed the
blazes on the tr 's, the signs of the road which our guide
had lost. Foll wing these, we made our way through
the wood, can : into and crossed a belt of burned larch
timber and beyond this dipped again into a small live
forest bordering the bottom of the mountains crowned
with the eternal snows. It grew dark so that we had
to camp for the night. The wind rose high and carried
in its grasp a great white sheet of snow that shut us
off from the horizon on every side and buried our camp
deep in its folds. Our horses stood round like white
ghosts, refusing to eat or to leave the circle round our
fire. The wind combed their manes and tails. Through

the niches in the mountains it roared and whistled. From somewhere in the distance came the low rumble of a pack of wolves, punctuated at intervals by the sharp individual barking that a favorable gust of wind threw up into high staccato.

As we lay by the fire, the Soyot came over to me and said: "Noyon, come with me to the *obo*. I want to show you something."

We went there and began to ascend the mountain. At the bottom of a very steep slope was laid up a large pile of stones and tree trunks, making a cone of some three metres in height. These *obo* are the Lamaite sacred signs set up at dangerous places, the altars to the bad demons, rulers of these places. Passing Soyots and Mongols pay tribute to the spirits by hanging on the branches of the trees in the *obo hatyk,* long streamers of blue silk, shreds torn from the lining of their coats or simply tufts of hair cut from their horses' manes; or by placing on the stones lumps of meat or cups of tea and salt.

"Look at it," said the Soyot. "The *hatyks* are torn off. The demons are angry, they will not allow us to pass, Noyon. . . . "

He caught my hand and with supplicating voice whispered: "Let us go back, Noyon; let us! The demons do not wish us to pass their mountains. For twenty years no one has dared to pass these mountains and all bold men who have tried have perished here. The demons fell upon them with snowstorm and cold. Look! It is beginning already. . . . Go back to our Noyon, wait for the warmer days and then. . . . "

I did not listen further to the Soyot but turned back

to the fire, which I could hardly see through the blinding snow. Fearing our guide might run away, I ordered a sentry to be stationed for the night to watch him. Later in the night I was awakened by the sentry, who said to me: "Maybe I am mistaken, but I think I heard a rifle."

What could I say to it? Maybe some stragglers like ourselves were giving a sign of their whereabouts to their lost companions, or perhaps the sentry had mistaken for a rifle shot the sound of some falling rock or frozen ice and snow. Soon I fell asleep again and suddenly saw in a dream a very clear vision. Out on the plain, blanketed deep with snow, was moving a line of riders. They were our pack horses, our Kalmuck and the funny pied horse with the Roman nose. I saw us descending from this snowy plateau into a fold in the mountains. Here some larch trees were growing, close to which gurgled a small, open brook. Afterwards I noticed a fire burning among the trees and then woke up.

It grew light. I shook up the others and asked them to prepare quickly so as not to lose time in getting under way. The storm was raging. The snow blinded us and blotted out all traces of the road. The cold also became more intense. At last we were in the saddles. The Soyot went ahead trying to make out the trail. As we worked higher the guide less seldom lost the way. Frequently we fell into deep holes covered with snow; we scrambled up over slippery rocks. At last the Soyot swung his horse round and, coming up to me, announced very positively: "I do not want to die with you and I will not go further."

My first motion was the swing of my whip back over

my head. I was so close to the "Promised Land" of Mongolia that this Soyot, standing in the way of fulfilment of my wishes, seemed to me my worst enemy. But I lowered my flourishing hand. Into my head flashed a quite wild thought.

"Listen," I said. "If you move your horses, you will receive a bullet in the back and you will perish not at the top of the mountain but at the bottom. And now I will tell you what will happen to us. When we shall have reached these rocks above, the wind will have ceased and the snowstorm will have subsided. The sun will shine as we cross the snowy plain above and afterwards we shall descend into a small valley where there are larches growing and a stream of open running water. There we shall light our fires and spend the night."

The Soyot began to tremble with fright.

"Noyon has already passed these mountains of Darkhat Ola?" he asked in amazement.

"No," I answered, "but last night I had a vision and I know that we shall fortunately win over this ridge."

"I will guide you!" exclaimed the Soyot, and, whipping his horse, led the way up the steep slope to the top of the ridge of eternal snows.

As we were passing along the narrow edge of a precipice, the Soyot stopped and attentively examined the trail.

"Today many shod horses have passed here!" he cried through the roar of the storm. "Yonder on the snow the lash of a whip has been dragged. These are not Soyots."

The solution of this enigma appeared instantly. A volley rang out. One of my companions cried out, as he caught hold of his right shoulder; one pack horse fell dead with a bullet behind his ear. We quickly tumbled out of our saddles, lay down behind the rocks and began to study the situation. We were separated from a parallel spur of the mountain by a small valley about one thousand paces across. There we made out about thirty riders already dismounted and firing at us. I had never allowed any fighting to be done until the initiative had been taken by the other side. Our enemy fell upon us unawares and I ordered my company to answer.

"Aim at the horses!" cried Colonel Ostrovsky. Then he ordered the Tartar and Soyot to throw our own animals. We killed six of theirs and probably wounded others, as they got out of control. Also our rifles took toll of any bold man who showed his head from behind his rock. We heard the angry shouting and maledictions of Red soldiers who shot up our position more and more animatedly.

Suddenly I saw our Soyot kick up three of the horses and spring into the saddle of one with the others in leash behind. Behind him sprang up the Tartar and the Kalmuck. I had already drawn my rifle on the Soyot but, as soon as I saw the Tartar and Kalmuck on their lovely horses behind him, I dropped my gun and knew all was well. The Reds let off a volley at the trio but they made good their escape behind the rocks and disappeared. The firing continued more and more lively and I did not know what to do. From our side we shot rarely, saving our cartridges. Watching carefully the enemy, I noticed two black points on the snow high above the Reds. They slowly approached our antagonists and finally were hidden from view behind some sharp hillocks. When they emerged from these, they were right on the edge of some overhanging rocks at the foot of which the Reds lay concealed from us. By this time I had no doubt that these were the heads of two men. Suddenly these men rose up and I watched them flourish and throw something that was followed by two deafening roars which re-echoed across the mountain valley. Immediately a third explosion was followed by wild shouts and disorderly firing among the Reds. Some of the horses rolled down the slope into the snow below and the soldiers, chased by our shots, made off as fast as they could down into the valley out of which we had come.

Afterward the Tartar told me the Soyot had proposed to guide them around behind the Reds to fall upon their rear with the bombs. When I had bound up the wounded shoulder of the officer and we had taken the pack off the killed animal, we continued our journey. Our position was complicated. We had no doubt that the Red detachment came up from Mongolia. Therefore, were there Red troops in Mongolia? What was their strength? Where might we meet them? Consequently, Mongolia was no more the Promised Land? Very sad thoughts took possession of us.

But Nature pleased us. The wind gradually fell. The storm ceased. The sun more and more frequently broke through the scudding clouds. We were traveling upon a high, snow-covered plateau, where in one place the wind blew it clean and in another piled it high with drifts which caught our horses and held them so that they could hardly extricate themselves at times. We had to dismount and wade through the white piles up to our waists and often a man or horse was down and had to be helped to his feet. At last the descent began and at sunset we stopped in the small larch grove, spent the night at the fire among the trees and drank the tea boiled in the water carried from the open mountain brook. In various places we came across the tracks of our recent antagonists.

Everything, even Nature herself and the angry demons of Darkhat Ola, had helped us: but we were not gay, because again before us lay the dread uncertainty that threatened us with new and possibly destructive dangers.

CHAPTER XIV

THE RIVER OF THE DEVIL

ULAN TAIGA with Darkhat Ola lay behind us. We went forward very rapidly because the Mongol plains began here, free from the impediments of mountains. Everywhere splendid grazing lands stretched away. In places there were groves of larch. We crossed some very rapid streams but they were not deep and they had hard beds. After two days of travel over the Darkhat plain we began meeting Soyots driving their cattle rapidly toward the northwest into Orgarkha Ola. They communicated to us very unpleasant news.

The Bolsheviki from the Irkutsk district had crossed the Mongolian border, captured the Russian colony at Khathyl on the southern shore of Lake Kosogol and turned off south toward Muren Kure, a Russian settlement beside a big Lamaite monastery sixty miles south of Kosogol. The Mongols told us there were no Russian troops between Khathyl and Muren Kure, so we decided to pass between these two points to reach Van Kure farther to the east. We took leave of our Soyot guide and, after having sent three scouts in advance, moved forward. From the mountains around the Kosogol we admired the splendid view of this broad Alpine lake. It was set like a sapphire in the old gold of the surrounding hills, chased with lovely bits of rich dark forestry. At night we approached Khathyl with great precaution and stopped on the shore of the river that flows from Kosogol, the Yaga or Egingol. We found a Mongol who agreed to transport us to the other bank of the frozen stream and to lead us by a safe road between Khathyl and Muren Kure. Everywhere along the shore of the river were found large *obo* and small shrines to the demons of the stream.

"Why are there so many *obo?*" we asked the Mongol.

"It is the River of the Devil, dangerous and crafty," replied the Mongol. "Two days ago a train of carts went through the ice and three of them with five soldiers were lost."

We started to cross. The surface of the river resembled a thick piece of looking-glass, being clear and without snow. Our horses walked very carefully but some fell and floundered before they could regain their feet. We were leading them by the bridle. With bowed heads and trembling all over they kept their frightened eyes ever on the ice at their feet. I looked down and understood their fear. Through the cover of one foot of transparent ice one could clearly see the bottom of the river. Under the lighting of the moon all the stones, the holes and even some of the grasses were distinctly visible, even though the depth was ten metres and more. The Yaga rushed under the ice with a furious speed, swirling and marking its course with long bands of foam and bubbles. Suddenly I jumped and stopped as though fastened to the spot. Along the surface of the river ran the boom of a cannon, followed by a second and a third.

"Quicker, quicker!" cried our Mongol, waving us forward with his hand.

Another cannon boom and a crack ran right close to us. The horses swung back on their haunches in protest, reared and fell, many of them striking their heads severely on the ice. In a second it opened up two feet wide, so that I could follow its jagged course along the surface. Immediately up out of the opening the water spread over the ice with a rush.

"Hurry, hurry!" shouted the guide.

With great difficulty we forced our horses to jump over this cleavage and to continue on further. They trembled and disobeyed and only the strong lash forced them to forget this panic of fear and go on.

When we were safe on the farther bank and well into the woods, our Mongol guide recounted to us how the river at times opens in this mysterious way and leaves great areas of clear water. All the men and animals on the river at such times must perish. The furious current of cold water will always carry them down under the ice. At other times a crack has been known to pass right under a horse and, where he fell in with his front feet in the attempt to get back to the other side, the crack has closed up and ground his legs or feet right off.

The valley of Kosogol is the crater of an extinct volcano. Its outlines may be followed from the high west shore of the lake. However, the Plutonic force still acts and, asserting the glory of the Devil, forces the Mongols to build *obo* and offer sacrifices at his shrines. We spent all the night and all the next day hurrying away eastward to avoid a meeting with the

Reds and seeking good pasturage for our horses. At about nine o'clock in the evening a fire shone out of the distance. My friend and I made toward it with the feeling that it was surely a Mongol *yurta* beside which we could camp in safety. We traveled over a mile before making out distinctly the lines of a group of *yurtas*. But nobody came out to meet us and, what astonished us more, we were not surrounded by the angry black Mongolian dogs with fiery eyes. Still, from the distance we had seen the fire and so there must be someone there. We dismounted from our horses and approached on foot. From out of the *yurta* rushed two Russian soldiers, one of whom shot at me with his pistol but missed me and wounded my horse in the back through the saddle. I brought him to earth with my Mauser and the other was killed by the butt end of my friend's rifle. We examined the bodies and found in their pockets the papers of soldiers of the Second Squadron of the Communist Interior Defence. Here we spent the night. The owners of the *yurtas* had evidently run away, for the Red soldiers had collected and packed in sacks the property of the Mongols. Probably they were just planning to leave, as they were fully dressed. We acquired two horses, which we found in the bushes, two rifles and two automatic pistols with cartridges. In the saddle bags we also found tea, tobacco, matches and cartridges—all of these valuable supplies to help us keep further hold on our lives.

Two days later we were approaching the shore of the River Uri when we met two Russian riders, who were the Cossacks of a certain Ataman Sutunin, acting against the Bolsheviki in the valley of the River Selenga. They were riding to carry a message from Sutunin to Kaigoro-doff, chief of the Anti-Bolsheviki in the Altai region. They informed us that along the whole Russian-Mongolian border the Bolshevik troops were scattered; also that Communist agitators had penetrated to Kiakhta, Ulankom and Kobdo and had persuaded the Chinese authorities to surrender to the Soviet authorities all the refugees from Russia. We knew that in the neighborhood of Urga and Van Kure engagements were taking place between the Chinese troops and the detachments of the Anti-Bolshevik Russian General Baron Ungern Sternberg and Colonel Kazagrandi, who were fighting for the independence of Outer Mongolia. Baron Ungern had now been twice defeated, so that the Chinese were carrying on high-handed in Urga, suspecting all foreigners of having relations with the Russian General.

We realized that the whole situation was sharply reversed. The route to the Pacific was closed. Reflecting very carefully over the problem, I decided that we had but one possible exit left. We must avoid all Mongolian cities with Chinese administration, cross Mongolia from north to south, traverse the desert in the southern part of the Principality of Jassaktu Khan, enter the Gobi in the western part of Inner Mongolia, strike as rapidly as possible through sixty miles of Chinese territory in the Province of Kansu and penetrate into Tibet. Here I hoped to search out one of the English Consuls and with his help to reach some English port in India. I understood thoroughly all the difficulties incident to such an enterprise but I had no other choice. It only remained to make this last foolish attempt or to perish without doubt at the hands of the Bolsheviki or languish in a

Chinese prison. When I announced my plan to my companions, without in any way hiding from them all its
dangers and quixotism, all of them answered very quickly
and shortly: "Lead us! We will follow."

One circumstance was distinctly in our favor. We
did not fear hunger, for we had some supplies of tea,
tobacco and matches and a surplus of horses, saddles,
rifles, overcoats and boots, which were an excellent cur-
rency for exchange. So then we began to initiate the
plan of the new expedition. We should start to the
south, leaving the town of Uliassutai on our right and
taking the direction of Zaganluk, then pass through the
waste lands of the district of Balir of Jassaktu Khan,
cross the Naron Khuhu Gobi and strike for the mountains of Boro. Here we should be able to take a long
rest to recuperate the strength of our horses and of ourselves. The second section of our journey would be
the passage through the western part of Inner Mongolia,
through the Little Gobi, through the lands of the Torguts,
over the Khara Mountains, across Kansu, where our road
must be chosen to the west of the Chinese town of
Suchow. From there we should have to enter the Dominion of Kuku Nor and then work on southward to the
head waters of the Yangtze River. Beyond this I had
but a hazy notion, which however I was able to verify
from a map of Asia in the possession of one of the
officers, to the effect that the mountain chains to the
west of the sources of the Yangtze separated that river
system from the basin of the Brahmaputra in Tibet
Proper, where I expected to be able to find English
assistance.

CHAPTER XV

THE MARCH OF GHOSTS

IN no other way can I describe the journey from the
River Ero to the border of Tibet. About eleven
hundred miles through the snowy steppes, over mountains and across deserts we traveled in forty-eight days.
We hid from the people as we journeyed, made short
stops in the most desolate places, fed for whole weeks
on nothing but raw, frozen meat in order to avoid
attracting attention by the smoke of fires. Whenever
we needed to purchase a sheep or a steer for our supply
department, we sent out only two unarmed men who
represented to the natives that they were the workmen
of some Russian colonists. We even feared to shoot,
although we met a great herd of antelopes numbering
as many as five thousand head. Behind Balir in the lands
of the Lama Jassaktu Khan, who had inherited his throne
as a result of the poisoning of his brother at Urga by
order of the Living Buddha, we met wandering Russian
Tartars who had driven their herds all the way from
Altai and Abakan. They welcomed us very cordially,
gave us oxen and thirty-six bricks of tea. Also they
saved us from inevitable destruction, for they told us
that at this season it was utterly impossible for horses
to make the trip across the Gobi, where there was no
grass at all. We must buy camels by exchanging for

them our horses and some other of our bartering supplies. One of the Tartars the next day brought to their camp a rich Mongol with whom he drove the bargain for this trade. He gave us nineteen camels and took all our horses, one rifle, one pistol and the best Cossack saddle. He advised us by all means to visit the sacred Monastery of Narabanchi, the last Lamaite monastery on the road from Mongolia to Tibet. He told us that the Holy Hutuktu, "the Incarnate Buddha," would be greatly offended if we did not visit the monastery and his famous "Shrine of Blessings," where all travelers going to Tibet always offered prayers. Our Kalmuck Lamaite supported the Mongol in this. I decided to go there with the Kalmuck. The Tartars gave me some big silk *hatyk* as presents and loaned us four splendid horses. Although the monastery was fifty-five miles distant, by nine o'clock in the evening I entered the *yurta* of this holy Hutuktu.

He was a middle-aged, clean shaven, spare little man, laboring under the name of Jclyb Djamsrap Hutuktu. He received us very cordially and was greatly pleased with the presentation of the *hatyk* and with my knowledge of the Mongol etiquette in which my Tartar had been long and persistently instructing me. He listened to me most attentively and gave valuable advice about the road, presenting me then with a ring which has since opened for me the doors of all Lamaite monasteries. The name of this Hutuktu is highly esteemed not only in all Mongolia but in Tibet and in the Lamaite world of China. We spent the night in his splendid *yurta* and on the following morning visited the shrines where they were conducting very solemn services with the music of gongs, tom-toms and whistling. The Lamas with their deep voices were intoning the prayers while the lesser priests answered with their antiphonies. The sacred phrase: *"Om! Mani padme Hung!"* was endlessly repeated.

The Hutuktu wished us success, presented us with a large yellow *hatyk* and accompanied us to the monastery gate. When we were in our saddles he said:

"Remember that you are always welcome guests here. Life is very complicated and anything may happen. Perhaps you will be forced in future to re-visit distant Mongolia and then do not miss Narabanchi Kure."

That night we returned to the Tartars and the next day continued our journey. As I was very tired, the slow, easy motion of the camel was welcome and restful to me. All the day I dozed off at intervals to sleep. It turned out to be very disastrous for me; for, when my camel was going up the steep bank of a river, in one of my naps I fell off and hit my head on a stone, lost consciousness and woke up to find my overcoat covered with blood. My friends surrounded me with their frightened faces. They bandaged my head and we started off again. I only learned long afterwards from a doctor who examined me that I had cracked my skull as the price of my siesta.

We crossed the eastern ranges of the Altai and the Karlik Tag, which are the most oriental sentinels the great Tian Shan system throws out into the regions of the Gobi; and then traversed from the north to the south the entire width of the Khuhu Gobi. Intense cold ruled all this time and fortunately the frozen sands gave us better speed. Before passing the Khara range, we exchanged our rocking-chair steeds for horses, a deal in which the Torguts skinned us badly like the true "old clothes men" they are.

Skirting around these mountains we entered Kansu. It was a dangerous move, for the Chinese were arresting all refugees and I feared for my Russian fellow-travelers. During the days we hid in the ravines, the forests and bushes, making forced marches at night. Four days we thus used in this passage of Kansu. The few Chinese peasants we did encounter were peaceful appearing and most hospitable. A marked sympathetic interest surrounded the Kalmuck, who could speak a bit of Chinese, and my box of medicines. Everywhere we found many ill people, chiefly afflicted with eye troubles, rheumatism and skin diseases.

As we were approaching Nan Shan, the northeast branch of the Altyn Tag (which is in turn the east branch of the Pamir and Karakhorum system), we overhauled a large caravan of Chinese merchants going to Tibet and joined them. For three days we were winding through the endless ravine-like valleys of these mountains and ascending the high passes. But we noticed that the Chinese knew how to pick the easiest routes for caravans over all these difficult places. In a state of semi-consciousness I made this whole journey toward the large group of swampy lakes, feeding the Koko Nor and a whole network of large rivers. From fatigue and constant nervous strain, probably helped by the blow on my head, I began suffering from sharp attacks of chills and fever, burning up at times and then chattering so with my teeth that I frightened my horse who several times threw me from the saddle. I raved, cried out at times and even wept. I called my family and instructed them how they must come to me. I remember as though through a dream how I was taken from the horse by my companions, laid on the ground, supplied with Chinese brandy and, when I recovered a little, how they said to me:

"The Chinese merchants are heading for the west and we must travel south."

"No! To the north," I replied very sharply.

"But no, to the south," my companions assured me.

"God and the Devil!" I angrily ejaculated, "we have just swum the Little Yenisei and Algyak is to the north!"

"We are in Tibet," remonstrated my companions. "We must reach the Brahmaputra."

Brahmaputra. . . . Brahmaputra. . . . This word revolved in my fiery brain, made a terrible noise and commotion. Suddenly I remembered everything and opened my eyes. I hardly moved my lips and soon I again lost consciousness. My companions brought me to the monastery of Sharkhe, where the Lama doctor quickly brought me round with a solution of *fatil* or Chinese ginseng. In discussing our plans he expressed grave doubt as to whether we would get through Tibet but he did not wish to explain to me the reason for his doubts.

CHAPTER XVI

IN MYSTERIOUS TIBET

A FAIRLY broad road led out from Sharkhe through the mountains and on the fifth day of our two weeks' march to the south from the monastery we emerged into the great bowl of the mountains in whose center lay the large lake of Koko Nor. If Finland deserves the ordinary title of the "Land of Ten Thousand Lakes," the dominion of Koko Nor may certainly with justice be called the "Country of a Million Lakes." We skirted this lake on the west between it and Doulan Kitt, zig-zagging between the numerous swamps, lakes and small rivers, deep and miry. The water was not here covered with ice and only on the tops of the mountains did we feel the cold winds sharply. We rarely met the natives of the country and only with greatest difficulty did our Kalmuck learn the course of the road from the occasional shepherds we passed. From the eastern shore of the Lake of Tassoun we worked round to a monastery on the further side, where we stopped for a short rest. Besides ourselves there was also another group of guests in the holy place. These were Tibetans. Their behavior was very impertinent and they refused to speak with us. They were all armed, chiefly with the Russian military rifles and were draped with crossed bandoliers of cartridges with two or three pistols stowed beneath belts with more cartridges sticking out. They examined us very sharply and we readily realized that they were estimating our martial strength. After they had left on that same day I ordered our Kalmuck to inquire from the High Priest of the temple exactly who they were. For a long time the monk gave evasive answers but when I showed him the ring of Hutuktu Narabanchi and presented him with a large yellow *hatyk,* he became more communicative.

"Those are bad people," he explained. "Have a care of them."

However, he was not willing to give their names, explaining his refusal by citing the Law of Buddhist lands against pronouncing the name of one's father, teacher or chief. Afterwards I found out that in North Tibet there exists the same custom as in North China. Here and there bands of *hunghutze* wander about. They appear at the headquarters of the leading trading firms and at the monasteries, claim tribute and after their collections become the protectors of the district. Probably this Tibetan monastery had in this band just such protectors.

When we continued our trip, we frequently noticed single horsemen far away or on the horizon, apparently studying our movements with care. All our attempts to approach them and enter into conversation with them were entirely unsuccessful. On their speedy little horses they disappeared like shadows. As we reached the steep and difficult Pass on the Hamshan and were preparing to spend the night there, suddenly far up on a ridge above us appeared about forty horsemen with entirely white mounts and without formal introduction or warn-

ing spattered us with a hail of bullets. Two of our
officers fell with a cry. One had been instantly killed
while the other lived some few minutes. I did not allow
my men to shoot but instead I raised a white flag and
started forward with the Kalmuck for a parley. At
first they fired two shots at us but then ceased firing
and sent down a group of riders from the ridge toward
us. We began the parley. The Tibetans explained that
Hamshan is a holy mountain and that here one must not
spend the night, advising us to proceed farther where
we could consider ourselves in safety. They inquired
from us whence we came and whither we were going,
stated in answer to our information about the purpose
of our journey that they knew the Bolsheviki and considered them the liberators of the people of Asia from
the yoke of the white race. I certainly did not want to
begin a political quarrel with them and so turned back
to our companions. Riding down the slope toward our
camp, I waited momentarily for a shot in the back but
the Tibetan *hunghutze* did not shoot.

We moved forward, leaving among the stones the
bodies of two of our companions as sad tribute to the
difficulties and dangers of our journey. We rode all
night, with our exhausted horses constantly stopping and
some lying down under us, but we forced them ever
onward. At last, when the sun was at its zenith, we
finally halted. Without unsaddling our horses, we gave
them an opportunity to lie down for a little rest. Before us lay a broad, swampy plain, where was evidently
the sources of the river Ma-chu. Not far beyond lay
the Lake of Aroung Nor. We made our fire of cattle
dung and began boiling water for our tea. Again with-

out any warning the bullets came raining in from all sides. Immediately we took cover behind convenient rocks and waited developments. The firing became faster and closer, the raiders appeared on the whole circle round us and the bullets came ever in increasing numbers. We had fallen into a trap and had no hope but to perish. We realized this clearly. I tried anew to begin the parley; but when I stood up with my white flag, the answer was only a thicker rain of bullets and unfortunately one of these, ricocheting off a rock, struck me in the left leg and lodged there. At the same moment another one of our company was killed. We had no other choice and were forced to begin fighting. The struggle continued for about two hours. Besides myself three others received slight wounds. We resisted as long as we could. The *hunghutze* approached and our situation became desperate.

"There's no choice," said one of my associates, a very expert Colonel. "We must mount and ride for it. . . anywhere."

"Anywhere. . . . " It was a terrible word! We consulted for but an instant. It was apparent that with this band of cut-throats behind us the farther we went into Tibet, the less chance we had of saving our lives.

We decided to return to Mongolia. But how? That we did not know. And thus we began our retreat. Firing all the time, we trotted our horses as fast as we could toward the north. One after another three of my companions fell. There lay my Tartar with a bullet through his neck. After him two young and fine stalwart officers were carried from their saddles with cries of death, while their scared horses broke out across the plain in wild fear, perfect pictures of our distraught selves. This emboldened the Tibetans, who became more and more audacious. A bullet struck the buckle on the ankle strap of my right foot and carried it, with a piece of leather and cloth, into my leg just above the ankle. My old and much tried friend, the agronome, cried out as he grasped his shoulder and then I saw him wiping and bandaging as best as he could his bleeding forehead. A second afterward our Kalmuck was hit twice right through the palm of the same hand, so that it was entirely shattered. Just at this moment fifteen of the *hunghutze* rushed against us in a charge.

"Shoot at them with volley fire!" commanded our Colonel.

Six robber bodies lay on the turf, while two others of the gang were unhorsed and ran scampering as fast as they could after their retreating fellows. Several minutes later the fire of our antagonists ceased and they raised a white flag. Two riders came forward toward us. In the parley it developed that their chief had been wounded through the chest and they came to ask us to "render first aid." At once I saw a ray of hope. I took my box of medicines and my groaning, cursing, wounded Kalmuck to interpret for me.

"Give that devil some cyanide of potassium," urged my companions.

But I devised another scheme.

We were led to the wounded chief. There he lay on the saddle cloths among the rocks, represented to us to be a Tibetan but I at once recognized him from his cast of countenance to be a Sart or Turcoman, probably from the southern part of Turkestan. He looked at me with a begging and frightened gaze. Examining him, I found the bullet had passed through his chest from left to right, that he had lost much blood and was very weak. Conscientiously I did all that I could for him. In the first place I tried on my own tongue all the medicines to be used on him, even the iodoform, in order to demonstrate that there was no poison among them. I cauterized the wound with iodine, sprinkled it with iodoform and applied the bandages. I ordered that the wounded man be not touched nor moved and that he be left right where he lay. Then I taught a Tibetan how the dressing must be changed and left with him medicated cotton, bandages and a little iodoform. To the patient, in whom the fever was already developing, I gave a big dose of aspirin and left several tablets of quinine with them. Afterwards, addressing myself to the bystanders through my Kalmuck, I said very solemnly:

"The wound is very dangerous but I gave to your Chief very strong medicine and hope that he will recover. One condition, however, is necessary: the bad demons which have rushed to his side for his unwarranted attack upon us innocent travelers will instantly kill him, if another shot is let off against us. You must not even keep a single cartridge in your rifles."

With these words I ordered the Kalmuck to empty his rifle and I, at the same time, took all the cartridges out of my Mauser. The Tibetans instantly and very servilely followed my example.

"Remember that I told you: 'Eleven days and eleven nights do not move from this place and do not charge your rifles.' Otherwise the demon of death will snatch off your Chief and will pursue you!"—and with these words I solemnly drew forth and raised above their heads the ring of Hutuktu Narabanchi.

I returned to my companions and calmed them. I told them we were safe against further attack from the robbers and that we must only guess the way to reach Mongolia. Our horses were so exhausted and thin that on their bones we could have hung our overcoats. We spent two days here, during which time I frequently visited my patient. It also gave us opportunity to bandage our own fortunately light wounds and to secure a little rest; though unfortunately I had nothing but a jackknife with which to dig the bullet out of my left calf and the shoemaker's accessories from my right ankle. Inquiring from the brigands about the caravan roads, we soon made our way out to one of the main routes and had the good fortune to meet there the caravan of the young Mongol Prince Pounzig, who was on a holy mission carrying a message from the Living Buddha in Urga to the Dalai Lama in Lhasa. He helped us to purchase horses, camels and food.

With all our arms and supplies spent in barter during the journey for the purchase of transport and food, we returned stripped and broken to the Narabanchi Monastery, where we were welcomed by the Hutuktu.

"I knew you would come back," said he. "The divinations revealed it all to me."

With six of our little band left behind us in Tibet to pay the eternal toll of our dash for the south we returned but twelve to the Monastery and waited there two weeks to re-adjust ourselves and learn how events would again set us afloat on this turbulent sea to steer for any port that Destiny might indicate. The officers enlisted in the detachment which was then being formed in Mongolia to fight against the destroyers of their native land, the Bolsheviki. My original companion and I prepared to continue our journey over Mongolian plains with whatever further adventures and dangers might come in the struggle to escape to a place of safety.

And now, with the scenes of that trying march so vividly recalled, I would dedicate these chapters to my gigantic, old and ruggedly tried friend, the agronome, to my Russian fellow-travelers, and especially, to the sacred memory of those of our companions whose bodies lie cradled in the sleep among the mountains of Tibet—Colonel Ostrovsky, Captains Zuboff and Turoff, Lieutenant Pisarjevsky, Cossack Vernigora and Tartar Mahomed Spirin. Also here I express my deep thanks for help and friendship to the Prince of Soldjak, Hereditary Noyon Ta Lama and to the Kampo Gelong of Narabanchi Monastery, the honorable Jelyb Djamsrap Hutuktu.

Part II

THE LAND OF DEMONS

Part II

THE LAND OF DEMONS

CHAPTER XVII

MYSTERIOUS MONGOLIA

IN the heart of Asia lies the enormous, mysterious and
rich country of Mongolia. From somewhere on the
snowy slopes of the Tian Shan and from the hot sands
of Western Zungaria to the timbered ridges of the Sayan
and to the Great Wall of China it stretches over a huge
portion of Central Asia. The cradle of peoples, his-
tories and legends; the native land of bloody conquerors,
who have left here their capitals covered by the sand of
the Gobi, their mysterious rings and their ancient nomad
laws; the states of monks and evil devils, the country of
wandering tribes administered by the descendants of
Jenghiz Khan and Kublai Khan—Khans and Princes of
the Junior lines: that is Mongolia.

Mysterious country of the cults of Rama, Sakkia-
Mouni, Djonkapa and Paspa, cults guarded by the very
person of the living Buddha—Buddha incarnated in the
third dignitary of the Lamaite religion—Bogdo Gheghen
in Ta Kure or Urga; the land of mysterious doctors,

prophets, sorcerers, fortune-tellers and witches; the land
of the sign of the swastika; the land which has not forgotten the thoughts of the long deceased great potentates
of Asia and of half of Europe: that is Mongolia.

The land of nude mountains, of plains burned by the
sun and killed by the cold, of ill cattle and ill people; the
nest of pests, anthrax and smallpox; the land of boiling
hot springs and of mountain passes inhabited by demons;
of sacred lakes swarming with fish; of wolves, rare species of deer and mountain goats, marmots in millions,
wild horses, wild donkeys and wild camels that have
never known the bridle, ferocious dogs and rapacious
birds of prey which devour the dead bodies cast out on the
plains by the people: that is Mongolia.

The land whose disappearing primitive people gaze
upon the bones of their forefathers whitening in the
sands and dust of their plains; where are dying out the
people who formerly conquered China, Siam, Northern
India and Russia and broke their chests against the iron
lances of the Polish knights, defending then all the Christian world against the invasion of wild and wandering
Asia: that is Mongolia.

The land swelling with natural riches, producing nothing, in need of everything, destitute and suffering from
the world's cataclysm: that is Mongolia.

In this land, by order of Fate, after my unsuccessful
attempt to reach the Indian Ocean through Tibet, I spent
half a year in the struggle to live and to escape. My old
and faithful friend and I were compelled, willy-nilly, to
participate in the exceedingly important and dangerous
events transpiring in Mongolia in the year of grace 1921.
Thanks to this, I came to know the calm, good and honest

Mongolian people; I read their souls, saw their sufferings and hopes; I witnessed the whole horror of their oppression and fear before the face of Mystery, there where Mystery pervades all life.   I watched the rivers during the severe cold break with a rumbling roar their chains of ice; saw lakes cast up on their shores the bones of human beings; heard unknown wild voices in the mountain ravines; made out the fires over miry swamps of the will-o'-the-wisps; witnessed burning lakes; gazed upward to mountains whose peaks could not be scaled; came across great balls of writhing snakes in the ditches in winter; met with streams which are eternally frozen, rocks like petrified caravans of camels, horsemen and carts; and over all saw the barren mountains whose folds looked like the mantle of Satan, which the glow of the evening sun drenched with blood.

"Look up there!" cried an old shepherd, pointing to the slope of the cursed Zagastai.   "That is no mountain. It is *he* who lies in his red mantle and awaits the day when he will rise again to begin the fight with the good spirits."

And as he spoke I recalled the mystic picture of the noted painter Vroubel.   The same nude mountains with the violet and purple robes of Satan, whose face is half covered by an approaching grey cloud.   Mongolia is a terrible land of mystery and demons.   Therefore it is no wonder that here every violation of the ancient order of life of the wandering nomad tribes is transformed into streams of red blood and horror, ministering to the demonic pleasure of Satan couched on the bare mountains and robed in the grey cloak of dejection and sadness, or in the purple mantle of war and vengeance.

After returning from the district of Koko Nor to Mongolia and resting a few days at the Narabanchi Monastery, we went to live in Uliassutai, the capital of Western Outer Mongolia. It is the last purely Mongolian town to the west. In Mongolia there are but three purely Mongolian towns, Urga, Uliassutai and Ulankom. The fourth town, Kobdo, has an essentially Chinese character, being the center of Chinese administration in this district inhabited by the wandering tribes only nominally recognizing the influence of either Peking or Urga. In Uliassutai and Ulankom, besides the unlawful Chinese commissioners and troops, there were stationed Mongolian governors or "Saits," appointed by the decree of the Living Buddha.

When we arrived in that town, we were at once in the sea of political passions. The Mongols were protesting in great agitation against the Chinese policy in their country; the Chinese raged and demanded from the Mongolians the payment of taxes for the full period since the autonomy of Mongolia had been forcibly extracted from Peking; Russian colonists who had years before settled near the town and in the vicinity of the great monasteries or among the wandering tribes had separated into factions and were fighting against one another; from Urga came the news of the struggle for the maintenance of the independence of Outer Mongolia, led by the Russian General, Baron Ungern von Sternberg; Russian officers and refugees congregated in detachments, against which the Chinese authorities protested but which the Mongols welcomed; the Bolsheviki, worried by the formation of White detachments in Mongolia, sent their troops to the borders of Mongolia; from Irkutsk and

Chita to Uliassutai and Urga envoys were running from the Bolsheviki to the Chinese commissioners with various proposals of all kinds; the Chinese authorities in Mongolia were gradually entering into secret relations with the Bolsheviki and in Kiakhta and Ulankom delivered to them the Russian refugees, thus violating recognized international law; in Urga the Bolsheviki set up a Russian communistic municipality; Russian Consuls were inactive; Red troops in the region of Kosogol and the valley of the Selenga had encounters with Anti-Bolshevik officers; the Chinese authorities established garrisons in the Mongolian towns and sent punitive expeditions into the country; and, to complete the confusion, the Chinese troops carried out house-to-house searches, during which they plundered and stole.

Into what an atmosphere we had fallen after our hard and dangerous trip along the Yenisei, through Urianhai, Mongolia, the lands of the Turguts, Kansu and Koko Nor!

"Do you know," said my old friend to me, "I prefer strangling Partisans and fighting with the *hunghutze* to listening to news and more anxious news!"

He was right; for the worst of it was that in this bustle and whirl of facts, rumours and gossip the Reds could approach troubled Uliassutai and take everyone with their bare hands. We should very willingly have left this town of uncertainties but we had no place to go. In the north were the hostile Partisans and Red troops; to the south we had already lost our companions and not a little of our own blood; to the west raged the Chinese administrators and detachments; and to the east a war had broken out, the news of which, in spite of the attempts of the Chinese authorities at secrecy, had filtered through and had testified to the seriousness of the situation in this part of Outer Mongolia. Consequently we had no choice but to remain in Uliassutai. Here also were living several Polish soldiers who had escaped from the prison camps in Russia, two Polish families and two American firms, all in the same plight as ourselves. We joined together and made our own intelligence department, very carefully watching the evolution of events. We succeeded in forming good connections with the Chinese commissioner and with the Mongolian Sait, which greatly helped us in our orientation.

What was behind all these events in Mongolia? The very clever Mongol Sait of Uliassutai gave me the following explanation.

"According to the agreements between Mongolia, China and Russia of October 21, 1912, of October 23, 1913, and of June 7, 1915, Outer Mongolia was accorded independence and the Moral Head of our 'Yellow Faith,' His Holiness the Living Buddha, became the Suzerain of the Mongolian people of Khalkha or Outer Mongolia with the title of 'Bogdo Djebtsung Damba Hutuktu Khan.' While Russia was still strong and carefully watched her policy in Asia, the Government of Peking kept the treaty; but, when, at the beginning of the war with Germany, Russia was compelled to withdraw her troops from Siberia, Peking began to claim the return of its lost rights in Mongolia. It was because of this that the first two treaties of 1912 and 1913 were supplemented by the convention of 1915. However, in 1916, when all the forces of Russia were pre-occupied in the unsuccessful war and afterwards when the first Russian revo-

lution broke out in February, 1917, overthrowing the
Romanoff Dynasty, the Chinese Government openly re-
took Mongolia. They changed all the Mongolian ministers and Saits, replacing them with individuals friendly
to China; arrested many Mongolian autonomists and
sent them to prison in Peking; set up their administration
in Urga and other Mongol towns; actually removed His
Holiness Bogdo Khan from the affairs of administration;
made him only a machine for signing Chinese decrees;
and at last introduced into Mongolia their troops. From
that moment there developed an energetic flow of Chinese
merchants and coolies into Mongolia. The Chinese began
to demand the payment of taxes and dues from 1912.
The Mongolian population were rapidly stripped of their
wealth and now in the vicinities of our towns and monasteries you can see whole settlements of beggar Mongols
living in dugouts. All our Mongol arsenals and treas-
uries were requisitioned. All monasteries were forced to
pay taxes; all Mongols working for the liberty of their
country were persecuted; through bribery with Chinese
silver, orders and titles the Chinese secured a following
among the poorer Mongol Princes. It is easy to understand how the governing class, His Holiness, Khans,
Princes, and high Lamas, as well as the ruined and oppressed people, remembering that the Mongol rulers had
once held Peking and China in their hands and under
their reign had given her the first place in Asia, were
definitely hostile to the Chinese administrators acting
thus. Insurrection was, however, impossible. We had
no arms. All our leaders were under surveillance and
every movement by them toward an armed resistance
would have ended in the same prison at Peking where

eighty of our Nobles, Princes and Lamas died from hunger and torture after a previous struggle for the liberty of Mongolia. Some abnormally strong shock was necessary to drive the people into action. This was given by the Chinese administrators, General Cheng Yi and General Chu Chi-hsiang. They announced that His Holiness Bogdo Khan was under arrest in his own palace, and they recalled to his attention the former decree of the Peking Government—held by the Mongols to be unwarranted and illegal—that His Holiness was the last Living Buddha. This was enough. Immediately secret relations were made between the people and their Living God, and plans were at once elaborated for the liberation of His Holiness and for the struggle for liberty and freedom of our people. We were helped by the great Prince of the Buriats, Djam Bolon, who began parleys with General Ungern, then engaged in fighting the Bolsheviki in Transbaikalia, and invited him to enter Mongolia and help in the war against the Chinese. Then our struggle for liberty began."

Thus the Sait of Uliassutai explained the situation to me. Afterwards I heard that Baron Ungern, who had agreed to fight for the liberty of Mongolia, directed that the mobilization of the Mongolians in the northern districts be forwarded at once and promised to enter Mongolia with his own small detachment, moving along the River Kerulen. Afterwards he took up relations with the other Russian detachment of Colonel Kazagrandi and, together with the mobilized Mongolian riders, began the attack on Urga. Twice he was defeated but on the third of February, 1921, he succeeded in capturing the town and replaced the Living Buddha on the throne of the Khans.

At the end of March, however, these events were still unknown in Uliassutai. We knew neither of the fall of Urga nor of the destruction of the Chinese army of nearly 15,000 in the battles of Maimachen on the shore of the Tola and on the roads between Urga and Ude. The Chinese carefully concealed the truth by preventing anybody from passing westward from Urga. However, rumours existed and troubled all. The atmosphere became more and more tense, while the relations between the Chinese on the one side and the Mongolians and Russians on the other became more and more strained. At this time the Chinese Commissioner in Uliassutai was Wang Tsao-tsun and his advisor, Fu Hsiang, both very young and inexperienced men. The Chinese authorities had dismissed the Uliassutai Sait, the prominent Mongolian patriot, Prince Chultun Beyle, and had appointed a Lama Prince friendly to China, the former Vice-Minister of War in Urga. Oppression increased. The searching of Russian officers' and colonists' houses and quarters commenced, open relations with the Bolsheviki followed and arrest and beatings became common. The Russian officers formed a secret detachment of sixty men so that they could defend themselves. However, in this detachment disagreements soon sprang up between Lieutenant-Colonel M. M. Michailoff and some of his officers. It was evident that in the decisive moment the detachment must separate into factions.

We foreigners in council decided to make a thorough reconnaissance in order to know whether there was danger of Red troops arriving. My old companion and I agreed

to do this scouting.   Prince Chultun Beyle gave us a very
good guide—an old Mongol named Tzeren, who spoke
and read Russian perfectly.   He was a very interesting
personage, holding the position of interpreter with the
Mongolian authorities and sometimes with the Chinese
Commissioner.   Shortly before he had been sent as a
special envoy to Peking with very important despatches
and this incomparable horseman had made the journey
between Uliassutai and Peking, that is 1,800 miles, in nine
days, incredible as it may seem.   He prepared himself for
the journey by binding all his abdomen and chest, legs,
arms and neck with strong cotton bandages to protect
himself from the wracks and strains of such a period in
the saddle.   In his cap he bore three eagle feathers as a
token that he had received orders to fly like a bird. Armed
with a special document called a *tzara*, which gave him
the right to receive at all post stations the best horses, one
to ride and one fully saddled to lead as a change, together
with two *oulatchen* or guards to accompany him and
bring back the horses from the next station or *ourton*, he
made the distance of from fifteen to thirty miles between
stations at full gallop, stopping only long enough to have
the horses and guards changed before he was off again.
Ahead of him rode one *oulatchen* with the best horses
to enable him to announce and prepare in advance the
complement of steeds at the next station.   Each *oulatchen*
had three horses in all, so that he could swing from one
that had given out and release him to graze until his return to pick him up and lead or ride him back home.   At
every third *ourton*, without leaving his saddle, he received
a cup of hot green tea with salt and continued his race
southward.   After seventeen or eighteen hours of such

riding he stopped at the *ourton* for the night or what was left of it, devoured a leg of boiled mutton and slept. Thus he ate once a day and five times a day had tea; and so he traveled for nine days!

With this servant we moved out one cold winter morning in the direction of Kobdo, just over three hundred miles, because from there we had received the disquieting rumours that the Red troops had entered Ulankom and that the Chinese authorities had handed over to them all the Europeans in the town. We crossed the River Dzaphin on the ice. It is a terrible stream. Its bed is full of quicksands, which in summer suck in numbers of camels, horses and men. We entered a long, winding valley among the mountains covered with deep snow and here and there with groves of the black wood of the larch. About halfway to Kobdo we came across the *yurta* of a shepherd on the shore of the small Lake of Baga Nor, where evening and a strong wind whirling gusts of snow in our faces easily persuaded us to stop. By the *yurta* stood a splendid bay horse with a saddle richly ornamented with silver and coral. As we turned in from the road, two Mongols left the *yurta* very hastily; one of them jumped into the saddle and quickly disappeared in the plain behind the snowy hillocks. We clearly made out the flashing folds of his yellow robe under the great outer coat and saw his large knife sheathed in a green leather scabbard and handled with horn and ivory. The other man was the host of the *yurta,* the shepherd of a local prince, Novontziran. He gave signs of great pleasure at seeing us and receiving us in his *yurta*.

"Who was the rider on the bay horse?" we asked.

He dropped his eyes and was silent.

"Tell us," we insisted. "If you do not wish to speak his name, it means that you are dealing with a bad character."

"No! No!" he remonstrated, flourishing his hands. "He is a good, great man; but the law does not permit me to speak his name."

We at once understood that the man was either the chief of the shepherd or some high Lama. Consequently we did not further insist and began making our sleeping arrangements. Our host set three legs of mutton to boil for us, skillfully cutting out the bones with his heavy knife. We chatted and learned that no one had seen Red troops around this region but in Kobdo and in Ulankom the Chinese soldiers were oppressing the population, and were beating to death with the bamboo Mongol men who were defending their women against the ravages of these Chinese troops. Some of the Mongols had retreated to the mountains to join detachments under the command of Kaigordoff, an Altai Tartar officer who was supplying them with weapons.

CHAPTER XVIII

THE MYSTERIOUS LAMA AVENGER

WE rested soundly in the *yurta* after the two days of travel which had brought us one hundred seventy miles through the snow and sharp cold. Round the evening meal of juicy mutton we were talking freely and carelessly when suddenly we heard a low, hoarse voice:

"Sayn—Good evening!"

We turned around from the brazier to the door and saw a medium height, very heavy set Mongol in deerskin overcoat and cap with side flaps and the long, wide tying strings of the same material. Under his girdle lay the same large knife in the green sheath which we had seen on the departing horseman.

"Amoursayn," we answered.

He quickly untied his girdle and laid aside his overcoat. He stood before us in a wonderful gown of silk, yellow as beaten gold and girt with a brilliant blue sash. His cleanly shaven face, short hair, red coral rosary on the left hand and his yellow garment proved clearly that before us stood some high Lama Priest,—with a big Colt under his blue sash!

I turned to my host and Tzeren and read in their faces fear and veneration. The stranger came over to the brazier and sat down.

"Let's speak Russian," he said and took a bit of meat.

The conversation began. The stranger began to find fault with the Government of the Living Buddha in Urga.

"There they liberate Mongolia, capture Urga, defeat the Chinese army and here in the west they give us no news of it. We are without action here while the Chinese kill our people and steal from them. I think that Bogdo Khan might send us envoys. How is it the Chinese can send their envoys from Urga and Kiakhta to Kobdo, asking for assistance, and the Mongol Government cannot do it? Why?"

"Will the Chinese send help to Urga?" I asked.

Our guest laughed hoarsely and said: "I caught all the envoys, took away their letters and then sent them back . . . into the ground."

He laughed again and glanced around peculiarly with his blazing eyes. Only then did I notice that his cheekbones and eyes had lines strange to the Mongols of Central Asia. He looked more like a Tartar or a Kirghiz. We were silent and smoked our pipes.

"How soon will the detachment of Chahars leave Uliassutai?" he asked.

We answered that we had not heard about them. Our guest explained that from Inner Mongolia the Chinese authorities had sent out a strong detachment, mobilized from among the most warlike tribe of Chahars, which wander about the region just outside the Great Wall. Its chief was a notorious *hunghutze* leader promoted by the Chinese Government to the rank of captain on promising that he would bring under subjugation to the Chinese authorities all the tribes of the districts of Kobdo and

Urianhai. When he learned whither we were going and for what purpose, he said he could give us the most accurate news and relieve us from the necessity of going farther.

"Besides that, it is very dangerous," he said, "because Kobdo will be massacred and burned. I know this positively."

When he heard of our unsuccessful attempt to pass through Tibet, he became attentive and very sympathetic in his bearing toward us and, with evident feeling of regret, expressed himself strongly:

"Only I could have helped you in this enterprise, but not the Narabanchi Hutuktu. With my *laissez-passer* you could have gone anywhere in Tibet. I am Tushegoun Lama."

Tushegoun Lama! How many extraordinary tales I had heard about him. He is a Russian Kalmuck, who because of his propaganda work for the independence of the Kalmuck people made the acquaintance of many Russian prisons under the Czar and, for the same cause, added to his list under the Bolsheviki. He escaped to Mongolia and at once attained to great influence among the Mongols. It was no wonder, for he was a close friend and pupil of the Dalai Lama in Potala (Lhasa), was the most learned among the Lamites, a famous thaumaturgist and doctor. He occupied an almost independent position in his relationship with the Living Buddha and achieved to the leadership of all the old wandering tribes of Western Mongolia and Zungaria, even extending his political domination over the Mongolian tribes of Turkestan. His influence was irresistible, based as it was on his great control of mysterious science, as he expressed it; but I was also told that it has its foundation largely in the panicky fear which he could produce in the Mongols. Everyone who disobeyed his orders perished. Such an one never knew the day or the hour when, in his *yurta* or beside his galloping horse on the plains, the strange and powerful friend of the Dalai Lama would appear. The stroke of a knife, a bullet or strong fingers strangling the neck like a vise accomplished the justice of the plans of this miracle worker.

Without the walls of the *yurta* the wind whistled and roared and drove the frozen snow sharply against the stretched felt. Through the roar of the wind came the sound of many voices in mingled shouting, wailing and laughter. I felt that in such surroundings it were not difficult to dumbfound a wandering nomad with miracles, because Nature herself had prepared the setting for it. This thought had scarcely time to flash through my mind before Tushegoun Lama suddenly raised his head, looked sharply at me and said:

"There is very much unknown in Nature and the skill of using the unknown produces the miracle; but the power is given to few. I want to prove it to you and you may tell me afterwards whether you have seen it before or not."

He stood up, pushed back the sleeves of his yellow garment, seized his knife and strode across to the shepherd.

"Michik, stand up!" he ordered.

When the shepherd had risen, the Lama quickly unbuttoned his coat and bared the man's chest. I could not yet understand what was his intention, when suddenly the Tushegoun with all his force struck his knife into the chest of the shepherd. The Mongol fell all covered with blood, a splash of which I noticed on the yellow silk of the Lama's coat.

"What have you done?" I exclaimed.

"Sh! Be still," he whispered turning to me his now quite blanched face.

With a few strokes of the knife he opened the chest of the Mongol and I saw the man's lungs softly breathing and the distinct palpitations of the heart. The Lama touched these organs with his fingers but no more blood appeared to flow and the face of the shepherd was quite calm. He was lying with his eyes closed and appeared to be in deep and quiet sleep. As the Lama began to open his abdomen, I shut my eyes in fear and horror; and, when I opened them a little while later, I was still more dumbfounded at seeing the shepherd with his coat still open and his breast normal, quietly sleeping on his side and Tushegoun Lama sitting peacefullly by the brazier, smoking his pipe and looking into the fire in deep thought.

"It is wonderful!" I confessed. "I have never seen anything like it!"

"About what are you speaking?" asked the Kalmuck.

"About your demonstration or 'miracle,' as you call it," I answered.

"I never said anything like that," refuted the Kalmuck, with coldness in his voice.

"Did you see it?" I asked of my companion.

"What?" he queried in a dozing voice.

I realized that I had become the victim of the hypnotic power of Tushegoun Lama; but I preferred this to seeing an innocent Mongolian die, for I had not believed that Tushegoun Lama, after slashing open the bodies of his victims, could repair them again so readily.

The following day we took leave of our hosts. We decided to return, inasmuch as our mission was accomplished; and Tushegoun Lama explained to us that he would "move through space." He wandered over all Mongolia, lived both in the single, simple *yurta* of the shepherd and hunter and in the splendid tents of the princes and tribal chiefs, surrounded by deep veneration and panic-fear, enticing and cementing to him rich and poor alike with his miracles and prophecies. When bidding us adieu, the Kalmuck sorcerer slyly smiled and said:

"Do not give any information about me to the Chinese authorities."

Afterwards he added: "What happened to you yesterday evening was a futile demonstration. You Europeans will not recognize that we dark-minded nomads possess the powers of mysterious science. If you could only see the miracles and power of the Most Holy Tashi Lama, when at his command the lamps and candles before the ancient statue of Buddha light themselves and when the *ikons* of the gods begin to speak and prophesy! But there exists a more powerful and more holy man. . ."

"Is it the King of the World in Agharti?" I interrupted.

He stared and glanced at me in amazement.

"Have you heard about him?" he asked, as his brows knit in thought.

After a few seconds he raised his narrow eyes and said: "Only one man knows his holy name; only one man now living was ever in Agharti. That is I. This is the reason why the Most Holy Dalai Lama has honored me and why the Living Buddha in Urga fears me. But in vain, for I shall never sit on the Holy Throne of the highest priest in Lhasa nor reach that which has come down from Jenghiz Khan to the Head of our yellow Faith. I am no monk. I am a warrior and avenger.'

He jumped smartly into the saddle, whipped his horse and whirled away, flinging out as he left the common Mongolian phrase of adieu: *"Sayn! Sayn-bayna!"*

On the way back Tzeren related to us the hundreds of legends surrounding Tushegoun Lama. One tale especially remained in my mind. It was in 1911 or 1912 when the Mongols by armed force tried to attain their liberty in a struggle with the Chinese. The general Chinese headquarters in Western Mongolia was Kobdo, where they had about ten thousand soldiers under the command of their best officers. The command to capture Kobdo was sent to Hun Baldon, a simple shepherd who had distinguished himself in fights with the Chinese and received from the Living Buddha the title of Prince of Hun. Ferocious, absolutely without fear and possessing gigantic strength, Baldon had several times led to the attack his poorly armed Mongols but each time had been forced to retreat after losing many of his men under the machine-gun fire. Unexpectedly Tushegoun Lama arrived. He collected all the soldiers and then said to them:

"You must not fear death and must not retreat. You are fighting and dying for Mongolia, for which the gods have appointed a great destiny. See what the fate of Mongolia will be!"

He made a great sweeping gesture with his hand and all the soldiers saw the country round about set with rich *yurtas* and pastures covered with great herds of horses and cattle. On the plains appeared numerous horsemen on richly saddled steeds. The women were gowned in the finest of silk with massive silver rings in their ears and precious ornaments in their elaborate head dresses Chinese merchants led an endless caravan of merchandise up to distinguished looking Mongol Saits, surrounded by the gaily dressed *tzirik* or soldiers and proudly negotiating with the merchants for their wares.

Shortly the vision disappeared and Tushegoun began to speak.

"Do not fear death! It is a release from our labor on earth and the path to the state of constant blessings. Look to the East! Do you see your brothers and friends who have fallen in battle?"

"We see, we see!" the Mongol warriors exclaimed in astonishment, as they all looked upon a great group of dwellings which might have been *yurtas* or the arches of temples flushed with a warm and kindly light. Red and yellow silk were interwoven in bright bands that covered the walls and floor, everywhere the gilding on pillars and walls gleamed brightly; on the great red altar burned the thin sacrificial candles in gold candelabra, beside the massive silver vessels filled with milk and nuts; on soft pillows about the floor sat the Mongols who had fallen in the previous attack on Kobdo. Before them stood low, lacquered tables laden with many dishes of steaming, succulent flesh of the lamb and the kid, with high jugs of wine and tea, with plates of *borsuk,* a kind of sweet, rich cakes, with aromatic *zatouran* covered with sheep's fat, with bricks of dried cheese, with dates, raisins and nuts. These fallen soldiers smoked golden pipes and chatted gaily.

This vision in turn also disappeared and before the

gazing Mongols stood only the mysterious Kalmuck with his hand upraised.

"To battle and return not without victory! I am with you in the fight."

The attack began. The Mongols fought furiously, perished by the hundreds but not before they had rushed into the heart of Kobdo. Then was re-enacted the long forgotten picture of Tartar hordes destroying European towns. Hun Baldon ordered carried over him a triangle of lances with brilliant red streamers, a sign that he gave up the town to the soldiers for three days. Murder and pillage began. All the Chinese met their death there. The town was burned and the walls of the fortress destroyed. Afterwards Hun Baldon came to Uliassutai and also destroyed the Chinese fortress there. The ruins of it still stand with the broken embattlements and towers, the useless gates and the remnants of the burned official quarters and soldiers' barracks.

CHAPTER XIX

WILD CHAHARS

AFTER our return to Uliassutai we heard that disquieting news had been received by the Mongol Sait
from Muren Kure. The letter stated that Red Troops were
pressing Colonel Kazagrandi very hard in the region of
Lake Kosogol. The Sait feared the advance of the Red
troops southward to Uliassutai. Both the American firms
liquidated their affairs and all our friends were prepared
for a quick exit, though they hesitated at the thought of
leaving the town, as they were afraid of meeting the detachment of Chahars sent from the east. We decided
to await the arrival of this detachment, as their coming
could change the whole course of events. In a few days
they came, two hundred warlike Chahar brigands under
the command of a former Chinese *hunghutze*. He was a
tall, skinny man with hands that reached almost to his
knees, a face blackened by wind and sun and mutilated
with two long scars down over his forehead and cheek,
the making of one of which had also closed one of his
hawklike eyes, topped off with a shaggy coonskin cap—
such was the commander of the detachment of Chahars.
A personage very dark and stern, with whom a night
meeting on a lonely street could not be considered a
pleasure by any bent of the imagination.

The detachment made camp within the destroyed fortress, near to the single Chinese building that had not been razed and which was now serving as headquarters for the Chinese Commissioner. On the very day of their arrival the Chahars pillaged a Chinese *dugun* or trading house not half a mile from the fortress and also offended the wife of the Chinese Commissioner by calling her a "traitor." The Chahars, like the Mongols, were quite right in their stand, because the Chinese Commissioner Wang Tsao-tsun had on his arrival in Uliassutai followed the Chinese custom of demanding a Mongolian wife. The servile new Sait had given orders that a beautiful and suitable Mongolian girl be found for him. One was so run down and placed in his *yamen*, together with her big wrestling Mongol brother who was to be a guard for the Commissioner but who developed into the nurse for the little white Pekingese pug which the official presented to his new wife.

Burglaries, squabbles and drunken orgies of the Chahars followed, so that Wang Tsoa-tsun exerted all his efforts to hurry the detachment westward to Kobdo and farther into Urianhai.

One cold morning the inhabitants of Uliassutai rose to witness a very stern picture. Along the main street of the town the detachment was passing. They were riding on small, shaggy ponies, three abreast; were dressed in warm blue coats with sheepskin overcoats outside and crowned with the regulation coonskin caps; armed from head to foot. They rode with wild shouts and cheers, very greedily eyeing the Chinese shops and the houses of the Russian colonists. At their head rode the one-eyed *hunghutze* chief with three horsemen behind him in white overcoats, who carried waving banners and blew what may have been meant for music through great conch shells. One of the Chahars could not resist and so jumped out of his saddle and made for a Chinese shop along the street. Immediately the anxious cries of the Chinese merchants came from the shop. The *hunghutze* swung round, noticed the horse at the door of the shop and realized what was happening. Immediately he reined his horse and made for the spot. With his raucous voice he called the Chahar out. As he came, he struck him full in the face with his whip and with all his strength. Blood flowed from the slashed cheek. But the Chahar was in the saddle in a second without a murmur and galloped to his place in the file. During this exit of the Chahars all the people were hidden in their houses, anxiously peeping through cracks and corners of the windows. But the Chahars passed peacefully out and only when they met a caravan carrying Chinese wine about six miles from town did their native tendency display itself again in pillaging and emptying several containers. Somewhere in the vicinity of Hargana they were ambushed by Tushe-goun Lama and so treated that never again will the plains of Chahar welcome the return of these warrior sons who were sent out to conquer the Soyot descendants of the ancient Tuba.

The day the column left Uliassutai a heavy snow fell, so that the road became impassable. The horses first were up to their knees, tired out and stopped. Some Mongol horsemen reached Uliassutai the following day after great hardship and exertion, having made only twenty-five miles in forty-eight hours. Caravans were compelled to stop along the routes. The Mongols would not consent even to attempt journeys with oxen and yaks which made but ten or twelve miles a day. Only camels could be used but there were too few and their drivers did **not** feel that they could make the first railway station of Kuku-Hoto, which was about fourteen hundred miles away. We were forced again to wait: for which? Death or salvation? Only our own energy and force could save us. Consequently my friend and I started out, supplied with a tent, stove and food, for a new reconnaissance along the shore of Lake Kosogol, whence the Mongol Sait expected the new invasion of Red troops.

CHAPTER XX

THE DEMON OF JAGISSTAI

OUR small group consisting of four mounted and one pack camel moved northward along the valley of the River Boyagol in the direction of the Tarbagatai Mountains. The road was rocky and covered deep with snow. Our camels walked very carefully, sniffing out the way as our guide shouted the "Ok! Ok!" of the camel drivers to urge them on. We left behind us the fortress and Chinese *dugun,* swung round the shoulder of a ridge and, after fording several times an open stream, began the ascent of the mountain. The scramble was hard and dangerous. Our camels picked their way most cautiously, moving their ears constantly, as is their habit in such stress. The trail zigzagged into mountain ravines, passed over the tops of ridges, slipped back down again into shallower valleys but ever made higher and higher altitudes. At one place under the grey clouds that tipped the ridges we saw away up on the wide expanse of snow some black spots.

"Those are the *obo,* the sacred signs and altars for the bad demons watching this pass," explained the guide. "This pass is called Jagisstai. Many very old tales about it have been kept alive, ancient as these mountains themselves."

We encouraged him to tell us some of them.

The Mongol, rocking on his camel and looking carefully all around him, began his tale.

"It was long ago, very long ago. . . . The grandson of the great Jenghiz Khan sat on the throne of China and ruled all Asia. The Chinese killed their Khan and wanted to exterminate all his family but a holy old Lama slipped the wife and little son out of the palace and carried them off on swift camels beyond the Great Wall, where they sank into our native plains. The Chinese made a long search for the trails of our refugees and at last found where they had gone. They despatched a strong detachment on fleet horses to capture them. Sometimes the Chinese nearly came up with the fleeing heir of our Khan but the Lama called down from Heaven a deep snow, through which the camels could pass while the horses were inextricably held. This Lama was from a distant monastery. We shall pass this hospice of Jahantsi Kure. In order to reach it one must cross over the Jagisstai. And it was just here the old Lama suddenly became ill, rocked in his saddle and fell dead. Ta Sin Lo, the widow of the Great Khan, burst into tears; but, seeing the Chinese riders galloping there below across the valley, pressed on toward the pass. The camels were tired, stopping every moment, nor did the woman know how to stimulate and drive them on. The Chinese riders came nearer and nearer. Already she heard their shouts of joy, as they felt within their grasp the prize of the mandarins for the murder of the heir of the Great Khan. The heads of the mother and the son would be brought to Peking and exposed on the Ch'ien Mên for the mockery and insults of the people. The frightened mother lifted her little son toward heaven and exclaimed:

" 'Earth and Gods of Mongolia, behold the offspring
of the man who has glorified the name of the Mongols
from one end of the world to the other! Allow not this
very flesh of Jenghiz Khan to perish!'

"At this moment she noticed a white mouse sitting
on a rock nearby. It jumped to her knees and said:

" 'I am sent to help you. Go on calmly and do not
fear. The pursuers of you and your son, to whom is
destined a life of glory, have come to the last bourne of
their lives.'

"Ta Sin Lo did not see how one small mouse could
hold in check three hundred men. The mouse jumped
back to the ground and again spoke:

" 'I am the demon of ᴛᴀʀbagatai, Jagasstai. I am
mighty and beloved of the Gods but, because you doubted
the powers of the miracle-speaking mouse, from this day
the Jagasstai will be dangerous for the good and bad
alike.'

"The Khan's widow and son were saved but Jagasstai
has ever remained merciless. During the journey over
this pass one must always be on one's guard. The demon
of the mountain is ever ready to lead the traveler to
destruction."

All the tops of the ridges of the Tarbagatai are thickly
dotted with the *obo* of rocks and branches. In one place
there was even erected a tower of stones as an altar to
propitiate the Gods for the doubts of Ta Sin Lo. Evidently the demon expected us. When we began our
ascent of the main ridge, he blew into our faces with a
sharp, cold wind, whistled and roared and afterwards
began casting over us whole blocks of snow torn off
the drifts above. We could not distinguish anything

around us, scarcely seeing the camel immediately in front.
Suddenly I felt a shock and looked about me. Nothing
unusual was visible. I was seated comfortably between
two leather saddle bags filled with meat and bread but
. . . I could not see the head of my camel. He had
disappeared. It seemed that he had slipped and fallen
to the bottom of a shallow ravine, while the bags which
were slung across his back without straps had caught on
a rock and stopped with myself there in the snow. This
time the demon of Jagasstai only played a joke but one
that did not satisfy him. He began to show more and
more anger. With furious gusts of wind he almost
dragged us and our bags from the camels and nearly
knocked over our humped steeds, blinded us with frozen
snow and prevented us from breathing. Through long
hours we dragged slowly on in the deep snow, often falling over the edge of the rocks. At last we entered a
small valley where the wind whistled and roared with
a thousand voices. It had grown dark. The Mongol
wandered around searching for the trail and finally came
back to us, flourishing his arms and saying:

"We have lost the road. We must spend the night
here. It is very bad because we shall have no wood for
our stove and the cold will grow worse."

With great difficulties and with frozen hands we managed to set up our tent in the wind, placing in it the now
useless stove. We covered the tent with snow, dug deep,
long ditches in the drifts and forced our camels to lie
down in them by shouting the "Dzuk! Dzuk!" command
to kneel. Then we brought our packs into the tent.

My companion rebelled against the thought of spend-
ing a cold night with a stove hard by.

"I am going out to look for firewood," said he very
decisively; and at that took up the ax and started.   He
returned after an hour with a big section of a telegraph
pole.

"You, Jenghiz Khans," said he, rubbing his frozen
hands, "take your axes and go up there to the left on
the mountain and you will find the telegraph poles that
have been cut down.   I made acquaintance with the old
Jagasstai and he showed me the poles."

Just a little way from us the line of the Russian tele-
graphs passed, that which had connected Irkutsk with
Uliassutai before the days of the Bolsheviki and which
the Chinese had commanded the Mongols to cut down
and take the wire.   These poles are now the salvation of
travelers crossing the pass.   Thus we spent the night in a
warm tent, supped well from hot meat soup with vermi-
celli, all in the very center of the dominion of the angered
Jagasstai.   Early the next morning we found the road
not more than two or three hundred paces from our tent
and continued our hard trip over the ridge of Tarbagatai.
At the head of the Adair River valley we noticed a flock
of the Mongolian crows with carmine beaks circling
among the rocks.   We approached the place and discovered the recently fallen bodies of a horse and rider.
What had happened to them was difficult to guess.   They
lay close together; the bridle was wound around the right
wrist of the man; no trace of knife or bullet was found.
It was impossible to make out the features of the man.
His overcoat was Mongolian but his trousers and under
jacket were not of the Mongolian pattern.   We asked
ourselves what had happened to him.

Our Mongol bowed his head in anxiety and said in

hushed but assured tones: "It is the vengeance of Jagasstai. The rider did not make sacrifice at the southern
obo and the demon has strangled him and his horse."

At last Tarbagatai was behind us. Before us lay the
valley of the Adair. It was a narrow zigzagging plain
following along the river bed between close mountain
ranges and covered with a rich grass. It was cut into
two parts by the road along which the prostrate telegraph
poles now lay, as the stumps of varying heights and long
stretches of wire completed the débris. This destruction
of the telegraph line between Irkutsk and Uliassutai was
necessary and incident to the aggressive Chinese policy
in Mongolia.

Soon we began to meet large herds of sheep, which
were digging through the snow to the dry but very
nutritious grass. In some places yaks and oxen were
seen on the high slopes of the mountains. Only once,
however, did we see a shepherd, for all of them, spying
us first, had made off to the mountains or hidden in the
ravines. We did not even discover any *yurtas* along the
way. The Mongols had also concealed all their movable
homes in the folds of the mountains out of sight and
away from the reach of the strong winds. Nomads are
very skilful in choosing the places for their winter dwellings. I had often in winter visited the Mongolian *yurtas*
set in such sheltered places that, as I came off the windy
plains, I felt as though I were in a conservatory. Once
we came up to a big herd of sheep. But as we approached
most of the herd gradually withdrew, leaving one part
that remained unmoved as the other worked off across
the plains. From this section soon about thirty of forty
head emerged and went scrambling and leaping right up

the mountain side. I took up my glasses and began to observe them. The part of the herd that remained behind
were common sheep; the large section that had drawn
off over the plain were Mongolian antelopes (*gazella
gutturosa*); while the few that had taken to the mountain
were the big horned sheep (*ovis argali*). All this company had been grazing together with the domestic sheep
on the plains of the Adair, which attracted them with its
good grass and clear water. In many places the river
was not frozen and in some places I saw great clouds
of steam over the surface of the open water. In the
meantime some of the antelopes and the mountain sheep
began looking at us.

"Now they will soon begin to cross our trail," laughed
the Mongol; "very funny beasts. Sometimes the antelopes course for miles in their endeavor to outrun and
cross in front of our horses and then, when they have
done so, go loping quietly off."

I had already seen this strategy of the antelopes and
I decided to make use of it for the purpose of the hunt.
We organized our chase in the following manner. We
let one Mongol with the pack camel proceed as we had
been traveling and the other three of us spread out like
a fan headed toward the herd on the right of our true
course. The herd stopped and looked about puzzled, for
their etiquette required that they should cross the path
of all four of these riders at once. Confusion began.
They counted about three thousand heads. All this army
began to run from one side to another but without forming any distinct groups. Whole squadrons of them ran
before us and then, noticing another rider, came coursing
back and made anew the same manœuvre. One group

of about fifty head rushed in two rows toward my point. When they were about a hundred and fifty paces away I shouted and fired. They stopped at once and began to whirl round in one spot, running into one another and even jumping over one another. Their panic cost them dear, for I had time to shoot four times to bring down two beautiful heads. My friend was even more fortunate than I, for he shot only once into the herd as it rushed past him in parallel lines and dropped two with the same bullet.

Meanwhile the *argali* had gone farther up the mountainside and taken stand there in a row like so many soldiers, turning to gaze at us. Even at this distance I could clearly distinguish their muscular bodies with their majestic heads and stalwart horns. Picking up our prey, we overtook the Mongol who had gone on ahead and continued our way. In many places we came across the carcasses of sheep with necks torn and the flesh of the sides eaten off.

"It is the work of wolves," said the Mongol. "They are always hereabout in large numbers."

We came across several more herds of antelope, which ran along quietly enough until they had made a comfortable distance ahead of us and then with tremendous leaps and bounds crossed our bows like the proverbial chicken on the road. Then, after a couple of hundred paces at this speed, they stopped and began to graze quite calmly. Once I turned my camel back and the whole herd immediately took up the challenge again, coursed along parallel with me until they had made sufficient distance for their ideas of safety and then once more rushed across the road ahead of me as though it were paved with red hot stones, only to assume their previous calmness and graze back on the same side of the trail from which our column had first started them. On another occasion I did this three times with a particular herd and laughed long and heartily at their stupid customs.

We passed a very unpleasant night in this valley. We stopped on the shore of the frozen stream in a spot where we found shelter from the wind under the lee of a high shore. In our stove we did have a fire and in our kettle boiling water. Also our tent was warm and cozy. We were quietly resting with pleasant thoughts of supper to soothe us, when suddenly a howling and laughter as though from some inferno burst upon us from just outside the tent, while from the other side of the valley came the long and doleful howls in answer.

"Wolves," calmly explained the Mongol, who took my revolver and went out of the tent. He did not return for some time but at last we heard a shot and shortly after he entered.

"I scared them a little," said he. "They had congregated on the shore of the Adair around the body of a camel."

"And they have not touched our camels?" we asked.

"We shall make a bonfire behind our tent; then they will not bother us."

After our supper we turned in but I lay awake for a long time listening to the crackle of the wood in the fire, the deep sighing breaths of the camels and the distant howling of the packs of wolves; but finally, even with all these noises, fell asleep. How long I had been asleep I did not know when suddenly I was awakened by a strong blow in the side. I was lying at the very edge of the tent and someone from outside had, without the least ceremony, pushed strongly against me. I thought it was one of the camels chewing the felt of the tent. I took my Mauser and struck the wall. A sharp scream was followed by the sound of quick running over the pebbles. In the morning we discovered the tracks of wolves approaching our tent from the side opposite to the fire and followed them to where they had begun to dig under the tent wall; but evidently one of the would-be robbers was forced to retreat with a bruise on his head from the handle of the Mauser.

Wolves and eagles are the servants of Jagasstai, the Mongol very seriously instructed us. However, this does not prevent the Mongols from hunting them. Once in the camp of Prince Baysei I witnessed such a hunt. The Mongol horsemen on the best of his steeds overtook the wolves on the open plain and killed them with heavy bamboo sticks or *tashur*. A Russian veterinary surgeon taught the Mongols to poison wolves with strychnine but the Mongols soon abandoned this method because of its danger to the dogs, the faithful friends and allies of the nomad. They do not, however, touch the eagles and hawks but even feed them. When the Mongols are slaughtering animals they often cast bits of meat up into the air for the hawks and eagles to catch in flight, just as we throw a bit of meat to a dog. Eagles and hawks fight and drive away the magpies and crows, which are very dangerous for cattle and horses, because they scratch and peck at the smallest wound or abrasion on the backs of the animals until they make them into uncurable areas which they continue to harass.

CHAPTER XXI

THE NEST OF DEATH

O UR camels were trudging to a slow but steady measure on toward the north. We were making twenty-
five to thirty miles a day as we approached a small
monastery that lay to the left of our route. It was in
the form of a square of large buildings surrounded by
a high fence of thick poles. Each side had an opening
in the middle leading to the four entrances of the temple
in the center of the square. The temple was built with
the red lacquered columns and the Chinese style roofs
and dominated the surrounding low dwellings of the
Lamas. On the opposite side of the road lay what appeared to be a Chinese fortress but which was in reality
a trading compound or *dugun,* which the Chinese always
build in the form of a fortress with double walls a few
feet apart, within which they place their houses and shops
and usually have twenty or thirty traders fully armed for
any emergency. In case of need these *duguns* can be
used as blockhouses and are capable of withstanding long
sieges. Between the *dugun* and the monastery and nearer
to the road I made out the camp of some nomads. Their
horses and cattle were nowhere to be seen. Evidently
the Mongols had stopped here for some time and had left
their cattle in the mountains. Over several *yurtas* waved

multi-colored triangular flags, a sign of the presence of disease. Near some *yurtas* high poles were stuck into the ground with Mongol caps at their tops, which indicated that the host of the *yurta* had died. The packs of dogs wandering over the plain showed that the dead bodies lay somewhere near, either in the ravines or along the banks of the river.

As we approached the camp, we heard from a distance the frantic beating of drums, the mournful sounds of the flute and shrill, mad shouting. Our Mongol went forward to investigate for us and reported that several Mongolian families had come here to the monastery to seek aid from the Hutuktu Jahansti who was famed for his miracles of healing. The people were stricken with leprosy and black smallpox and had come from long distances only to find that the Hutuktu was not at the monastery but had gone to the Living Buddha in Urga. Consequently they had been forced to invite the witch doctors. The people were dying one after another. Just the day before they had cast on the plain the twenty-seventh man.

Meanwhile, as we talked, the witch doctor came out of one of the *yurtas*. He was an old man with a cataract on one eye and with a face deeply scarred by smallpox. He was dressed in tatters with various colored bits of cloth hanging down from his waist. He carried a drum and a flute. We could see froth on his blue lips and madness in his eyes. Suddenly he began to whirl round and dance with a thousand prancings of his long legs and writhings of his arms and shoulders, still beating the drum and playing the flute or crying and raging at intervals, ever accelerating his movements until at last with pallid face and bloodshot eyes he fell on the snow, where he continued to writhe and give out his incoherent cries. In this manner the doctor treated his patients, frightening with his madness the bad devils that carry disease. Another witch doctor gave his patients dirty, muddy water, which I learned was the water from the bath of the very person of the Living Buddha who had washed in it his "divine" body born from the sacred flower of the lotus.

"Om! Om!" both witches continuously screamed.

While the doctors fought with the devils, the ill people were left to themselves. They lay in high fever under the heaps of sheepskins and overcoats, were delirious, raved and threw themselves about. By the braziers squatted adults and children who were still well, indifferently chatting, drinking tea and smoking. In all the *yurtas* I saw the diseased and the dead and such misery and physical horrors as cannot be described.

And I thought: "Oh, Great Jenghiz Khan! Why did you with your keen understanding of the whole situation of Asia and Europe, you who devoted all your life to the glory of the name of the Mongols, why did you not give to your own people, who preserve their old morality, honesty and peaceful customs, the enlightenment that would have saved them from such death? Your bones in the mausoleum at Karakorum being destroyed by the centuries that pass over them must cry out against the rapid disappearance of your formerly great people, who were feared by half the civilized world!"

Such thoughts filled my brain when I saw this camp of the dead tomorrow and when I heard the groans, shoutings and raving of dying men, women and children. Somewhere in the distance the dogs were howling mournfully, and monotonously the drum of the tired witch rolled.

"Forward!" I could not witness longer this dark horror, which I had no means or force to eradicate. We quickly passed on from the ominous place. Nor could we shake the thought that some horrible invisible spirit was following us from this scene of terror. "The devils of disease?" "The pictures of horror and misery?" "The souls of men who have been sacrificed on the altar of darkness of Mongolia?" An inexplicable fear penetrated into our consciousness from whose grasp we could not release ourselves. Only when we had turned from the road, passed over a timbered ridge into a bowl in the mountains from which we could see neither Jahantsi Kure, the *dugun* nor the squirming grave of dying Mongols could we breathe freely again.

Presently we discovered a large lake. It was Tisingol. Near the shore stood a large Russian house, the telegraph station between Kosogol and Uliassutai.

CHAPTER XXII

AMONG THE MURDERERS

A S we approached the telegraph station, we were met by a blonde young man who was in charge of the office, Kanine by name. With some little confusion he offered us a place in his house for the night. When we entered the room, a tall, lanky man rose from the table and indecisively walked toward us, looking very attentively at us the while.

"Guests . . ." explained Kanine. "They are going to Khathyl. Private persons, strangers, foreigners . . ."

"A-h," drawled the stranger in a quiet, comprehending tone.

While we were untying our girdles and with difficulty getting out of our great Mongolian coats, the tall man was animatedly whispering something to our host. As we approached the table to sit down and rest, I overheard him say: "We are forced to postpone it," and saw Kanine simply nod in answer.

Several other people were seated at the table, among them the assistant of Kanine, a tall blonde man with a white face, who talked like a Gatling gun about everything imaginable. He was half crazy and his semi-madness expressed itself when any loud talking, shouting or sudden sharp report led him to repeat the words of the one to whom he was talking at the time or to relate in a mechanical, hurried manner stories of what was happening around him just at this particular juncture. The wife of Kanine, a pale, young, exhausted-looking woman with frightened eyes and a face distorted by fear, was also there and near her a young girl of fifteen with cropped hair and dressed like a man, as well as the two small sons of Kanine. We made acquaintance with all of them. The tall stranger called himself Gorokoff, a Russian colonist from Samgaltai, and presented the short-haired girl as his sister. Kanine's wife looked at us with plainly discernible fear and said nothing, evidently displeased over our being there. However, we had no choice and consequently began drinking tea and eating our bread and cold meat.

Kanine told us that ever since the telegraph line had been destroyed all his family and relatives had felt very keenly the poverty and hardship that naturally followed. The Bolsheviki did not send him any salary from Irkutsk, so that he was compelled to shift for himself as best he could. They cut and cured hay for sale to the Russian colonists, handled private messages and merchandise from Khathyl to Uliassutai and Samgaltai, bought and sold cattle, hunted and in this manner managed to exist. Gorokoff announced that his commercial affairs compelled him to go to Khathyl and that he and his sister would be glad to join our caravan. He had a most unprepossessing, angry-looking face with colorless eyes that always avoided those of the person with whom he was speaking. During the conversation we asked Kanine if there were Russian colonists near by, to which he answered with knitted brow and a look of disgust on his face:

"There is one rich old man, Bobroff, who lives a *verst*

away from our station; but I would not advise you to visit him. He is a miserly, inhospitable old fellow who does not like guests."

During these words of her husband Madame Kanine dropped her eyes and contracted her shoulders in something resembling a shudder. Gorokoff and his sister smoked along indifferently. I very clearly remarked all this as well as the hostile tone of Kanine, the confusion of his wife and the artificial indifference of Gorokoff; and I determined to see the old colonist given such a bad name by Kanine. In Uliassutai I knew two Bobroffs. I said to Kanine that I had been asked to hand a letter personally to Bobroff and, after finishing my tea, put on my overcoat and went out.

The house of Bobroff stood in a deep sink in the mountains, surrounded by a high fence over which the low roofs of the houses could be seen. A light shone through the window. I knocked at the gate. A furious barking of dogs answered me and through the cracks of the fence I made out four huge black Mongol dogs, showing their teeth and growling as they rushed toward the gate. Inside the court someone opened the door and called out: "Who is there?"

I answered that I was traveling through from Uliassutai. The dogs were first caught and chained and I was then admitted by a man who looked me over very carefully and inquiringly from head to foot. A revolver handle stuck out of his pocket. Satisfied with his observations and learning that I knew his relatives, he warmly welcomed me to the house and presented me to his wife, a dignified old woman, and to his beautiful little adopted daughter, a girl of five years. She had been found on the plain beside the dead body of her mother exhausted in her attempt to escape from the Bolsheviki in Siberia.

Bobroff told me that the Russian detachment of Kazagrandi had succeeded in driving the Red troops away from the Kosogol and that we could consequently continue our trip to Khathyl without danger.

"Why did you not stop with me instead of with those brigands?" asked the old fellow.

I began to question him and received some very important news. It seemed that Kanine was a Bolshevik, the agent of the Irkutsk Soviet, and stationed here for purposes of observation. However, now he was rendered harmless, because the road between him and Irkutsk was interrupted. Still from Biisk in the Altai country had just come a very important commissar.

"Gorokoff?" I asked.

"That's what he calls himself," replied the old fellow; "but I am also from Biisk and I know everyone there. His real name is Pouzikoff and the short-haired girl with him is his mistress. He is the commissar of the 'Cheka' and she is the agent of this establishment. Last August the two of them shot with their revolvers seventy bound officers from Kolchak's army. Villainous, cowardly murderers! Now they have come here for a reconnaissance. They wanted to stay in my house but I knew them too well and refused them place."

"And you do not fear him?" I asked, remembering the different words and glances of these people as they sat at the table in the station.

"No," answered the old man. "I know how to defend myself and my family and I have a protector too—my son, such a shot, a rider and a fighter as does not exist in all Mongolia. I am very sorry that you will not make the acquaintance of my boy. He has gone off to the herds and will return only tomorrow evening."

We took most cordial leave of each other and I promised to stop with him on my return.

"Well, what yarns did Bobroff tell you about us?" was the question with which Kanine and Gorokoff met me when I came back to the station.

"Nothing about you," I answered, "because he did not even want to speak with me when he found out that I was staying in your house. What is the trouble between you?" I asked of them, expressing complete astonishment on my face.

"It is an old score," growled Gorokoff.

"A malicious old churl," Kanine added in agreement, the while the frightened, suffering-laden eyes of his wife again gave expression to terrifying horror, as if she momentarily expected a deadly blow. Gorokoff began to pack his luggage in preparation for the journey with us the following morning. We prepared our simple beds in an adjoining room and went to sleep. I whispered to my friend to keep his revolver handy for anything that might happen but he only smiled as he dragged his revolver and his ax from his coat to place them under his pillow.

"This people at the outset seemed to me very suspicious," he whispered. "They are cooking up something crooked. Tomorrow I shall ride behind this Gorokoff and shall prepare for him a very faithful one of my bullets, a little dum-dum."

The Mongols spent the night under their tent in the

open court beside their camels, because they wanted to be near to feed them. About seven o'clock we started. My friend took up his post as rear guard to our caravan, keeping all the time behind Gorokoff, who with his sister, both armed from tip to toe, rode splendid mounts.

"How have you kept your horses in such fine condition coming all the way from Samgaltai?" I inquired as I looked over their fine beasts.

When he answered that these belonged to his host, I realized that Kanine was not so poor as he made out; for any rich Mongol would have given him in exchange for one of these lovely animals enough sheep to have kept his household in mutton for a whole year.

Soon we came to a large swamp surrounded by dense brush, where I was much astonished by seeing literally hundreds of white *kuropatka* or partridges. Out of the water rose a flock of duck with a mad rush as we hove in sight. Winter, cold driving wind, snow and wild ducks! The Mongol explained it to me thus:

"This swamp always remains warm and never freezes. The wild ducks live here the year round and the *kuropatka* too, finding fresh food in the soft warm earth."

As I was speaking with the Mongol I noticed over the swamp a tongue of reddish-yellow flame. It flashed and disappeared at once but later, on the farther edge, two further tongues ran upward. I realized that here was the real will-o'-the-wisp surrounded by so many thousands of legends and explained so simply by chemistry as merely a flash of methane or swamp gas generated by the putrefying of vegetable matter in the warm damp earth.

"Here dwell the demons of Adair, who are in perpetual war with those of Muren," explained the Mongol.

"Indeed," I thought, "if in prosaic Europe in our days the inhabitants of our villages believe these flames to be some wild sorcery, then surely in the land of mystery they must be at least the evidences of war between the demons of two neighboring rivers!"

After passing this swamp we made out far ahead of us a large monastery. Though this was some half mile off the road, the Gorokoffs said they would ride over to it to make some purchases in the Chinese shops there. They quickly rode away, promising to overtake us shortly, but we did not see them again for a while. They slipped away without leaving any trail but we met them later in very unexpected circumstances of fatal portent for them. On our part we were highly satisfied that we were rid of them so soon and, after they were gone, I imparted to my friend the information gleaned from Bobroff the evening before.

CHAPTER XXIII

ON A VOLCANO

THE following evening we arrived at Khathyl, a small Russian settlement of ten scattered houses in the valley of the Egingol or Yaga, which here takes its waters from the Kosogol half a mile above the village. The Kosogol is a huge Alpine lake, deep and cold, eighty-five miles in length and from ten to thirty in width. On the western shore live the Darkhat Soyots, who call it Hubsugul, the Mongols, Kosogol. Both the Soyots and Mongols consider this a terrible and sacred lake. It is very easy to understand this prejudice because the lake lies in a region of present volcanic activity, where in the summer on perfectly calm sunny days it sometimes lashes itself into great waves that are dangerous not only to the native fishing boats but also to the large Russian passenger steamers that ply on the lake. In winter also it sometimes entirely breaks up its covering of ice and gives off great clouds of steam. Evidently the bottom of the lake is sporadically pierced by discharging hot springs or, perhaps, by streams of lava. Evidence of some great underground convulsion like this is afforded by the mass of killed fish which at times dams the outlet river in its shallow places. The lake is exceedingly rich in fish, chiefly varieties of trout and salmon, and is famous for its wonderful "white fish," which was previously sent all over Siberia and even down into Manchuria so far as Moukden. It is fat and remarkably tender and produces fine caviar. Another variety in the lake is the white *khayrus* or trout, which in the migration season, contrary to the customs of most fish, goes down stream into the Yaga, where it sometimes fills the river from bank to bank with swarms of backs breaking the surface of the water. However, this fish is not caught, because it is infested with worms and is unfit for food. Even cats and dogs will not touch it. This is a very interesting phemonenon and was being investigated and studied by Professor Dorogostaisky of the University at Irkutsk when the coming of the Bolsheviki interrupted his work.

In Khathyl we found a panic. The Russian detachment of Colonel Kazagrandi, after having twice defeated the Bolsheviki and well on its march against Irkutsk, was suddenly rendered impotent and scattered through internal strife among the officers. The Bolsheviki took advantage of this situation, increased their forces to one thousand men and began a forward movement to recover what they had lost, while the remnants of Colonel Kazagrandi's detachment were retreating on Khathyl, where he determined to make his last stand against the Reds. The inhabitants were loading their movable property with their families into carts and scurrying away from the town, leaving all their cattle and horses to whomsoever should have the power to seize and hold them. One party intended to hide in the dense larch forest and the mountain ravines not far away, while another party made southward for Muren Kure and Uliassutai. The morning following our arrival the Mongol official received word that the Red troops had outflanked Colonel Kazagrandi's men and were approaching Khathyl. The Mongol loaded his documents and his servants on eleven camels and left his *yamen*. Our Mongol guides, without ever saying a word to us, secretly slipped off with him and left us without camels. Our situation thus became desperate. We hastened to the colonists who had not yet got away to bargain with them for camels, but they had previously, in anticipation of trouble, sent their herds to distant Mongols and so could do nothing to help us. Then we betook ourselves to Dr. V. G. Gay, a veterinarian living in the town, famous throughout Mongolia for his battle against rinderpest. He lived here with his family and after being forced to give up his government work became a cattle dealer. He was a most interesting person, clever and energetic, and the one who had been appointed under the Czarist régime to purchase all the meat supplies from Mongolia for the Russian Army on the German Front. He organized a huge enterprise in Mongolia but when the Bolsheviki seized power in 1917 he transferred his allegiance and began to work with them. Then in May, 1918, when the Kolchak forces drove the Bolsheviki out of Siberia, he was arrested and taken for trial. However, he was released because he was looked upon as the single individual to organize this big Mongolian enterprise and he handed to Admiral Kolchak all the supplies of meat and the silver formerly received from the Soviet commissars. At this time Gay had been serving as the chief organizer and supplier of the forces of Kazagrandi.

When we went to him, he at once suggested that we take the only thing left, some poor, broken-down horses which would be able to carry us the sixty miles to Muren

Kure, where we could secure camels to return to Ulias-sutai. However, even these were being kept some distance from the town so that we should have to spend the night there, the night in which the Red troops were expected to arrive. Also we were much astonished to see that Gay was remaining there with his family right up to the time of the expected arrival of the Reds. The only others in the town were a few Cossacks, who had been ordered to stay behind to watch the movements of the Red troops. The night came. My friend and I were prepared either to fight or, in the last event, to commit suicide. We stayed in a small house near the Yaga, where some workmen were living who could not, and did not feel it necessary to, leave. They went up on a hill from which they could scan the whole country up to the range from behind which the Red detachment must appear. From this vantage point in the forest one of the workmen came running in and cried out:

"Woe, woe to us! The Reds have arrived. A horseman is galloping fast through the forest road. I called to him but he did not answer me. It was dark but I knew the horse was a strange one."

"Do not babble so!" said another of the workmen. "Some Mongol rode by and you jumped to the conclusion that he was a Red."

"No, it was not a Mongol," he replied. "The horse was shod. I heard the sound of iron shoes on the road. Woe to us!"

"Well," said my friend, "it seems that this is our finish. It is a silly way for it all to end."

He was right. Just then there was a knock at our door but it was that of the Mongol bringing us three horses for our escape. Immediately we saddled them, packed the third beast with our tent and food and rode off at once to take leave of Gay.

In his house we found the whole war council. Two or three colonists and several Cossacks had galloped from the mountains and announced that the Red detachment was approaching Khathyl but would remain for the night in the forest, where they were building campfires. In fact, through the house windows we could see the glare of the fires. It seemed very strange that the enemy should await the morning there in the forest when they were right on the village they wished to capture.

An armed Cossack entered the room and announced that two armed men from the detachment were approaching. All the men in the room pricked up their ears. Outside were heard the horses' hoofs followed by men's voices and a knock at the door.

"Come in," said Gay.

Two young men entered, their moustaches and beards white and their cheeks blazing red from the cold. They were dressed in the common Siberian overcoat with the big Astrakhan caps, but they had no weapons. Questions began. It developed that it was a detachment of White peasants from the Irkutsk and Yakutsk districts who had been fighting with the Bolsheviki. They had been defeated somewhere in the vicinity of Irkutsk and were now trying to make a junction with Kazagrandi. The leader of this band was a socialist, Captain Vassilieff, who had suffered much under the Czar because of his tenets.

Our troubles had vanished but we decided to start immediately to Muren Kure, as we had gathered our information and were in a hurry to make our report. We started. On the road we overtook three Cossacks who were going out to bring back the colonists who were fleeing to the south. We joined them and, dismounting, we all led our horses over the ice. The Yaga was mad. The subterranean forces produced underneath the ice great heaving waves which with a swirling roar threw up and tore loose great sections of ice, breaking them into small blocks and sucking them under the unbroken downstream field. Cracks ran like snakes over the surface in different directions. One of the Cossacks fell into one of these but we had just time to save him. He was forced by his ducking in such extreme cold to turn back to Khathyl. Our horses slipped about and fell several times. Men and animals felt the presence of death which hovered over them and momentarily threatened them with destruction. At last we made the farther bank and continued southward down the valley, glad to have left the geological and figurative volcanoes behind us. Ten miles farther on we came up with the first party of refugees. They had spread a big tent and made a fire inside, filling it with warmth and smoke. Their camp was made beside the establishment of a large Chinese trading house, where the owners refused to let the colonists come into their amply spacious buildings, even though there were children, women and invalids among the refugees. We spent but half an hour here. The road as we continued was easy, save in places where the snow lay deep. We crossed the fairly high divide between the Egingol and Muren. Near the pass one very unexpected event occurred to us. We crossed the mouth of a fairly wide valley whose upper end was covered with a dense wood. Near this wood we noticed two horsemen, evidently watching us. Their manner of sitting in their saddles and the character of their horses told us that they were not Mongols. We began shouting and waving to them; but they did not answer. Out of the wood emerged a third and stopped to look at us. We decided to interview them and, whipping up our horses, galloped toward them. When we were about one thousand yards from them, they slipped from their saddles and opened on us with a running fire. Fortunately we rode a little apart and thus made a poor target for them. We jumped off our horses, dropped prone on the ground and prepared to fight. However, we did not fire because we thought it might be a mistake on their part, thinking that we were Reds. They shortly made off. Their shots from the European rifles had given us further proof that they were not Mongols. We waited until they had disappeared into the woods and then went forward to investigate their tracks, which we found were those of shod horses, clearly corroborating the earlier evidence that they were not Mongols. Who could they have been? We never found out; yet what a different relationship they might have borne to our lives, had their shots been true!

After we had passed over the divide, we met the Russian colonist D. A. Teternikoff from Muren Kure, who invited us to stay in his house and promised to secure camels for us from the Lamas. The cold was intense and heightened by a piercing wind. During the day we froze to the bone but at night thawed and warmed up nicely by our tent stove. After two days we entered the valley of Muren and from afar made out the square of the Kure with its Chinese roofs and large red temples.

Nearby was a second square, the Chinese and Russian settlement. Two hours more brought us to the house of our hospitable companion and his attractive young wife who feasted us with a wonderful luncheon of tasty dishes. We spent five days at Muren waiting for the camels to be engaged. During this time many refugees arrived from Khathyl because Colonel Kazagrandi was gradually falling back upon the town. Among others there were two Colonels, Plavako and Maklakoff, who had caused the disruption of the Kazagrandi force. No sooner had the refugees appeared in Muren Kure than the Mongolian officials announced that the Chinese authorities had ordered them to drive out all Russian refugees.

"Where can we go now in winter with women and children and no homes of our own?" asked the distraught refugees.

"That is of no moment to us," answered the Mongolian officials. "The Chinese authorities are angry and have ordered us to drive you away. We cannot help you at all."

The refugees had to leave Muren Kure and so erected their tents in the open not far away. Plavako and Maklakoff bought horses and started out for Van Kure. Long afterwards I learned that both had been killed by the Chinese along the road.

We secured three camels and started out with a large group of Chinese merchants and Russian refugees to make Uliassutai, preserving the warmest recollections of our courteous hosts, T. V. and D. A. Teternikoff. For the trip we had to pay for our camels the very high price of 33 *lan* of the silver bullion which had been supplied us by an American firm in Uliassutai, the equivalent roughly of 2.7 pounds of the white metal.

CHAPTER XXIV

A BLOODY CHASTISEMENT

BEFORE long we struck the road which we had travelled coming north and saw again the kindly rows of chopped down telegraph poles which had once so warmly protected us. Over the timbered hillocks north of the valley of Tisingol we wended just as it was growing dark. We decided to stay in Bobroff's house and our companions thought to seek the hospitality of Kanine in the telegraph station. At the station gate we found a soldier with a rifle, who questioned us as to who we were and whence we had come and, being apparently satisfied, whistled out a young officer from the house.

"Lieutenant Ivanoff," he introduced himself. "I am staying here with my detachment of White Partisans."

He had come from near Irkutsk with his following of ten men and had formed a connection with Lieutenant-Colonel Michailoff at Uliassutai, who commanded him to take possession of this blockhouse.

"Enter, please," he said hospitably.

I explained to him that I wanted to stay with Bobroff, whereat he made a despairing gesture with his hand and said:

"Don't trouble yourself. The Bobroffs are killed and their house burned."

I could not keep back a cry of horror.

The Lieutenant continued: "Kanine and the Pouzikoffs killed them, pillaged the place and afterwards burned the house with their dead bodies in it. Do you want to see it?"

My friend and I went with the Lieutenant and looked over the ominous site. Blackened uprights stood among charred beams and planks while crockery and iron pots and pans were scattered all around. A little to one side under some felt lay the remains of the four unfortunate individuals. The Lieutenant first spoke:

"I reported the case to Uliassutai and received word back that the relatives of the deceased would come with two officers, who would investigate the affair. That is why I cannot bury the bodies."

"How did it happen?" we asked, oppressed by the sad picture.

"It was like this," he began. "I was approaching Tisingol at night with my ten soldiers. Fearing that there might be Reds here, we sneaked up to the station and looked into the windows. We saw Pouzikoff, Kanine and the short-haired girl, looking over and dividing clothes and other things and weighing lumps of silver. I did not at once grasp the significance of all this; but, feeling the need for continued caution, ordered one of my soldiers to climb the fence and open the gate. We rushed into the court. The first to run from the house was Kanine's wife, who threw up her hands and shrieked in fear: "I knew that misfortune would come of all this!" and then fainted. One of the men ran out of a side door to a shed in the yard and there tried to get over the fence. I had not noticed him but one of my soldiers caught him. We were met at the door by Kanine, who was white and trembling. I realized that something important had taken place, placed them all under arrest, ordered the men tied and placed a close guard. All my questions were met with silence save by Madame Kanine who cried: 'Pity, pity for the children! They are innocent!' as she dropped on her knees and stretched out her hands in supplication to us. The short-haired girl laughed out of impudent eyes and blew a puff of smoke into my face. I was forced to threaten them and said:

" 'I know that you have committed some crime, but you do not want to confess. If you do not, I shall shoot the men and take the women to Uliassutai to try them there.'

"I spoke with definiteness of voice and intention, for they roused my deepest anger. Quite to my surprise the short-haired girl first began to speak.

" 'I want to tell you about everything,' she said.

"I ordered ink, paper and pen brought me. My soldiers were the witnesses. Then I prepared the protocol of the confession of Pouzikoff's wife. This was her dark and bloody tale.

" 'My husband and I are Bolshevik commissars and we have been sent to find out how many White officers are hidden in Mongolia. But the old fellow Bobroff knew us. We wanted to go away but Kanine kept us, telling us that Bobroff was rich and that he had for a long time wanted to kill him and pillage his place. We agreed to join him. We decoyed the young Bobroff to come and play cards with us. When he was going home my husband stole along behind and shot him. Afterwards we all went to Bobroff's place. I climbed upon the fence and threw some poisoned meat to the dogs, who were dead in a few minutes. Then we all climbed over. The first person to emerge from the house was Bobroff's wife. Pouzikoff, who was hidden behind the door, killed her with his ax. The old fellow we killed with a blow of the ax as he slept. The little girl ran out into the room as she heard the noise and Kanine shot her in the head with buckshot. Afterwards we looted the house and burned it, even destroying the horses and cattle. Later all would have been completely burned, so that no traces remained, but you suddenly arrived and these stupid fellows at once betrayed us.'

"It was a dastardly affair," continued the Lieutenant, as we returned to the station. "The hair raised on my head as I listened to the calm description of this young woman, hardly more than a girl. Only then did I fully realize what depravity Bolshevism had brought into the world, crushing out faith, fear of God and conscience. Only then did I understand that all honest people must fight without compromise against this most dangerous enemy of mankind, so long as life and strength endure."

As we walked I noticed at the side of the road a black spot. It attracted and fixed my attention.

"What is that?" I asked, pointing to the spot.

"It is the murderer Pouzikoff whom I shot," answered the Lieutenant. "I would have shot both Kanine and the wife of Pouzikoff but I was sorry for Kanine's wife and children and I haven't learned the lesson of shooting women. Now I shall send them along with you under the surveillance of my soldiers to Uliassutai. The same result will come, for the Mongols who try them for the murder will surely kill them."

This is what happened at Tisingol, on whose shores the

will-o'-the-wisp flits over the marshy pools and near which runs the cleavage of over two hundred miles that the last earthquake left in the surface of the land. Maybe it was out of this cleavage that Pouzikoff, Kanine and the others who have sought to infect the whole world with horror and crime made their appearance from the land of the inferno. One of Lieutenant Ivanoff's soldiers, who was always praying and pale, called them all "the servants of Satan."

Our trip from Tisingol to Uliassutai in the company of these criminals was very unpleasant. My friend and I entirely lost our usual strength of spirit and healthy frame of mind. Kanine persistently brooded and thought while the impudent woman laughed, smoked and joked with the soldiers and several of our companions. At last we crossed the Jagisstai and in a few hours descried at first the fortress and then the low adobe houses huddled on the plain, which we knew to be Uliassutai.

CHAPTER XXV

HARASSING DAYS

ONCE more we found ourselves in the whirl of events. During our fortnight away a great deal had happened here. The Chinese Commissioner Wang Tsao-tsun had sent eleven envoys to Urga but none had returned. The situation in Mongolia remained far from clear. The Russian detachment had been increased by the arrival of new colonists and secretly continued its illegal existence, although the Chinese knew about it through their omnipresent system of spies. In the town no Russian or foreign citizens left their houses and all remained armed and ready to act. At night armed sentinels stood guard in all their court-yards. It was the Chinese who induced such precautions. By order of their Commissioner all the Chinese merchants with stocks of rifles armed their staffs and handed over any surplus guns to the officials, who with these formed and equipped a force of two hundred coolies into a special garrison of gamins. Then they took possession of the Mongolian arsenal and distributed these additional guns among the Chinese vegetable farmers in the *nagan hushun,* where there was always a floating population of the lowest grade of transient Chinese laborers. This trash of China now felt themselves strong, gathered together in excited discussions and evidently were preparing for some outburst of aggression. At night the coolies transported many boxes of cartridges from the Chinese shops to the *nagan hushun* and the behaviour of the Chinese mob became unbearably audacious.   These coolies and gamins impertinently stopped and searched people right on the streets and sought to provoke fights that would allow them to take anything they wanted. Through secret news we received from certain Chinese quarters we learned that the Chinese were preparing a *pogrom* for all the Russians and Mongols in Uliassutai. We fully realized that it was only necessary to fire one single house at the right part of the town and the entire settlement of wooden buildings would go up in flames. The whole population prepared to defend themselves, increased the sentinels in the compounds, appointed leaders for certain sections of the town, organized a special fire brigade and prepared horses, carts and food for a hasty flight.   The situation became worse when news arrived from Kobdo that the Chinese there had made a *pogrom,* killing some of the inhabitants and burning the whole town after a wild looting orgy.   Most of the people got away to the forests on the mountains but it was at night and consequently without warm clothes and without food. During the following days these mountains around Kobdo heard many cries of misfortune, woe and death.   The severe cold and hunger killed off the women and children out under the open sky of the Mongolian winter.   This news was soon known to the Chinese.   They laughed in mockery and soon organized a big meeting at the *nagan hushun* to discuss letting the mob and gamins loose on the town.

A young Chinese, the son of a cook of one of the colonists, revealed this news.   We immediately decided

to make an investigation.   A Russian officer and my
friend joined me with this young Chinese as a guide for
a trip to the outskirts of the town.   We feigned simply
a stroll but were stopped by the Chinese sentinel on the
side of the city toward the *nagan hushun* with an impertinent command that no one was allowed to leave the
town.   As we spoke with him, I noticed that between the
town and the *nagan hushun* Chinese guards were stationed all along the way and that streams of Chinese were
moving in that direction.   We saw at once it was impossible to reach the meeting from this approach, so we
chose another route.   We left the city from the eastern
side and passed along by the camp of the Mongolians
who had been reduced to beggary by the Chinese imposi-
tions.   There also they were evidently anxiously awaiting
the turn of events, for, in spite of the lateness of the hour,
none had gone to sleep.   We slipped out on the ice and
worked around by the river to the *nagan hushun*.   As we
passed free of the city we began to ، ۱eak cautiously along,
taking advantage of every bit of cover.   We were armed
with revolvers and hand grenades and knew that a small
detachment had been prepared in the town to come to our
aid, if we should be in danger.   First the young Chinese
stole forward with my friend following him like a
shadow, constantly reminding him that he would strangle
him like a mouse if he made one move to betray us.   I
fear the young guide did not greatly enjoy the trip with
my gigantic friend puffing all too loudly with the unusual
exertions.   At last the fences of *nagan hushun* were in
sight and nothing between us and them save the open
plain, where our group would have been easily spotted;
so that we decided to crawl up one by one, save that the

Chinese was retained in the society of my trusted friend. Fortunately there were many heaps of frozen manure on the plain, which we made use of as cover to lead us right up to our objective point, the fence of the enclosures. In the shadow of this we slunk along to the courtyard where the voices of the excited crowd beckoned us. As we took good vantage points in the darkness for listening and making observations, we remarked two extraordinary things in our immediate neighborhood.

Another invisible guest was present with us at the Chinese gathering. He lay on the ground with his head in a hole dug by the dogs under the fence. He was perfectly still and evidently had not heard our advance. Nearby in a ditch lay a white horse with his nose muzzled and a little further away stood another saddled horse tied to a fence.

In the courtyard there was a great hubbub. About two thousand men were shouting, arguing and flourishing their arms about in wild gesticulations. Nearly all were armed with rifles, revolvers, swords and axes. In among the crowd circulated the gamins, constantly talking, handing out papers, explaining and assuring. Finally a big, broad-shouldered Chinese mounted the well combing, waved his rifle about over his head and opened a tirade in strong, sharp tones.

"He is assuring the people," said our interpreter, "that they must do here what the Chinese have done in Kobdo and must secure from the Commissioner the assurance of an order to his guard not to prevent the carrying out of their plans. Also that the Chinese Commissioner must demand from the Russians all their weapons. 'Then we shall take vengeance on the Russians for their Blagoveschensk crime when they drowned three thousand Chinese in 1900. You remain here while I go to the Commissioner and talk with him.' "

He jumped down from the well and quickly made his way to the gate toward the town. At once I saw the man who was lying with his head under the fence draw back out of his hole, take his white horse from the ditch and then run over to untie the other horse and lead them both back to our side, which was away from the city. He left the second horse there and hid himself around the corner of the *hushun*. The spokesman went out of the gate and, seeing his horse over on the other side of the enclosure, slung his rifle across his back and started for his mount. He had gone about half way when the stranger behind the corner of the fence suddenly galloped out and in a flash literally swung the man clear from the ground up across the pommel of his saddle, where we saw him tie the mouth of the semi-strangled Chinese with a cloth and dash off with him toward the west away from the town.

"Who do you suppose he is?" I asked of my friend, who answered up at once: "It must be Tushegoun Lama. . . ."

His whole appearance did strongly remind me of this mysterious Lama avenger and his manner of addressing himself to his enemy was a strict replica of that of Tushegoun. Late in the night we learned that some time after their orator had gone to seek the Commissioner's cooperation in their venture, his head had been flung over the fence into the midst of the waiting audience and that eight gamins had disappeared on their way from the *hushun* to the town without leaving trace or trail. This event terrorized the Chinese mob and calmed their heated spirits.

The next day we received very unexpected aid. A young Mongol galloped in from Urga, his overcoat torn, his hair all dishevelled and fallen to his shoulders and a revolver prominent beneath his girdle. Proceeding directly to the market where the Mongols are always gathered, without leaving his saddle he cried out:

"Urga is captured by our Mongols and *Chiang Chün* Baron Ungern! Bogdo Hutuktu is once more our Khan! Mongols, kill the Chinese and pillage their shops! Our patience is exhausted!"

Through the crowd rose the roar of excitement. The rider was surrounded with a mob of insistent questioners. The old Mongol Sait, Chultun Beyli, who had been dismissed by the Chinese, was at once informed of this news and asked to have the messenger brought to him. After questioning the man he arrested him for inciting the people to riot, but he refused to turn him over to the Chinese authorities. I was personally with the Sait at the time and heard his decision in the matter. When the Chinese Commissioner, Wang Tsao-tsun, threatened the Sait for disobedience to his authority, the old man simply fingered his rosary and said:

"I believe the story of this Mongol in its every word and I apprehend that you and I shall soon have to reverse our relationship."

I felt that Wang Tsao-tsun also accepted the correctness of the Mongol's story, because he did not insist further. From this moment the Chinese disappeared from the streets of Uliassutai as though they never had been, and synchronously the patrols of the Russian officers and

of our foreign colony took their places.   The panic among
the Chinese was heightened by the receipt of a letter containing the news that the Mongols and Altai Tartars
under the leadership of the Tartar officer Kaigorodoff
pursued the Chinese who were making off with their
booty from the sack of Kobdo and overtook and annihi-
lated them on the borders of Sinkiang.   Another part of
the letter told how General Bakitch and the six thousand
men who had been interned with him by the Chinese
authorities on the River Amyl had received arms and
started to join with Ataman Annenkoff, who had been
interned in Kuldja, with the ultimate intention of linking
up with Baron Ungern.   This rumour proved to be wrong
because neither Bakitch nor Annenkoff entertained this
intention, because Annenkoff had been transported by the
Chinese into the Depths of Turkestan.   However, the
news produced veritable stupefaction among the Chinese.

   Just at this time there arrived at the house of the
Bolshevist Russian colonist Bourdukoff three Bolshevik
agents from Irkutsk named Saltikoff, Freimann and
Novak, who started an agitation among the Chinese authorities to get them to disarm the Russian officers and
hand them over to the Reds.   They persuaded the Chinese Chamber of Commerce to petition the Irkutsk Soviet
to send a detachment of Reds to Uliassutai for the protection of the Chinese against the White detachments.
Freimann brought with him communistic pamphlets in
Mongolian and instructions to begin the reconstruction
of the telegraph line to Irkutsk.   Bourdukoff also received
some messages from the Bolsheviki.   This quartette developed their policy very successfully and soon saw
Wang Tsao-tsun fall in with their schemes.   Once more

the days of expecting a *pogrom* in Uliassutai returned to us. The Russian officers anticipated attempts to arrest them. The representative of one of the American firms went with me to the Commissioner for a parley. We pointed out to him the illegality of his acts, inasmuch as he was not authorized by his Government to treat with the Bolsheviki when the Soviet Government had not been recognized by Peking. Wang Tsao-tsun and his advisor Fu Hsiang were palpably confused at finding we knew of his secret meetings with the Bolshevik agents. He assured us that his guard was sufficient to prevent any such *pogrom*. It was quite true that his guard was very capable, as it consisted of well trained and disciplined soldiers under the command of a serious-mind-d and well educated officer; but, what could eighty soldiers do against a mob of three thousand coolies, one thousand armed merchants and two hundred gamins? We strongly registered our apprehensions and urged him to avoid any bloodshed, pointing out that the foreign and Russian population were determined to defend themselves to the last moment. Wang at once ordered the establishment of strong guards on the streets and thus made a very interesting picture with all the Russian, foreign and Chinese patrols moving up and down throughout the whole town. Then we did not know there were three hundred more sentinels on duty, the men of Tushegoun Lama hidden nearby in the mountains.

Once more the picture changed very sharply and suddenly. The Mongolian Sait received news through the Lamas of the nearest monastery that Colonel Kazagrandi, after fighting with the Chinese irregulars, had captured Van Kure and had formed there Russian-Mongolian brigades of cavalry, mobilizing the Mongols by the order of the Living Buddha and the Russians by order of Baron Ungern. A few hours later it became known that in the large monastery of Dzain the Chinese soldiers had killed the Russian Captain Barsky and as a result some of the troops of Kazagrandi attacked and swept the Chinese out of the place. At the taking of Van Kure the Russians arrested a Korean Communist who was on his way from Moscow with gold and propaganda to work in Korea and America. Colonel Kazagrandi sent this Korean with his freight of gold to Baron Ungern. After receiving this news the chief of the Russian detachment in Uliassutai arrested all the Bolsheviki agents and passed judgment upon them and upon the murderers of the Bobroffs. Kanine, Madame Pouzikoff and Freimann were shot. Regarding Saltikoff and Novak some doubt sprang up and, moreover, Saltikoff escaped and hid, while Novak, under advice from Lieutenant Colonel Michailoff, left for the west. The chief of the Russian detachment gave out orders for the mobilization of the Russian colonists and openly took Uliassutai under his protection with the tacit agreement of the Mongolian authorities. The Mongol Sait, Chultun Beyli, convened a council of the neighboring Mongolian Princes, the soul of which was the noted Mongolian patriot, Hun Jap Lama. The Princes quickly formulated their demands upon the Chinese for the complete evacuation of the territory subject to the Sait Chultun Beyli. Out of it grew parleys, threats and friction between the various Chinese and Mongolian elements. Wang Tsao-tsun proposed his scheme of settlement, which some of the Mongolian Princes accepted; but Jap Lama at the decisive moment threw the Chinese document to the ground, drew his knife and swore that he would die by his own hand rather than set it as a seal upon this treacherous agreement. As a result the Chinese proposals were rejected and the antagonists began to prepare themselves for the struggle. All the armed Mongols were summoned from Jassaktu Khan, Sain-Noion Khan and the dominion of Jahantsi Lama. The Chinese authorities placed their four machine guns and prepared to defend the fortress. Continuous deliberations were held by both the Chinese and Mongols. Finally, our old acquaintance Tzeren came to me as one of the unconcerned foreigners and handed to me the joint requests of Wang Tsao-tsun and Chultun Beyli to try to pacify the two elements and to work out a fair agreement between them. Similar requests were handed to the representative of an American firm. The following evening we held the first meeting of the arbitrators and the Chinese and Mongolian representatives. It was passionate and stormy, so that we foreigners lost all hope of the success of our mission. However, at midnight when the speakers were tired, we secured agreement on two points: the Mongols announced that they did not want to make war and that they desired to settle this matter in such a way as to retain the friendship of the great Chinese people; while the Chinese Commissioner acknowledged that China had violated the treaties by which full independence had been legally granted to Mongolia.

These two points formed for us the groundwork of the next meeting and gave us the starting points for urging reconciliation. The deliberations continued for three days and finally turned so that we foreigners could propose our suggestions for an agreement. Its chief provisions were that the Chinese authorities should surrender administrative powers, return the arms to the Mongolians, disarm the two hundred gamins and leave the country; and that the Mongols on their side should give free and honorable passage of their country to the Commissioner with his armed guard of eighty men. This Chinese-Mongolian Treaty of Uliassutai was signed and sealed by the Chinese Commissioners, Wang Tsao-tsun and Fu Hsiang, by both Mongolian Saits, by Hun Jap Lama and other Princes, as well as by the Russian and Chinese Presidents of the Chambers of Commerce and by us foreign arbitrators. The Chinese officials and convoy began at once to pack up their belongings and prepare for departure. The Chinese merchants remained in Uliassutai because Sait Chultun Beyli, now having full authority and power, guaranteed their safety. The day of departure for the expedition of Wang Tsao-tsun arrived. The camels with their packs already filled the *yamen* court-yard and the men only awaited the arrival of their horses from the plains. Suddenly the news spread everywhere that the herd of horses had been stolen during the night and run off toward the south. Of two soldiers that had been sent out to follow the tracks of the herd only one came back with the news that the other had been killed. Astonishment spread over the whole town while among the Chinese it turned to open panic. It perceptibly increased when some Mongols from a distant *ourton* to the east came in and announced that in various places along the post road to Urga they had discovered the bodies of sixteen of the soldiers whom Wang Tsao-tsun had sent out with letters for Urga. The mystery of these events will soon be explained.

The chief of the Russian detachment received a letter from a Cossack Colonel, V. N. Domojiroff, containing the order to disarm immediately the Chinese garrison, to arrest all Chinese officials for transport to Baron Ungern at Urga, to take control of Uliassutai, by force if necessary, and to join forces with his detachment. At the very same time a messenger from the Narabanchi Hutuktu galloped in with a letter to the effect that a Russian detachment under the leadership of Hun Boldon and Colonel Domojiroff from Urga had pillaged some Chinese firms and killed the merchants, had come to the Monastery and demanded horses, food and shelter. The Hutuktu asked for help because the ferocious conqueror of Kobdo, Hun Boldon, could very easily pillage the unprotected isolated monastery. We strongly urged Colonel Michailoff not to violate the sealed treaty and discountenance all the foreigners and Russians who had taken part in making it, for this would but be to imitate the Bolshevik principle of making deceit the leading rule in all acts of state. This touched Michailoff and he answered Domojiroff that Uliassutai was already in his hands without a fight; that over the building of the former Russian Consulate the tri-color flag of Russia was flying; the gamins had been disarmed but that the other orders could not be carried out, because their execution would violate the Chinese-Mongolian treaty just signed in Uliassutai.

Daily several envoys traveled from Narabanchi Hutuktu to Uliassutai. The news became more and more disquieting. The Hutuktu reported that Hun Boldon was mobilizing the Mongolian beggars and horse stealers, arming and training them; that the soldiers were taking the sheep of the monastery; that the *"Noyon"* Domojiroff was aıways drunk; and that the protests of the Hutuktu were answered with jeers and scolding. The messengers gave very indefinite information regarding the strength of the detachment, some placing it at about thirty while others stated that Domojiroff said he had eight hundred in all. We could not understand it at all and soon the messengers ceased coming. All the letters of the Sait remained unanswered and the envoys did not return. There seemed to be no doubt that the men had been killed or captured.

Prince Chultun Beyli determined to go himself. He took with him the Russian and Chinese Presidents of the Chambers of Commerce and two Mongolian officers. Three days elapsed without receiving any news from him whatever. The Mongols began to get worried. Then the Chinese Commissioner and Hun Jap Lama addressed a request to the foreigner group to send some one to Narabanchi, in order to try to resolve the controversy there and to persuade Domojiroff to recognize the treaty and not permit the "great insult of violation" of a covenant between the two great peoples. Our group asked me once more to accomplish this mission *pro bono publico*. I had assigned me as interpreter a fine young Russian colonist, the nephew of the murdered Bobroff, a splendid rider as well as a cool, brave man. Lt.-Colonel Michailoff gave me one of his officers to accompany me. Supplied with an express *tzara* for the post horses and guides, we traveled rapidly over the way which was now familiar to me to find my old friend, Jelib Djamsrap Huktuktu of Narabanchi. Although there were deep snow in some places, we made from one hundred to one hundred and fifteen miles per day.

CHAPTER XXVI

THE BAND OF WHITE HUNGHUTZES

W E arrived at Narabanchi late at night on the third
day out. As we were approaching, we noticed
several riders who, as soon as they had seen us, galloped
quickly back to the monastery. For some time we looked
for the camp of the Russian detachment without finding
it. The Mongols led us into the monastery, where the
Hutuktu immediately received me. In his *yurta* sat
Chultun Beyli. There he presented me with *hatyks* and
said to me: "The very God has sent you here to us in this
difficult moment."

It seems Domojiroff had arrested both the Presidents
of the Chambers of Commerce and had threatened to
shoot Prince Chultun. Both Domojiroff and Hun Boldon
had no documents legalizing their activities. Chultun
Beyli was preparing to fight with them.

I asked them to take me to Domojiroff. Through the
dark I saw four big *yurtas* and two Mongol sentinels with
Russian rifles. We entered the Russian *"Noyon's"* tent.
A very strange picture was presented to our eyes. In the
middle of the *yurta* the brazier was burning. In the usual
place for the altar stood a throne, on which the tall, thin,
grey-haired Colonel Domojiroff was seated. He was only
in his undergarments and stockings, was evidently a little
drunk and was telling stories. Around the brazier lay

twelve young men in various picturesque poses. My officer companion reported to Domojiroff about the events in Uliassutai and during the conversation I asked Domojiroff where his detachment was encamped. He laughed and answered, with a sweep of his hand: "This is my detachment." I pointed out to him that the form of his orders to us in Uliassutai had led us to believe that he must have a large company with him. Then I informed him that Lt.-Colonel Michailoff was preparing to cross swords with the Bolshevik force approaching Uliassutai.

"What?" he exclaimed with fear and confusion, "the Reds?"

We spent the night in his *yurta* and, when I was ready to lie down, my officer whispered to me:

"Be sure to keep your revolver handy," to which I laughed and said:

"But we are in the center of a White detachment and therefore in perfect safety!"

"Uh-huh!" answered my officer and finished the response with one eye closed.

The next day I invited Domojiroff to walk with me over the plain, when I talked very frankly with him about what had been happening. He and Hun Boldon had received orders from Baron Ungern simply to get into touch with General Bakitch, but instead they began pillaging Chinese firms along the route and he had made up his mind to become a great conqueror. On the way he had run across some of the officers who deserted Colonel Kazagrandi and formed his present band. I succeeded in persuading Domojiroff to arrange matters peacefully with Chultun Beyli and not to violate the treaty. He immediately went ahead to the monastery. As I returned,

I met a tall Mongol with a ferocious face, dressed in a blue silk outercoat—it was Hun Boldon. He introduced himself and spoke with me in Russian. I had only time to take off my coat in the tent of Domojiroff when a Mongol came running to invite me to the *yurta* of Hun Boldon. The Prince lived just beside me in a splendid blue *yurta*. Knowing the Mongolian custom, I jumped into the saddle and rode the ten paces to his door. Hun Boldon received me with coldness and pride.

"Who is he?" he inquired of the interpreter, pointing to me with his finger.

I understood his desire to offend me and I answered in the same manner, thrusting out my finger toward him and turning to the interpreter with the same question in a slightly more unpleasant tone:

"Who is he? High Prince and warrior or shepherd and brute?"

Boldon at once became confused and, with trembling voice and agitation in his whole manner, blurted out to me that he would not allow me to interfere in his affairs and would shoot every man who dared to run counter to his orders. He pounded on the low table with his fist and then rose up and drew his revolver. But I was much traveled among the nomads and had studied them thoroughly—Princes, Lamas, shepherds and brigands. I grasped my whip and, striking it on the table with all my strength, I said to the interpreter:

"Tell him that he has the honor to speak with neither Mongol nor Russian but with a foreigner, a citizen of a great and free state. Tell him he must first learn to be a man and then he can visit me and we can talk together."

I turned and went out. Ten minutes later Hun Boldon

entered my *yurta* and offered his apologies. I persuaded him to parley with Chultun Beyli and not to offend the free Mongol people with his activities. That very night all was arranged. Hun Boldon dismissed his Mongols and left for Kobdo, while Domojiroff with his band started for Jassaktu Khan to arrange for the mobilization of the Mongols there. With the consent of Chultun Beyli he wrote to Wang Tsao-tsun a demand to disarm his guard, as all of the Chinese troops in Urga had been so treated; but this letter arrived after Wang had bought camels to replace the stolen horses and was on his way to the border. Later Lt.-Colonel Michailoff sent a detachment of fifty men under the command of Lieutenant Strigine to overhaul Wang and receive their arms.

CHAPTER XXVII

MYSTERY IN A SMALL TEMPLE

PRINCE CHULTUN BEYLI and I were ready to leave the Narabanchi Kure. While the Hutuktu was holding service for the Sait in the Temple of Blessing, I wandered around through the narrow alleyways between the walls of the houses of the various grades of Lama *Gelongs, Getuls, Chaidje* and *Rabdjampa;* of schools where the learned doctors of theology or *Maramba* taught together with the doctors of medicine or *Ta Lama;* of the residences for students called *Bandi;* of stores, archives and libraries. When I returned to the *yurta* of the Hutuktu, he was inside. He presented me with a large *hatyk* and proposed a walk around the monastery. His face wore a preoccupied expression from which I gathered that he had something he wished to discuss with me. As we went out of the *yurta,* the liberated President of the Russian Chamber of Commerce and a Russian officer joined us. The Hutuktu led us to a small building just back of a bright yellow stone wall.

"In that building once stopped the Dalai Lama and Bogdo Khan and we always paint the buildings yellow where these holy persons have lived. Enter!"

The interior of the building was arranged with splendor. On the ground floor was the dining-room, furnished with richly carved, heavy blackwood Chinese tables and

cabinets filled with porcelains and bronze. Above were
two rooms, the first a bed-room hung with heavy yellow
silk curtains; a large Chinese lantern richly set with colored stones hung by a thin bronze chain from the carved
wooden ceiling beam. Here stood a large square bed covered with silken pillows, mattresses and blankets. The
frame work of the bed was also of the Chinese blackwood
and carried, especially on the posts that held the roof-like
canopy, finely executed carvings with the chief motive the
conventional dragon devouring the sun. By the side
stood a chest of drawers completely covered with carvings
setting forth religious pictures. Four comfortable easy
chairs completed the furniture, save for the low oriental
throne which stood on a dais at the end of the room.

"Do you see this throne?" said the Hutuktu to me.
"One night in winter several horsemen rode into the
monastery and demanded that all the *Gelongs* and *Getuls*
with the Hutuktu and *Kanpo* at their head should congre-
gate in this room. Then one of the strangers mounted
the throne, where he took off his *bashlyk* or cap-like head
covering. All of the Lamas fell to their knees as they
recognized the man who had been long ago described in
the sacred bulls of Dalai Lama, Tashi Lama and Bogdo
Khan. He was the man to whom the whole world belongs
and who has penetrated into all the mysteries of Nature.
He pronounced a short Tibetan prayer, blessed all his
hearers and afterwards made predictions for the coming
half century. This was thirty years ago and in the in-
terim all his prophecies are being fulfilled. During his
prayers before that small shrine in the next room this
door opened of its own accord, the candles and lights
before the altar lighted themselves and the sacred braziers

without coals gave forth great streams of incense that filled the room. And then, without warning, the King of the World and his companions disappeared from among us. Behind him remained no trace save the folds in the silken throne coverings which smoothed themselves out and left the throne as though no one had sat upon it."

The Hutuktu entered the shrine, kneeled down, covering his eyes with his hands, and began to pray. I looked at the calm, indifferent face of the golden Buddha, over which the flickering lamps threw changing shadows, and then turned my eyes to the side of the throne. It was wonderful and difficult to believe but I really saw there the strong, muscular figure of a man with a swarthy face of stern and fixed expression about the mouth and jaws, thrown into high relief by the brightness of the eyes. Through his transparent body draped in white raiment I saw the Tibetan inscriptions on the back of the throne. I closed my eyes and opened them again. No one was there but the silk throne covering seemed to be moving.

"Nervousness," I thought. "Abnormal and over-emphasized impressionability growing out of the unusual surroundings and strains."

The Hutuktu turned to me and said: "Give me your *hatyk*. I have the feeling that you are troubled about those whom you love, and I want to pray for them. And you must pray also, importune God and direct the sight of your soul to the King of the World who was here and sanctified this place."

The Hutuktu placed the *hatyk* on the shoulder of the Buddha and, prostrating himself on the carpet before the altar, whispered the words of prayer. Then he raised his head and beckoned me to him with a slight movement of his hand.

"Look at the dark space behind the statue of Buddha and he will show your beloved to you."

Readily obeying his deep-voiced command, I began to look into the dark niche behind the figure of the Buddha. Soon out of the darkness began to appear streams of smoke or transparent threads. They floated in the air, becoming more and more dense and increasing in number, until gradually they formed the bodies of several persons and the outlines of various objects. I saw a room that was strange to me with my family there, surrounded by some whom I knew and others whom I did not. I recognized even the dress my wife wore. Every line of her dear face was clearly visible. Gradually the vision became too dark, dissipated itself into the streams of smoke and transparent threads and disappeared. Behind the golden Buddha was nothing but the darkness. The Hutuktu arose, took my *hatyk* from the shoulder of the Buddha and handed it to me with these words:

"Fortune is always with you and with your family. God's goodness will not forsake you."

We left the building of this unknown King of the World, where he had prayed for all mankind and had predicted the fate of peoples and states. I was greatly astonished to find that my companions had also seen my vision and to hear them describe to me in minute detail the appearance and the clothes of the persons whom I had seen in the dark niche behind the head of Buddha.*

* In order that I might have the evidence of others on this extraordinarily impressive vision, I asked them to make protocols or affidavits concerning what they saw. This they did and I now have these statements in my possession.

The Mongol officer also told me that Chultun Beyli had the day before asked the Hutuktu to reveal to him his fate in this important juncture of his life and in this crisis of his country but the Hutuktu only waved his hand in an expression of fear and refused. When I asked the Hutuktu for the reason of his refusal, suggesting to him that it might calm and help Chultun Beyli as the vision of my beloved had strengthened me, the Hutuktu knitted his brow and answered:

"No! The vision would not please the Prince. His fate is black. Yesterday I thrice sought his fortune on the burned shoulder blades and with the entrails of sheep and each time came to the same dire result, the same dire result! . . ."

He did not really finish speaking but covered his face with his hands in fear. He was convinced that the lot of Chultun Beyli was black as the night.

In an hour we were behind the low hills that hid the Narabanchi Kure from our sight.

CHAPTER XXVIII

THE BREATH OF DEATH

WE arrived at Uliassutai on the day of the return of the detachment which had gone out to disarm the convoy of Wang Tsao-tsun. This detachment had met Colonel Domojiroff, who ordered them not only to disarm but to pillage the convoy and, unfortunately, Lieutenant Strigine executed this illegal and unwarranted command. It was compromising and ignominious to see Russian officers and soldiers wearing the Chinese overcoats, boots and wrist watches which had been taken from the Chinese officials and the convoy. Everyone had Chinese silver and gold also from the loot. The Mongol wife of Wang Tsao-tsun and her brother returned with the detachment and entered a complaint of having been robbed by the Russians. The Chinese officials and their convoy, deprived of their supplies, reached the Chinese border only after great distress from hunger and cold. We foreigners were astounded that Lt.-Colonel Michailoff received Strigine with military honors but we caught the explanation of it later when we learned that Michailoff had been given some of the Chinese silver and his wife the handsomely decorated saddle of Fu Hsiang. Chultun Beyli demanded that all the weapons taken from the Chinese and all the stolen property be turned over to him, as it must later be returned to the Chinese authorities;

but Michailoff refused. Afterwards we foreigners cut off all contact with the Russian detachment. The relations between the Russians and Mongols became very strained. Several of the Russian officers protested against the acts of Michailoff and Strigine and controversies became more and more serious.

At this time, one morning in April, an extraordinary group of armed horsemen arrived at Uliassutai. They stayed at the house of the Bolshevik Bourdukoff, who gave them, so we were told, a great quantity of silver. This group explained that they were former officers in the Imperial Guard. They were Colonels Poletika, N. N. Philipoff and three of the latter's brothers. They announced that they wanted to collect all the White officers and soldiers then in Mongolia and China and lead them to Urianhai to fight the Bolsheviki; but that first they wanted to wipe out Ungern and return Mongolia to China. They called themselves the representatives of the Central Organization of the Whites in Russia.

The society of Russian officers in Uliassutai invited them to a meeting, examined their documents and interrogated them. Investigation proved that all the statements of these officers about their former connections were entirely wrong, that Poletika occupied an important position in the war commissariat of the Bolsheviki, that one of the Philipoff brothers was the assistant of Kameneff in his first attempt to reach England, that the Central White Organization in Russia did not exist, that the proposed fighting in Urianhai was but a trap for the White officers and that this group was in close relations with the Bolshevik Bourdukoff.

A discussion at once sprang up among the officers as to

what they should do with this group, which split the detachment into two distinct parties. Lt-Colonel Michailoff with several officers joined themselves to Poletika's group just as Colonel Domojiroff arrived with his detachment. He began to get in touch with both factions and to feel out the politics of the situation, finally appointing Poletika to the post of Commandant of Uliassutai and sending to Baron Ungern a full report of the events in the town. In this document he devoted much space to me, accusing me of standing in the way of the execution of his orders. His officers watched me continuously. From different quarters I received warnings to take great care. This band and its leader openly demanded to know what right this foreigner had to interfere in the affairs of Mongolia, one of Domojiroff's officers directly giving me the challenge in a meeting in the attempt to provoke a controversy. I quietly answered him:

"And on what basis do the Russian refugees interfere, they who have rights neither at home nor abroad?"

The officer made no verbal reply but in his eyes burned a definite answer. My huge friend who sat beside me noticed this, strode over toward him and, towering over him, stretched his arms and hands as though just waking from sleep and remarked: "I'm looking for a little boxing exercise."

On one occasion Domojiroff's men would have succeeded in taking me if I had not been saved by the watchfulness of our foreign group. I had gone to the fortress to negotiate with the Mongol Sait for the departure of the foreigners from Uliassutai. Chultun Beyli detained me for a long time, so that I was forced to return about nine in the evening. My horse was walking. Half a mile from the town three men sprang up out of the ditch and ran at me. I whipped up my horse but noticed several more men coming out of the other ditch as though to head me off. They, however, made for the other group and captured them and I heard the voice of a foreigner calling me back. There I found three of Domojiroff's officers surrounded by the Polish soldiers and other foreigners under the leadership of my old trusted agronome, who was occupied with tying the hands of the officers behind their backs so strongly that the bones cracked. Ending his work and still smoking his perpetual pipe, he announced in a serious and important manner: "I think it best to throw them into the river."

Laughing at his seriousness and the fear of Domojiroff's officers, I asked them why they had started to attack me. They dropped their eyes and were silent. It was an eloquent silence and we perfectly understood what they had proposed to do. They had revolvers hidden in their pockets.

"Fine!" I said, "All is perfectly clear. I shall release you but you must report to your sender that he will not welcome you back the next time. Your weapons I shall hand to the Commandant of Uliassutai."

My friend, using his former terrifying care, began to untie them, repeating over and over: "And I would have fed you to the fishes in the river!" Then we all returned to the town, leaving them to go their way.

Domojiroff continued to send envoys to Baron Ungern at Urga with requests for plenary powers and money and with reports about Michailoff, Chultun Beyli, Poletika, Philipoff and myself. With Asiatic cunning he was then maintaining good relations with all those for whom he was preparing death at the hands of the severe warrior, Baron Ungern, who was receiving only one-sided reports about all the happenings in Uliassutai. Our whole colony was greatly agitated. The officers split into different parties; the soldiers collected in groups and discussed the events of the day, criticising their chiefs, and under the influence of some of Domojiroff's men began making such statements as:

"We have now seven Colonels, who all want to be in command and are all quarreling among themselves. They all ought to be pegged down and given good sound thrashings. The one who could take the greatest number of blows ought to be chosen as our chief."

It was an ominous joke that proved the demoralization of the Russian detachment.

"It seems," my friend frequently observed, "that we shall soon have the pleasure of seeing a Council of Soldiers here in Uliassutai. God and the Devil! One thing here is very unfortunate—there are no forests near into which good Christian men may dive and get away from all these cursed Soviets. It's bare, frightfully bare, this wretched Mongolia, with no place for us to hide."

Really this possibility of the Soviet was approaching. On one occasion the soldiers captured the arsenal containing the weapons surrendered by the Chinese and carried them off to their barracks. Drunkenness, gambling and fighting increased. We foreigners, carefully watching events and in fear of a catastrophe, finally decided to leave Uliassutai, that caldron of passions, controversies and denunciations. We heard that the group of Poletika was also preparing to get out a few days later. We foreigners separated into two parties, one traveling by the old cara-

van route across the Gobi considerably to the south of
Urga to Kuku-Hoto or Kweihuacheng and Kalgan, and
mine, consisting of my friend, two Polish soldiers and
myself, heading for Urga via Zain Shabi, where Colonel
Kazagrandi had asked me in a recent letter to meet him.
Thus we left the Uliassutai where we had lived through
so many exciting events.

On the sixth day after our departure there arrived in
the town the Mongol-Buriat detachment under the command of the Buriat Vandaloff and the Russian Captain
Bezrodnoff. Afterwards I met them in Zain Shabi. It
was a detachment sent out from Urga by Baron Ungern
to restore order in Uliassutai and to march on to Kobdo.
On the way from Zain Shabi Bezrodnoff came across the
group of Poletika and Michailoff. He instituted a search
which disclosed suspicious documents in their baggage
and in that of Michailoff and his wife the silver and other
possessions taken from the Chinese. From this group of
sixteen he sent N. N. Philipoff to Baron Ungern, released
three others and shot the remaining twelve. Thus ended
in Zain Shabi the life of one party of Uliassutai refugees
and the activities of the group of Poletika. In Uliassutai
Bezrodnoff shot Chultun Beyli for the violation of the
treaty with the Chinese, and also some Bolshevist Russian
colonists; arrested Domojiroff and sent him to Urga; and
. . . restored order. The predictions about Chultun
Beyli were fulfilled.

I knew of Domojiroff's reports regarding myself but I
decided, nevertheless, to proceed to Urga and not to swing
round it, as Poletika had started to do when he was acci-
dentally captured by Bezrodnoff. I was accustomed now
to looking into the eyes of danger and I set out to meet the

terrible "bloody Baron." No one can decide his own fate. I did not think myself in the wrong and the feeling of fear had long since ceased to occupy a place in my *ménage*. On the way a Mongol rider who overhauled us brought the news of the death of our acquaintances at Zain Shabi. He spent the night with me in the *yurta* at the *ourton* and related to me the following legend of death.

"It was a long time ago when the Mongolians ruled over China. The Prince of Uliassutai, Beltis Van, was mad. He executed any one he wished without trial and no one dared to pass through his town. All the other Princes and rich Mongols surrounded Uliassutai, where Beltis raged, cut off communication on every road and allowed none to pass in or out. Famine developed in the town. They consumed all the oxen, sheep and horses and finally Beltis Van determined to make a dash with his soldiers through to the west to the land of one of his tribes, the Olets. He and his men all perished in the fight. The Princes, following the advice of the Hutuktu Buyantu, buried the dead on the slopes of the mountains surrounding Uliassutai. They buried them with incantations and exorcisings in order that Death by Violence might be kept from a further visitation to their land. The tombs were covered with heavy stones and the Hutuktu predicted that the bad demon of Death by Violence would only leave the earth when the blood of a man should be spilled upon the covering stone. Such a legend lived among us. Now it is fulfilled. The Russians shot there three Bolsheviki and the Chinese two Mongols. The evil spirit of Beltis Van broke loose from beneath the heavy stone and now mows down the people with his scythe. The noble Chultun Beyli has perished; the Rus-

sian Noyon Michailoff also has fallen; and death has
flowed out from Uliassutai all over our boundless plains.
Who shall be able to stem it now? Who shall tie the
ferocious hands? An evil time has fallen upon the Gods
and the Good Spirits. The Evil Demons have made war
upon the Good Spirits. What can man now do? Only
perish, only perish. . . ."

Part III

THE STRAINING HEART OF ASIA

Part III
THE STRAINING HEART OF ASIA

___

CHAPTER XXIX

ON THE ROAD OF GREAT CONQUERORS

THE great conqueror, Jenghiz Khan, the son of sad, stern, severe Mongolia, according to an old Mongolian legend "mounted to the top of Karasu Togol and with his eyes of an eagle looked to the west and the east. In the west he saw whole seas of human blood over which floated a bloody fog that blanketed all the horizon. There he could not discern his fate. But the gods ordered him to proceed to the west, leading with him all his warriors and Mongolian tribes. To the east he saw wealthy towns, shining temples, crowds of happy people, gardens and fields of rich earth, all of which pleased the great Mongol. He said to his sons: 'There in the west I shall be fire and sword, destroyer, avenging Fate; in the east I shall come as the merciful, great builder, bringing happiness to the people and to the land.' "

Thus runs the legend. I found much of truth in it. I had passed over much of his road to the west and always identified it by the old tombs and the impertinent monu-

ments of stone to the merciless conqueror. I saw also a
part of the eastern road of the hero, over which he
traveled to China. Once when we were making a trip out
of Uliassutai we stopped the night in Djirgalantu. The
old host of the *ourton,* knowing me from my previous
trip to Narabanchi, welcomed us very kindly and regaled
us with stories during our evening meal. Among other
things he led us out of the *yurta* and pointed out a mountain peak brightly lighted by the full moon and recounted
to us the story of one of the sons of Jenghiz, afterwards
Emperor of China, Indo-China and Mongolia, who had
been attracted by the beautiful scenery and grazing lands
of Djirgalantu and had founded here a town. This was
soon left without inhabitants, for the Mongol is a nomad
who cannot live in artificial cities. The plain is his house
and the world his town. For a time this town witnessed
battles between the Chinese and the troops of Jenghiz
Khan but afterwards it was forgotten. At present there
remains only a half-ruined tower, from which in the early
days the heavy rocks were hurled down upon the heads
of the enemy, and the dilapidated gate of Kublai, the
grandson of Jenghiz Khan. Against the greenish sky
drenched with the rays of the moon stood out the jagged
line of the mountains and the black silhouette of the tower
with its loopholes, through which the alternate scudding
clouds and light flashed.

When our party left Uliassutai, we traveled on lei-
surely, making thirty-five to fifty miles a day until we
were within sixty miles of Zain Shabi, where I took leave
of the others to go south to this place in order to keep my
engagement with Colonel Kazagrandi. The sun had just
risen as my single Mongol guide and I without any pack

animals began to ascend the low, timbered ridges, from the top of which I caught the last glimpses of my companions disappearing down the valley. I had no idea then of the many and almost fatal dangers which I should have to pass through during this trip by myself, which was destined to prove much longer than I had anticipated. As we were crossing a small river with sandy shores, my Mongol guide told me how the Mongolians came there during the summer to wash gold, in spite of the prohibitions of the Lamas. The manner of working the placer was very primitive but the results testified clearly to the richness of these sands. The Mongol lies flat on the ground, brushes the sand aside with a feather and keeps blowing into the little excavation so formed. From time to time he wets his finger and picks up on it a small bit of grain gold or a diminutive nugget and drops these into a little bag hanging under his chin. In such manner this primitive dredge wins about a quarter of an ounce or five dollars' worth of the yellow metal per day.

I determined to make the whole distance to Zain Shabi in a single day. At the *ourtons* I hurried them through the catching and saddling of the horses as fast as I could. At one of these stations about twenty-five miles from the monastery the Mongols gave me a wild horse, a big, strong white stallion. Just as I was about to mount him and had already touched my foot to the stirrup, he jumped and kicked me right on the leg which had been wounded in the Ma-chu fight. The leg soon began to swell and ache. At sunset I made out the first Russian and Chinese buildings and later the monastery at Zain. We dropped into the valley of a small stream which flowed along a mountain on whose peak were set white rocks forming the

words of a Tibetan prayer. At the bottom of this mountain was a cemetery for the Lamas, that is, piles of bones
and a pack of dogs. At last the monastery lay right below
us, a common square surrounded with wooden fences.
In the middle rose a large temple quite different from all
those of western Mongolia, not in the Chinese but in the
Tibetan style of architecture, a white building with per-
pendicular walls and regular rows of windows in black
frames, with a roof of black tiles and with a most unusual
damp course laid between the stone walls and the roof
timbers and made of bundles of twigs from a Tibetan tree
which never rots. Another small quadrangle lay a little to
the east and contained Russian buildings connected with
the monastery by telephone.

"That is the house of the Living God of Zain," the
Mongol explained, pointing to this smaller quadrangle.
"He likes Russian customs and manners."

To the north on a conical-shaped hill rose a tower that
recalled the Babylonian *zikkurat*. It was the temple where
the ancient books and manuscripts were kept and the
broken ornaments and objects used in the religious ceremonies together with the robes of deceased Hutuktus preserved. A sheer cliff rose behind this museum, which it
was impossible for one to climb. On the face of this were
carved images of the Lamaite gods, scattered about without any special order. They were from one to two and a
half metres high. At night the monks lighted lamps
before them, so that one could see these images of the
gods and goddesses from far away.

We entered the trading settlement. The streets were
deserted and from the windows only women and children
looked out. I stopped with a Russian firm whose other

branches I had known throughout the country. Much to my astonishment they welcomed me as an acquaintance. It appeared that the Hutuktu of Narabanchi had sent word to all the monasteries that, whenever I should come, they must all render me aid, inasmuch as I had saved the Narabanchi Monastery and, by the clear signs of the divinations, I was an incarnate Buddha beloved of the Gods. This letter of this kindly disposed Hutuktu helped me very much—perhaps I should even say more, that it saved me from death. The hospitality of my hosts proved of great and much needed assistance to me because my injured leg had swelled and was aching severely. When I took off my boot, I found my foot all covered with blood and my old wound re-opened by the blow. A *felcher* was called to assist me with treatment and bandaging, so that I was able to walk again three days later.

I did not find Colonel Kazagrandi at Zain Shabi. After destroying the Chinese gamins who had killed the local Commandant, he had returned via Van Kure. The new Commandment handed me the letter of Kazagrandi, who very cordially asked me to visit him after I had rested in Zain. A Mongolian document was enclosed in the letter giving me the right to receive horses and carts from herd to herd by means of the *"urga,"* which I shall later describe and which opened for me an entirely new vista of Mongolian life and country that I should otherwise never have seen. The making of this journey of over two hundred miles was a very disagreeable task for me; but evidently Kazagrandi, whom I had never met, had serious reasons for wishing this meeting.

At one o'clock the day after my arrival I was visited by

the local "Very God," *Gheghen* Pandita Hutuktu. A
more strange and extraordinary appearance of a god I
could not imagine. He was a short, thin young man of
twenty or twenty-two years with quick, nervous movements and with an expressive face lighted and dominated,
like the countenances of all the Mongol gods, by large,
frightened eyes. He was dressed in a blue silk Russian
uniform with yellow epaulets with the sacred sign of
Pandita Hutuktu, in blue silk trousers and high boots, all
surmounted by a white Astrakhan cap with a yellow
pointed top. At his girdle a revolver and sword were
slung. I did not know quite what to think of this disguised god. He took a cup of tea from the host and
began to talk with a mixture of Mongolian and Russian.

"Not far from my Kure is located the ancient mon-
astery of Erdeni Dzu, erected on the site of the ruins of
Karakorum, the ancient capital of Jenghiz Khan and
afterwards frequently visited by Kublai Kahn for sanc-
tuary and rest after his labors as Emperor of China,
India, Persia, Afghanistan, Mongolia and half of Europe.
Now only ruins and tombs remain to mark this former
'Garden of Beatific Days.' The pious monks of Baroun
Kure found in the underground chambers of the ruins
manuscripts that were much older than Erdeni Dzu itself.
In these my Maramba Meetchik-Atak found the prediction that the Hutuktu of Zain who should carry the title
of 'Pandita,' should be but twenty-one years of age, be
born in the heart of the lands of Jenghiz Khan and have
on his chest the natural sign of the swastika—such
Hutuktu would be honored by the people in the days of
a great war and trouble, would begin the fight with the
servants of Red evil and would conquer them and bring

order into the universe, celebrating this happy day in the
city with white temples and with the songs of ten thousand
bells. It is I, Pandita Hutuktu! The signs and symbols
have met in me. I shall destroy the Bolsheviki, the bad
'servants of the Red evil,' and in Moscow I shall rest from
my glorious and great work. Therefore I have asked
Colonel Kazagrandi to enlist me in the troops of Baron
Ungern and give me the chance to fight. The Lamas seek
to prevent me from going but who is the god here?"

He very sternly stamped his foot, while the Lamas and
guard who accompanied him reverently bowed their
heads.

As he left he presented me with a *hatyk* and, rummag-
ing through my saddle bags, I found a single article that
might be considered worthy as a gift for a Hutuktu, a
small bottle of osmiridium, this rare, natural concomitant
of platinum.

"This is the most stable and hardest of metals," I said.
"Let it be the sign of your glory and strength, Hutuktu!"

The Pandita thanked me and invited me to visit him.
When I had recovered a little, I went to his house, which
was arranged in European style: electric lights, push bells
and telephone. He feasted me with wine and sweets and
introduced me to two very interesting personages, one an
old Tibetan surgeon with a face deeply pitted by smallpox,
a heavy thick nose and crossed eyes. He was a peculiar
surgeon, consecrated in Tibet. His duties consisted in
treating and curing Hutuktus when they were ill and . . .
in poisoning them when they became too independent or
extravagant or when their policies were not in accord
with the wishes of the Council of Lamas of the Living
Buddha or the Dalai Lama. By now Pandita Hutuktu

probably rests in eternal peace on the top of some sacred mountain, sent thither by the solicitude of his extraordinary court physician. The martial spirit of Pandita Hutuktu was very unwelcome to the Council of Lamas, who protested against the adventuresomeness of this "Living God."

Pandita liked wine and cards. One day when he was in the company of Russians and dressed in a European suit, some Lamas came running to announce that divine service had begun and that the "Living God" must take his place on the altar to be prayed to but he had gone out from his abode and was playing cards! Without any confusion Pandita drew his red mantle of the Hutuktu over his European coat and long grey trousers and allowed the shocked Lamas to carry their "God" away in his palanquin.

Besides the surgeon-poisoner I met at the Hutuktu's a lad of thirteen years, whose youthfulness, red robe and cropped hair led me to suppose he was a *Bandi* or student servant in the home of the Hutuktu; but it turned out otherwise. This boy was the first *Hubilgan*, also an incarnate Buddha, an artful teller of fortunes and the successor of Pandita Hutuktu. He was drunk all the time and a great card player, always making side-splitting jokes that greatly offended the Lamas.

That same evening I made the acquaintance of the second *Hubilgan* who called on me, the real administrator of Zain Shabi, which is an independent dominion subject directly to the Living Buddha. This *Hubilgan* was a serious and ascetic man of thirty-two, well educated and deeply learned in Mongol lore. He knew Russian and read much in that language, being interested chiefly in the

life and stories of other peoples. He had a high respect
for the creative genius of the American people and said to
me:

"When you go to America, ask the Americans to come
to us and lead us out from the darkness that surrounds us.
The Chinese and Russians will lead us to destruction and
only the Americans can save us."

It is a deep satisfaction for me to carry out the request
of this influential Mongol, *Hubilgan*, and to urge his
appeal to the American people. Will you not save this
honest, uncorrupted but dark, deceived and oppressed
people? They should not be allowed to perish, for within
their souls they carry a great store of strong moral
forces. Make of them a cultured people, believing in the
verity of humankind; teach them to use the wealth of
their land; and the ancient people of Jenghiz Khan will
ever be your faithful friends.

When I had sufficiently recovered, the Hutuktu invited
me to travel with him to Erdeni Dzu, to which I willingly
agreed. On the following morning a light and comfortable carriage was brought for me. Our trip lasted five
days, during which we visited Erdeni Dzu, Karakorum,
Hoto-Zaidam and Hara-Balgasun. All these are the
ruins of monasteries and cities erected by Jenghiz Khan
and his successors, Ugadai Khan and Kublai in the thirteenth century. Now only the remnants of walls and
towers remain, some large tombs and whole books of
legends and stories.

"Look at these tombs!" said the Hutuktu to me.
"Here the son of Khan Uyuk was buried. This young
prince was bribed by the Chinese to kill his father but
was frustrated in his attempt by his own sister, who killed

him in her watchful care of her old father, the Emperor
and Khan. There is the tomb of Tsinilla, the beloved
spouse of Khan Mangu. She left the capital of China to
go to Khara Bolgasun, where she fell in love with the
brave shepherd Damcharen, who overtook the wind on
his steed and who captured wild yaks and horses with his
bare hands. The enraged Khan ordered his unfaithful
wife strangled but afterwards buried her with imperial
honors and frequently came to her tomb to weep for his
lost love."

"And what happened to Damcharen?" I inquired.

The Hutuktu himself did not know; but his old servant,
the real archive of legends, answered:

"With the aid of ferocious Chahar brigands he fought
with China for a long time. It is, however, unknown how
he died."

Among the ruins the monks pray at certain fixed times
and they also search for sacred books and objects concealed or buried in the débris. Recently they found here
two Chinese rifles and two gold rings and big bundles of
old manuscripts tied with leather thongs.

"Why did this region attract the powerful emperors
and Khans who ruled from the Pacific to the Adriatic?"
I asked myself. Certainly not these mountains and valleys covered with larch and birch, not these vast sands,
receding lakes and barren rocks. It seems that I found
the answer.

The great emperors, remembering the vision of Jenghiz
Khan, sought here new revelations and predictions of his
miraculous, majestic destiny, surrounded by the divine
honors, obeisance and hate. Where could they come into
touch with the gods, the good and bad spirits? Only

there where they abode. All the district of Zain with these ancient ruins is just such a place.

"On this mountain only such men can ascend as are born of the direct line of Jenghiz Khan," the Pandita explained to me. "Half way up the ordinary man suffocates and dies, if he ventures to go further. Recently Mongolian hunters chased a pack of wolves up this mountain and, when they came to this part of the mountainside, they all perished. There on the slopes of the mountain lie the bones of eagles, big horned sheep and the *kabarga* antelope, light and swift as the wind. There dwells the bad demon who possesses the book of human destinies."

"This is the answer," I thought.

In the Western Caucasus I once saw a mountain between Soukhoum Kale and Tuopsei where wolves, eagles and wild goats also perish, and where men would likewise perish if they did not go on horseback through this zone. There the earth breathes out carbonic acid gas through holes in the mountainside, killing all animal life. The gas clings to the earth in a layer about half a metre thick. Men on horseback pass above this and the horses always hold their heads way up and snuff and whinny in fear until they cross the dangerous zone. Here on the top of this mountain where the bad demon peruses the book of human destinies is the same phenomenon, and I realized the sacred fear of the Mongols as well as the stern attraction of this place for the tall, almost gigantic descendants of Jenghiz Khan. Their heads tower above the layers of poisonous gas, so that they can reach the top of this mysterious and terrible mountain. Also it is possible to explain this phenomenon geologically, because here in this region is the southern edge of the coal deposits which are the source of carbonic acid and swamp gases.

Not far from the ruins in the lands of Hun Doptchin Djamtso there is a small lake which sometimes burns with a red flame, terrifying the Mongols and herds of horses. Naturally this lake is rich with legends. Here a meteor formerly fell and sank far into the earth. In the hole this lake appeared. Now, it seems, the inhabitants of the subterranean passages, semi-man and semi-demon, are laboring to extract this "stone of the sky" from its deep bed and it is setting the water on fire as it rises and falls back in spite of their every effort. I did not see the lake myself but a Russian colonist told me that it may be petroleum on the lake that is fired either from the campfires of the shepherds or by the blazing rays of the sun.

At any rate all this makes it very easy to understand the attractions for the great Mongol potentates. The strongest impression was produced upon me by Karakorum, the place where the cruel and wise Jenghiz Khan lived and laid his gigantic plans for overrunning all the west with blood and for covering the east with a glory never before seen. Two Karakorums were erected by Jenghiz Khan, one here near Tatsa Gol on the Caravan Road and the other in Pamir, where the sad warriors buried the greatest of human conquerors in the mausoleum built by five hundred captives who were sacrificed to the spirit of the deceased when their work was done.

The warlike Pandita Hutuktu prayed on the ruins where the shades of these potentates who had ruled half the world wandered, and his soul longed for the chimerical exploits and for the glory of Jenghiz and Tamerlane.

On the return journey we were invited not far from

Zain to visit a very rich Mongol by the way. He had already prepared the *yurtas* suitable for Princes, ornamented with rich carpets and silk draperies. The Hutuktu accepted. We arranged ourselves on the soft pillows in the *yurtas* as the Hutuktu blessed the Mongol, touching his head with his holy hand, and received the *hatyks*. The host then had a whole sheep brought in to us, boiled in a huge vessel. The Hutuktu carved off one hind leg and offered it to me, while he reserved the other for himself. After this he gave a large piece of meat to the smallest son of the host, which was the sign that Pandita Hutuktu invited all to begin the feast. In a trice the sheep was entirely carved or torn up and in the hands of the banqueters. When the Hutuktu had thrown down by the brazier the white bones without a trace of meat left on them, the host on his knees withdrew from the fire a piece of sheepskin and ceremoniously offered it on both his hands to the Hutuktu. Pandita began to clean off the wool and ashes with his knife and, cutting it into thin strips, fell to eating this really tasty course. It is the covering from just above the breast bone and is called in Mongolian *tarach* or "arrow." When a sheep is skinned, this small section is cut out and placed on the hot coals, where it is broiled very slowly. Thus prepared it is considered the most dainty bit of the whole animal and is always presented to the guest of honor. It is not permissible to divide it, such is the strength of the custom and ceremony.

After dinner our host proposed a hunt for bighorns, a large herd of which was known to graze in the mountains within less than a mile from the *yurtas*. Horses with rich saddles and bridles were led up. All the elaborate harness of the Hutuktu's mount was ornamented with red and yellow bits of cloth as a mark of his rank. About fifty Mongol riders galloped behind us. When we left our horses, we were placed behind the rocks roughly three hundred paces apart and the Mongols began the encircling movement around the mountain. After about half an hour I noticed way up among the rocks something flash and soon made out a fine bighorn jumping with tremendous springs from rock to rock, and behind him a herd of some twenty odd head leaping like lightning over the ground. I was vexed beyond words when it appeared that the Mongols had made a mess of it and pushed the herd out to the side before having completed their circle. But happily I was mistaken. Behind a rock right ahead of the herd a Mongol sprang up and waved his hands. Only the big leader was not frightened and kept right on past the unarmed Mongol while all the rest of the herd swung suddenly round and rushed right down upon me. I opened fire and dropped two of them. The Hutuktu also brought down one as well as a musk antelope that came unexpectedly from behind a rock hard by. The largest pair of horns weighed about thirty pounds, but they were from a young sheep.

The day following our return to Zain Shabi, as I was feeling quite recovered, I decided to go on to Van Kure. At my leave-taking from the Hutuktu I received a large *hatyk* from him together with warmest expressions of thanks for the present I had given him on the first day of our acquaintance.

"It is a fine medicine!" he exclaimed. "After our trip I felt quite exhausted but I took your medicine and am now quite rejuvenated. Many, many thanks!"

The poor chap had swallowed my osmiridium. To be

sure it could not harm him; but to have helped him was wonderful. Perhaps doctors in the Occident may wish to try this new, harmless and very cheap remedy—only eight pounds of it in the whole world—and I merely ask that they leave me the patent rights for it for Mongolia, Barga, Sinkiang, Koko Nor and all the other lands of Central Asia.

An old Russian colonist went as guide for me. They gave me a big but light and comfortable cart hitched and drawn in a marvelous way. A straight pole four metres long was fastened athwart the front of the shafts. On either side two riders took this pole across their saddle pommels and galloped away with me across the plains. Behind us galloped four other riders with four extra horses.

CHAPTER XXX

ARRESTED!

ABOUT twelve miles from Zain we saw from a ridge a snakelike line of riders crossing the valley, which detachment we met half an hour later on the shore of a deep, swampy stream. The group consisted of Mongols, Buriats and Tibetans armed with Russian rifles. At the head of the column were two men, one of whom in a huge black Astrakhan and black felt cape with red Caucasian cowl on his shoulders blocked my road and, in a coarse, harsh voice, demanded of me: "Who are you, where are you from and where are you going?"

I gave also a laconic answer. They then said that they were a detachment of troops from Baron Ungern under the command of Captain Vandaloff. "I am Captain Bezrodnoff, military judge."

Suddenly he laughed loudly. His insolent, stupid face did not please me and, bowing to the officers, I ordered my riders to move.

"Oh no!" he remonstrated, as he blocked the road again. "I cannot allow you to go farther. I want to have a long and serious conversation with you and you will have to come back to Zain for it."

I protested and called attention to the letter of Colonel Kazagrandi, only to hear Bezrodnoff answer with coldness:

"This letter is a matter of Colonel Kazagrandi's and to bring you back to Zain and talk with you is my affair. Now give me your weapon."

But I could not yield to this demand, even though death were threatened.

"Listen," I said. "Tell me frankly. Is yours really a detachment fighting against the Bolsheviki or is it a Red contingent?"

"No, I assure you!" replied the Buriat officer Vandaloff, approaching me. "We have already been fighting the Bolsheviki for three years."

"Then I cannot hand you my weapon," I calmly replied. "I brought it from Soviet Siberia, have had many fights with this faithful weapon and now I am to be disarmed by White officers! It is an offence that I cannot allow."

With these words I threw my rifle and my Mauser into the stream. The officers were confused. Bezrodnoff turned red with anger.

"I freed you and myself from humiliation," I explained.

Bezrodnoff in silence turned his horse, the whole detachment of three hundred men passed immediately before me and only the last two riders stopped, ordered my Mongols to turn my cart round and then fell in behind my little group. So I was arrested! One of the horsemen behind me was a Russian and he told me that Bezrodnoff carried with him many death decrees. I was sure that mine was among them.

Stupid, very stupid! What was the use of fighting one's way through Red detachments, of being frozen and hungry, of almost perishing in Tibet only to die from a bullet of one of Bezrodnoff's Mongols? For such a pleasure it was not worth while to travel so long and so far! In every Siberian "Cheka" I could have had this end so joyfully accorded me.

When we arrived at Zain Shabi, my luggage was examined and Bezrodnoff began to question me in minutest detail about the events in Uliassutai. We talked about three hours, during which I tried to defend all the officers of Uliassutai, maintaining that one must not trust only the reports of Domojiroff. When our conversation was finished, the Captain stood up and offered his apologies for detaining me in my journey. Afterwards he presented me a fine Mauser with silver mountings on the handle and said:

"Your pride greatly pleased me. I beg you to receive this weapon as a memento of me."

The following morning I set out anew from Zain Shabi, having in my pocket the *laissez-passer* of Bezrodnoff for his outposts.

CHAPTER XXXI

TRAVELING BY "URGA"

ONCE more we traveled along the now known places, the mountain from which I espied the detachment of Bezrodnoff, the stream into which I had thrown my weapon, and soon all this lay behind us. At the first *ourton* we were disappointed because we did not find horses there. In the *yurtas* were only the host with two of his sons. I showed him my document and he exclaimed:

"Noyon has the right of '*urga*.' Horses will be brought very soon."

He jumped into his saddle, took two of my Mongols with him, providing them and himself with long thin poles, four or five metres in length, and fitted at the end with a loop of rope, and galloped away. My cart moved behind them. We left the road, crossed the plain for an hour and came upon a big herd of horses grazing there. The Mongol began to catch a quota of them for us with his pole and noose or *urga*, when out of the mountains nearby came galloping the owners of the herds. When the old Mongol showed my papers to them, they submissively acquiesced and substituted four of their men for those who had come with me thus far. In this manner the Mongols travel, not along the *ourton* or station road but directly from one herd to another, where the fresh

horses are caught and saddled and the new owners substituted for those of the last herd. All the Mongols so
effected by the right of *urga* try to finish their task as
rapidly as possible and gallop like mad for the nearest
herd in your general direction of travel to turn over their
task to their neighbor. Any traveler having this right of
urga can catch horses himself and, if there are no owners,
can force the former ones to carry on and leave the animals in the next herd he requisitions. But this happens
very rarely because the Mongol never likes to seek out his
animals in another's herd, as it always gives so many
chances for controversy.

It was from this custom, according to one explanation,
that the town of Urga took its name among outsiders.
By the Mongols themselves it is always referred to as
Ta Kure, "The Great Monastery." The reason the
Buriats and Russians, who were the first to trade into this
region, called it Urga was because it was the principal
destination of all the trading expeditions which crossed
the plains by this old method or right of travel. A second
explanation is that the town lies in a "loop" whose sides
are formed by three mountain ridges, along one of which
the River Tola runs like the pole or stick of the familiar
urga of the plains.

Thanks to this unique ticket of *urga* I crossed quite
untraveled sections of Mongolia for about two hundred
miles. It gave me the welcome opportunity to observe the
fauna of this part of the country. I saw many huge herds
of Mongolian antelopes running from five to six thousand, many groups of bighorns, *wapiti* and *kabarga* antelopes. Sometimes small herds of wild horses and wild
asses flashed as a vision on the horizon.

In one place I observed a big colony of marmots. All over an area of several square miles their mounds were scattered with the holes leading down to their runways below, the dwellings of the marmot. In and out among these mounds the greyish-yellow or brown animals ran in all sizes up to half that of an average dog. They ran heavily and the skin on their fat bodies moved as though it were too big for them. The marmots are splendid prospectors, always digging deep ditches, throwing out on the surface all the stones. In many places I saw mounds the marmots had made from copper ore and farther north some from minerals containing wolfram and vanadium. Whenever the marmot is at the entrance of his hole, he sits up straight on his hind legs and looks like a bit of wood, a small stump or a stone. As soon as he spies a rider in the distance, he watches him with great curiosity and begins whistling sharply. This curiosity of the marmots is taken advantage of by the hunters, who sneak up to their holes flourishing streamers of cloth on the tips of long poles. The whole attention of the small animals is concentrated on this small flag and only the bullet that takes his life explains to him the reason for this previously unknown object.

I saw a very exciting picture as I passed through a marmot colony near the Orkhon River. There were thousands of holes here so that my Mongols had to use all their skill to keep the horses from breaking their legs in them. I noticed an eagle circling high overhead. All of a sudden he dropped like a stone to the top of a mound, where he sat motionless as a rock. The marmot in a few minutes ran out of his hole to a neighbor's doorway. The eagle calmly jumped down from the top and with one wing closed the entrance to the hole. The rodent heard the noise, turned back and rushed to the attack, trying to break through to his hole where he had evidently left his family. The struggle began. The eagle fought with one free wing, one leg and his beak but did not withdraw the bar to the entrance. The marmot jumped at the rapacious bird with great boldness but soon fell from a blow on the head. Only then the eagle withdrew his wing, approached the marmot, finished him off and with difficulty lifted him in his talons to carry him away to the mountains for a tasty luncheon.

In the more barren places with only occasional spears of grass in the plain another species of rodent lives, called *imouran*, about the size of a squirrel. They have a coat the same color as the prairie and, running about it like snakes, they collect the seeds that are blown across by the wind and carry them down into their diminutive homes. The *imouran* has a truly faithful friend, the yellow lark of the prairie with a brown back and head. When he sees the *imouran* running across the plain, he settles on his back, flaps his wings in balance and rides well this swiftly galloping mount, who gaily flourishes his long shaggy tail. The lark during his ride skilfully and quickly catches the parasites living on the body of his friend, giving evidence of his enjoyment of his work with a short agreeable song. The Mongols call the *imouran* "the steed of the gay lark." The lark warns the *imouran* of the approach of eagles and hawks with three sharp whistles the moment he sees the aerial brigand and takes refuge himself behind a stone or in a small ditch. After this signal no *imouran* will stick his head out of his hole until the danger is past.

Thus the gay lark and his steed live in kindly neighborliness.

In other parts of Mongolia where there was very rich grass I saw another type of rodent, which I had previously come across in Urianhai. It is a gigantic black prairie rat with a short tail and lives in colonies of from one to two hundred. He is interesting and unique as the most skilful farmer among the animals in his preparation of his winter supply of fodder. During the weeks when the grass is most succulent he actually mows it down with swift jerky swings of his head, cutting about twenty or thirty stalks with his sharp long front teeth. Then he allows his grass to cure and later puts up his prepared hay in a most scientific manner. First he makes a mound about a foot high. Through this he pushes down into the ground four slanting stakes, converging toward the middle of the pile, and binds them close over the surface of the hay with the longest strands of grass, leaving the ends protruding enough for him to add another foot to the height of the pile, when he again binds the surface with more long strands—all this to keep his winter supply of food from blowing away over the prairie. This stock he always locates right at the door of his den to avoid long winter hauls. The horses and camels are very fond of this small farmer's hay, because it is always made from the most nutritious grass. The haycocks are so strongly made that one can hardly kick them to pieces.

Almost everywhere in Mongolia I met either single pairs or whole flocks of the greyish-yellow prairie partridges, *salga* or "partridge swallow," so called because they have long sharp tails resembling those of swallows and because their flight also is a close copy of that of the swallow. These birds are very tame or fearless, allowing men to come within ten or fifteen paces of them; but, when they do break, they go high and fly long distances without lighting, whistling all the time quite like swallows. Their general markings are light grey and yellow, though the males have pretty chocolate spots on the backs and wings, while their legs and feet are heavily feathered.

My opportunity to make these observations came from traveling through unfrequented regions by the *urga,* which, however, had its counterbalancing disadvantages. The Mongols carried me directly and swiftly toward my destination, receiving with great satisfaction the presents of Chinese dollars which I gave them. But after having made about five thousand miles on my Cossack saddle that now lay behind me on the cart all covered with dust like common merchandise, I rebelled against being wracked and torn by the rough riding of the cart as it was swung heedlessly over stones, hillocks and ditches by the wild horses with their equally wild riders, bounding and cracking and holding together only through its tenacity of purpose in demonstrating the cosiness and attractiveness of a good Mongol equipage! All my bones began to ache. Finally I groaned at every lunge and at last I suffered a very sharp attack of *ischias* or sciatica in my wounded leg. At night I could neither sleep, lie down nor sit with comfort and spent the whole night pacing up and down the plain, listening to the loud snoring of the inhabitants of the *yurta.* At times I had to fight the two huge black dogs which attacked me. The following day I could endure the wracking only until noon and was then forced to give up and lie down. The pain was unbearable. I could not move my leg nor my back and finally fell into a high fever. We were forced to stop and rest. I swallowed all my stock of aspirin and quinine but without relief. Before me was a sleepless night about which I could not think without weakening fear. We had stopped in the *yurta* for guests by the side of a small monastery. My Mongols invited the Lama doctor to visit me, who gave me two very bitter powders and assured me I should be able to continue in the morning. I soon felt a stimulated palpitation of the heart, after which the pain became even sharper. Again I spent the night without any sleep but when the sun arose the pain ceased instantly and, after an hour, I ordered them to saddle me a horse, as I was afraid to continue further in the cart.

While the Mongols were catching the horses, there came to my tent Colonel N. N. Philipoff, who told me that he denied all the accusations that he and his brother and Poletika were Bolsheviki and that Bezrodnoff allowed him to go to Van Kure to meet Baron Ungern, who was expected there. Only Philipoff did not know that his Mongol guide was armed with a bomb and that another Mongol had been sent on ahead with a letter to Baron Ungern. He did not know that Poletika and his brothers were shot at the same time in Zain Shabi. Philipoff was in a hurry and wanted to reach Van Kure that day. I left an hour after him.

CHAPTER XXXII

AN OLD FORTUNE TELLER

FROM this point we began traveling along the *ourton* road. In this region the Mongols had very poor and exhausted horses, because they were forced continuously to supply mounts to the numerous envoys of Dai-chin Van and of Colonel Kazagrandi. We were compelled to spend the night at the last *ourton* before Van Kure, where a stout old Mongol and his son kept the station. After our supper he took the shoulder-blade of the sheep, which had been carefully scraped clean of all the flesh, and, looking at me, placed this bone in the coals with some incantations and said:

"I want to tell your fortune. All my predictions come true."

When the bone had been blackened, he drew it out, blew off the ashes and began to scrutinize the surface very closely and to look through it into the fire. He continued his examination for a long time and then, with fear in his face, placed the bone back in the coals.

"What did you see?" I asked, laughing.

"Be silent!" he whispered. "I made out horrible signs."

He again took out the bone and began examining it all over, all the time whispering prayers and making strange movements. In a very solemn quiet voice he began his predictions.

"Death in the form of a tall white man with red hair will stand behind you and will watch you long and close. You will feel it and wait but Death will withdraw. . . . Another white man will become your friend. . . . Before the fourth day you will lose your acquaintances. They will die by a long knife. I already see them being eaten by the dogs. Beware of the man with a head like a saddle. He will strive for your death."

For a long time after the fortune had been told we sat smoking and drinking tea but still the old fellow looked at me only with fear. Through my brain flashed the thought that thus must his companions in prison look at one who is condemned to death.

The next morning we left the fortune teller before the sun was up, and, when we had made about fifteen miles, hove in sight of Van Kure. I found Colonel Kazagrandi at his headquarters. He was a man of good family, an experienced engineer and a splendid officer, who had distinguished himself in the war at the defence of the island of Moön in the Baltic and afterwards in the fight with the Bolsheviki on the Volga. Colonel Kazagrandi offered me a bath in a real tub, which had its habitat in the house of the president of the local Chamber of Commerce. As I was in this house, a tall young captain entered. He had long curly red hair and an unusually white face, though heavy and stolid, with large, steel-cold eyes and with beautiful, tender, almost girlish lips. But in his eyes there was such cold cruelty that it was quite unpleasant to look at his otherwise fine face. When he left the room, our host told me that he was Captain Veseloffsky, the adjutant of General Rezukhin, who was fighting against the Bolsheviki in the north of Mongolia.

They had just that day arrived for a conference with Baron Ungern.

After luncheon Colonel Kazagrandi invited me to his *yurta* and began discussing events in western Mongolia, where the situation had become very tense.

"Do you know Dr. Gay?" Kazagrandi asked me. "You know he helped me to form my detachment but Urga accuses him of being the agent of the Soviets."

I made all the defences I could for Gay. He had helped me and had been exonerated by Kolchak.

"Yes, yes, and I justified Gay in such a manner," said the Colonel, "but Rezukhin, who has just arrived today, has brought letters of Gay's to the Bolsheviki which were seized in transit. By order of Baron Ungern, Gay and his family have today been sent to the headquarters of Rezukhin and I fear that they will not reach this destination."

"Why?" I asked.

"They will be executed on the road!" answered Colonel Kazagrandi.

"What are we to do?" I responded. "Gay cannot be a Bolshevik, "because he is too well educated and too clever for it."

"I don't know; I don't know!" murmured the Colonel with a despondent gesture. "Try to speak with Rezukhin."

I decided to proceed at once to Rezukhin but just then Colonel Philipoff entered and began talking about the errors being made in the training of the soldiers. When I had donned my coat, another man came in. He was a small sized officer with an old green Cossack cap with a visor, a torn grey Mongol overcoat and with his right hand in a black sling tied around his neck. It was General Rezukhin, to whom I was at once introduced. During the conversation the General very politely and very skilfully inquired about the lives of Philipoff and myself during the last three years, joking and laughing with discretion and modesty. When he soon took his leave, I availed myself of the chance and went out with him.

He listened very attentively and politely to me and afterwards, in his quiet voice, said:

"Dr. Gay is the agent of the Soviets, disguised as a White in order the better to see, hear and know everything. We are surrounded by our enemies. The Russian people are demoralized and will undertake any treachery for money. Such is Gay. Anyway, what is the use of discussing him further? He and his family are no longer alive. Today my men cut them to pieces five kilometres from here."

In consternation and fear I looked at the face of this small, dapper man with such soft voice and courteous manners. In his eyes I read such hate and tenacity that I understood at once the trembling respect of all the officers whom I had seen in his presence. Afterwards in Urga I learned more of this General Rezukhin distinguished by his absolute bravery and boundless cruelty. He was the watchdog of Baron Ungern, ready to throw himself into the fire and to spring at the throat of anyone his master might indicate.

Only four days then had elapsed before "my acquaintances" died "by a long knife," so that one part of the prediction had been thus fulfilled. And now I have to await Death's threat to me. The delay was not long. Only two days later the Chief of the Asiatic Division of Cavalry arrived—Baron Ungern von Sternberg.

CHAPTER XXXIII

"DEATH FROM THE WHITE MAN WILL STAND BEHIND YOU"

"THE terrible general, the Baron," arrived quite unexpectedly, unnoticed by the outposts of Colonel Kazagrandi. After a talk with Kazagrandi the Baron invited Colonel N. N. Philipoff and me into his presence. Colonel Kazagrandi brought the word to me. I wanted to go at once but was detained about half an hour by the Colonel, who then sped me with the words:

"Now God help you! Go!"

It was a strange parting message, not reassuring and quite enigmatical. I took my Mauser and also hid in the cuff of my coat my cyanide of potassium. The Baron was quartered in the *yurta* of the military doctor. When I entered the court, Captain Veseloffsky came up to me. He had a Cossack sword and a revolver without its holster beneath his girdle. He went into the *yurta* to report my arrival.

"Come in," he said, as he emerged from the tent.

At the entrance my eyes were struck with the sight of a pool of blood that had not yet had time to drain down into the ground—an ominous greeting that seemed to carry the very voice of one just gone before me. I knocked.

"Come in!" was the answer in a high tenor. As I

passed the threshold, a figure in a red silk Mongolian coat rushed at me with the spring of a tiger, grabbed and shook my hand as though in flight across my path and then fell prone on the bed at the side of the tent.

"Tell me who you are! Hereabouts are many spies and agitators," he cried out in an hysterical voice, as he fixed his eyes upon me. In one moment I perceived his appearance and psychology. A small head on wide shoulders; blonde hair in disorder; a reddish bristling moustache; a skinny, exhausted face, like those on the old Byzantine ikons. Then everything else faded from view save a big, protruding forehead overhanging steely sharp eyes. These eyes were fixed upon me like those of an animal from a cave. My observations lasted for but a flash but I understood that before me was a very dangerous man ready for an instant spring into irrevocable action. Though the danger was evident, I felt the deepest offence.

"Sit down," he snapped out in a hissing voice, as he pointed to a chair and impatiently pulled at his moustache. I felt my anger rising through my whole body and I said to him without taking the chair:

"You have allowed yourself to offend me, Baron. My name is well enough known so that you cannot thus indulge yourself in such epithets. You can do with me as you wish, because force is on your side, but you cannot compel me to speak with one who gives me offence."

At these words of mine he swung his feet down off the bed and with evident astonishment began to survey me, holding his breath and pulling still at his moustache. Retaining my exterior calmness, I began to glance indifferently around the *yurta*, and only then I noticed General Rezukhin. I bowed to him and received his silent acknowledgment. After that I swung my glance back to the Baron, who sat with bowed head and closed eyes, from time to time rubbing his brow and mumbling to himself.

Suddenly he stood up and sharply said, looking past and over me:

"Go out! There is no need of more. . . ."

I swung round and saw Captain Veseloffsky with his white, cold face. I had not heard him enter. He did a formal "about face" and passed out of the door.

" 'Death from the white man' has stood behind me," I thought; "but has it quite left me?"

The Baron stood thinking for some time and then began to speak in jumbled, unfinished phrases.

"I ask your pardon. . . . You must understand there are so many traitors! Honest men have disappeared. I cannot trust anybody. All names are false and assumed; documents are counterfeited. Eyes and words deceive. . . . All is demoralized, insulted by Bolshevism. I just ordered Colonel Philipoff cut down, he who called himself the representative of the Russian White Organization. In the lining of his garments were found two secret Bolshevik codes. . . . When my officer flourished his sword over him, he exclaimed: 'Why do you kill me, *Tavarische?*' I cannot trust anybody. . . ."

He was silent and I also held my peace.

"I beg your pardon!" he began anew. "I offended you; but I am not simply a man, I am a leader of great forces and have in my head so much care, sorrow and woe!"

In his voice I felt there was mingled despair and sincerity. He frankly put out his hand to me. Again silence. At last I answered:

"What do you order me to do now, for I have neither counterfeit nor real documents? But many of your officers know me and in Urga I can find many who will testify that I could be neither agitator nor . . ."

"No need, no need!" interrupted the Baron. "All is clear, all is understood! I was in your soul and I know all. It is the truth which Hutuktu Narabanchi has written about you. What can I do for you?"

I explained how my friend and I had escaped from Soviet Russia in the effort to reach our native land and how a group of Polish soldiers had joined us in the hope of getting back to Poland; and I asked that help be given us to reach the nearest port.

"With pleasure, with pleasure. . . . I will help you all," he answered excitely. "I shall drive you to Urga in my motor car. Tomorrow we shall start and there in Urga we shall talk about further arrangements."

Taking my leave, I went out of the *yurta*. On arriving at my quarters, I found Colonel Kazagrandi in great anxiety walking up and down my room.

"Thanks be to God!" he exclaimed and crossed himself.

His joy was very touching but at the same time I thought that the Colonel could have taken much more active measures for the salvation of his guest, if he had been so minded. The agitation of this day had tired me and made me feel years older. When I looked in the mirror I was certain there were more white hairs on my head. At night I could not sleep for the flashing thoughts of the young, fine face of Colonel Philipoff, the pool of blood, the cold eyes of Captain Veseloffsky, the sound of Baron Ungern's voice with its tones of despair and woe, until finally I sank into a heavy stupor. I was awakened by Baron Ungern who came to ask pardon that he could not take me in his motor car, because he was obliged to take Daichin Van with him. But he informed me that he had left instructions to give me his own white camel and two Cossacks as servants. I had no time to thank him before he rushed out of my room.

Sleep then entirely deserted me, so I dressed and began smoking pipe after pipe of tobacco, as I thought: "How much easier to fight the Bolsheviki on the swamps of Seybi and to cross the snowy peaks of Ulan Taiga, where the bad demons kill all the travelers they can! There everything was simple and comprehensible, but here it is all a mad nightmare, a dark and foreboding storm!" I felt some tragedy, some horror in every movement of Baron Ungern, behind whom paced this silent, white-faced Veseloffsky and Death.

CHAPTER XXXIV.

THE HORROR OF WAR!

AT dawn of the following morning they led up the splendid white camel for me and we moved away. My company consisted of the two Cossacks, two Mongol soldiers and one Lama with two pack camels carrying the tent and food. I still apprehended that the Baron had it in mind not to dispose of me before my friends there in Van Kure but to prepare this journey for me under the guise of which it would be so easy to do away with me by the road. A bullet in the back and all would be finished. Consequently I was momentarily ready to draw my revolver and defend myself. I took care all the time to have the Cossacks either ahead of me or at the side. About noon we heard the distant honk of a motor car and soon saw Baron Ungern whizzing by us at full speed. With him were two adjutants and Prince Daichin Van. The Baron greeted me very kindly and shouted:

"Shall see you again in Urga!"

"Ah!" I thought, "evidently I shall reach Urga. So I can be at ease during my trip, and in Urga I have many friends beside the presence there of the bold Polish soldiers whom I had worked with in Uliassutai and who had outdistanced me in this journey."

After the meeting with the Baron my Cossacks became very attentive to me and sought to distract me with stories. They told me about their very severe struggles with the Bolsheviki in Transbaikalia and Mongolia, about the battle with the Chinese near Urga, about finding communistic passports on several Chinese soldiers from Moscow, about the bravery of Baron Ungern and how he would sit at the campfire smoking and drinking tea right on the battle line without ever being touched by a bullet. At one fight seventy-four bullets entered his overcoat, saddle and the boxes by his side and again left him untouched. This is one of the reasons for his great influence over the Mongols. They related how before the battle he had made a reconnaissance in Urga with only one Cossack and on his way back had killed a Chinese officer and two soldiers with his bamboo stick or *tashur;* how he had no outfit save one change of linen and one extra pair of boots; how he was always calm and jovial in battle and severe and morose in the rare days of peace; and how he was everywhere his soldiers were fighting.

I told them, in turn, of my escape from Siberia and with chatting thus the day slipped by very quickly. Our camels trotted all the time, so that instead of the ordinary eighteen to twenty miles per day we made nearly fifty. My mount was the fastest of them all. He was a huge white animal with a splendid thick mane and had been presented to Baron Ungern by some Prince of Inner Mongolia with two black sables tied on the bridle. He was a calm, strong, bold giant of the desert, on whose back I felt myself as though perched on the tower of a building. Beyond the Orkhon River we came across the first dead body of a Chinese soldier, which lay face up and arms outstretched right in the middle of the road.

When we had crossed the Burgut Mountains, we entered the Tola River valley, farther up which Urga is located. The road was strewn with the overcoats, shirts, boots, caps and kettles which the Chinese had thrown away in their flight; and marked by many of their dead. Further on the road crossed a morass, where on either side lay great mounds of the dead bodies of men, horses and camels with broken carts and military débris of every sort. Here the Tibetans of Baron Ungern had cut up the escaping Chinese baggage transport; and it was a 'strange and gloomy contrast to see the piles of dead besides the effervescing awakening life of spring. In every pool wild ducks of different kinds floated about; in the high grass the cranes performed their weird dance of courtship; on the lakes great flocks of swans and geese were swimming; through the swampy places like spots of light moved the brilliantly colored pairs of the Mongolian sacred bird, the *turpan* or "Lama goose"; on the higher dry places flocks of wild turkey gamboled and fought as they fed; flocks of the *salga* partridge whistled by; while on the mountain side not far away the wolves lay basking and turning in the lazy warmth of the sun, whining and occasionally barking like playful dogs.

Nature knows only life. Death is for her but an episode whose traces she rubs out with sand and snow or ornaments with luxuriant greenery and brightly colored bushes and flowers. What matters it to Nature if a mother at Chefoo or on the banks of the Yangtse offers her bowl of rice with burning incense at some shrine and prays for the return of her son that has fallen unknown for all time on the plains along the Tola, where his bones will dry beneath the rays of Nature's dissipating fire and be scattered by her winds over the sands of the prairie? It is splendid, this indifference of Nature to death, and her greediness for life!

On the fourth day we made the shores of the Tola well after nightfall. We could not find the regular ford and I forced my camel to enter the stream in the attempt to make a crossing without guidance. Very fortunately I found a shallow, though somewhat miry, place and we got over all right. This is something to be thankful for in fording a river with a camel; because, when your mount finds the water too deep, coming up around his neck, he does not strike out and swim like a horse will do but just rolls over on his side and floats, which is vastly inconvenient for his rider. Down by the river we pegged our tent.

Fifteen miles further on we crossed a battlefield, where the third great battle for the independence of Mongolia had been fought. Here the troops of Baron Ungern clashed with six thousand Chinese moving down from Kiakhta to the aid of Urga. The Chinese were completely defeated and four thousand prisoners taken. However, these surrendered Chinese tried to escape during the night. Baron Ungern sent the Transbaikal Cossacks and Tibetans in pursuit of them and it was their work which we saw on this field of death. There were still about fifteen hundred unburied and as many more interred, according to the statements of our Cossacks, who had participated in this battle. The killed showed terrible sword wounds; everywhere equipment and other débris were scattered about. The Mongols with their herds moved away from the neighborhood and their place was taken by the wolves which hid behind every stone and in every ditch as we passed. Packs of dogs that had become wild fought with the wolves over the prey.

At last we left this place of carnage to the cursed god of war. Soon we approached a shallow, rapid stream, where the Mongols slipped from their camels, took off their caps and began drinking. It was a sacred stream which passed beside the abode of the Living Buddha. From this winding valley we suddenly turned into another where a great mountain ridge covered with dark, dense forest loomed up before us.

"Holy Bogdo-Ol!" exclaimed the Lama. "The abode of the Gods which guard our Living Buddha!"

Bogdo-Ol is the huge knot which ties together here three mountain chains: Gegyl from the southwest, Gangyn from the south, and Huntu from the north. This mountain covered with virgin forest is the property of the Living Buddha. The forests are full of nearly all the varieties of animals found in Mongolia, but hunting is not allowed. Any Mongol violating this law is condemned to death, while foreigners are deported. Crossing the Bogdo-Ol is forbidden under penalty of death. This command was transgressed by only one man, Baron Ungern, who crossed the mountain with fifty Cossacks, penetrated to the palace of the Living Buddha, where the Pontiff of Urga was being held under arrest by the Chinese, and stole him.

CHAPTER XXXV

IN THE CITY OF LIVING GODS, OF 30,000 BUDDHAS AND 60,000 MONKS

AT last before our eyes the abode of the Living Buddha! At the foot of Bogdo-Ol behind white walls rose a white Tibetan building covered with greenish-blue tiles that glittered under the sunshine. It was richly set among groves of trees dotted here and there with the fantastic roofs of shrines and small palaces, while further from the mountain it was connected by a long wooden bridge across the Tola with the city of monks, sacred and revered throughout all the East as Ta Kure or Urga. Here besides the Living Buddha live whole throngs of secondary miracle workers, prophets, sorcerers and wonderful doctors. All these people have divine origin and are honored as living gods. At the left on the high plateau stands an old monastery with a huge, dark red tower, which is known as the "Temple Lamas City," containing a gigantic bronze gilded statue of Buddha sitting on the golden flower of the lotus; tens of smaller temples, shrines, obo, open altars, towers for astrology and the grey city of the Lamas consisting of single-storied houses and yurtas, where about 60,000 monks of all ages and ranks dwell; schools, sacred archives and libraries, the houses of Bandi and the inns for the honored guests from China, Tibet, and the lands of the Buriat and Kalmuck.

Down below the monastery is the foreign settlement where the Russian, foreign and richest Chinese merchants live and where the multi-colored and crowded oriental bazaar carries forward its bustling life. A kilometre away the greyish enclosure of Maimachen surrounds the remaining Chinese trading establishments, while farther on one sees a long row of Russian private houses, a hospital, church, prison and, last of all, the awkward four-storied red brick building that was formerly the Russian Consulate.

We were already within a short distance of the monastery, when I noticed several Mongol soldiers in the mouth of a ravine nearby, dragging back and concealing in the ravine three dead bodies.

"What are they doing?" I asked.

The Cossacks only smiled without answering. Suddenly they straightened up with a sharp salute. Out of the ravine came a small, stocky Mongolian pony with a short man in the saddle. As he passed us, I noticed the epaulets of a colonel and the green cap with a visor. He examined me with cold, colorless eyes from under dense brows. As he went on ahead, he took off his cap and wiped the perspiration from his bald head. My eyes were struck by the strange undulating line of his skull. It was the man "with the head like a saddle," against whom I had been warned by the old fortune teller at the last *ourton* outside Van Kure!

"Who is this officer?" I inquired.

Although he was already quite a distance in front of us, the Cossacks whispered: "Colonel Sepailoff, Commandant of Urga City."

Colonel Sepailoff, the darkest person on the canvas

of Mongolian events! Formerly a mechanician, afterwards a gendarme, he had gained quick promotion under
the Czar's régime. He was always nervously jerking and
wriggling his body and talking ceaselessly, making most
unattractive sounds in his throat and sputtering with
saliva all over his lips, his whole face often contracted
with spasms. He was mad and Baron Ungern twice appointed a commission of surgeons to examine him and
ordered him to rest in the hope he could rid the man of
his evil genius. Undoubtedly Sepailoff was a sadist. I
heard afterwards that he himself executed the condemned
people, joking and singing as he did his work. Dark,
terrifying tales were current about him in Urga. He
was a bloodhound, fastening his victims with the jaws
of death. All the glory of the cruelty of Baron Ungern
belonged to Sepailoff. Afterwards Baron Ungern once
told me in Urga that this Sepailoff annoyed him and that
Sepailoff could kill him just as well as others. Baron
Ungern feared Sepailoff, not as a man, but dominated by
his own superstition, because Sepailoff had found in
Transbaikalia a witch doctor who predicted the death of
the Baron if he dismissed Sepailoff. Sepailoff knew no
pardon for Bolshevik nor for any one connected with
the Bolsheviki in any way. The reason for his vengeful
spirit was that the Bolsheviki had tortured him in prison
and, after his escape, had killed all his family. He was
now taking his revenge.

I put up with a Russian firm and was at once visited
by my associates from Uliassutai, who greeted me with
great joy because they had been much exercised about
the events in Van Kure and Zain Shabi. When I had
bathed and spruced up, I went out with them on the

street. We entered the bazaar. The whole market was crowded. To the lively colored groups of men buying, selling and shouting their wares, the bright streamers of Chinese cloth, the strings of pearls, the earrings and bracelets gave an air of endless festivity; while on another side buyers were feeling of live sheep to see whether they were fat or not, the butcher was cutting great pieces of mutton from the hanging carcasses and everywhere these sons of the plain were joking and jesting. The Mongolian women in their huge coiffures and heavy silver caps like saucers on their heads were admiring the variegated silk ribbons and long chains of coral beads; an imposing big Mongol attentively examined a small herd of splendid horses and bargained with the Mongol *zahachine* or owner of the horses; a skinny, quick, black Tibetan, who had come to Urga to pray to the Living Buddha or, maybe, with a secret message from the other "God" in Lhasa, squatted and bargained for an image of the Lotus Buddha carved in agate; in another corner a big crowd of Mongols and Buriats had collected and surrounded a Chinese merchant selling finely painted snuff-bottles of glass, crystal, porcelain, amethyst, jade, agate and nephrite, for one of which made of a greenish milky nephrite with regular brown veins running through it and carved with a dragon winding itself around a bevy of young damsels the merchant was demanding of his Mongol inquirers ten young oxen; and everywhere Buriats in their long red coats and small red caps embroidered with gold helped the Tartars in black overcoats and black velvet caps on the back of their heads to weave the pattern of this Oriental human tapestry. Lamas formed the common background for it all, as they

wandered about in their yellow and red robes, with capes
picturesquely thrown over their shoulders and caps of
many forms, some like yellow mushrooms, others like the
red Phrygian bonnets or old Greek helmets in red. They
mingled with the crowd, chatting serenely and counting
their rosaries, telling fortunes for those who would hear
but chiefly searching out the rich Mongols whom they
could cure or exploit by fortune telling, predictions or
other mysteries of a city of 60,000 Lamas. Simultaneously religious and political espionage was being carried
out. Just at this time many Mongols were arriving from
Inner Mongolia and they were continuously surrounded
by an invisible but numerous network of watching Lamas.
Over the buildings around floated the Russian, Chinese
and Mongolian national flags with a single one of the
Stars and Stripes above a small shop in the market; while
over the nearby tents and *yurtas* streamed the ribbons,
the squares, the circles and triangles of the princes and
private persons afflicted or dying from smallpox and
leprosy. All were mingled and mixed in one bright mass
strongly lighted by the sun. Occasionally one saw the
soldiers of Baron Ungern rushing about in long blue
coats; Mongols and Tibetans in red coats with yellow
epaulets bearing the swastika of Jenghiz Khan and the
initials of the Living Buddha; and Chinese soldiers from
their detachment in the Mongolian army. After the defeat of the Chinese army two thousand of these braves
petitioned the Living Buddha to enlist them in his legions,
swearing fealty and faith to him. They were accepted
and formed into two regiments bearing the old Chinese
silver dragons on their caps and shoulders.

As we crossed this market, from around a corner came

a big motor car with the roar of a siren. There was Baron Ungern in the yellow silk Mongolian coat with a blue girdle. He was going very fast but recognized me at once, stopping and getting out to invite me to go with him to his *yurta*. The Baron lived in a small, simply arranged *yurta*, set up in the courtyard of a Chinese *hong*. He had his headquarters in two other *yurtas* nearby, while his servants occupied one of the Chinese *fang-tzu*. When I reminded him of his promise to help me to reach the open ports, the General looked at me with his bright eyes and spoke in French:

"My work here is coming to an end. In nine days I shall begin the war with the Bolsheviki and shall go into the Transbaikal. I beg that you will spend this time here. For many years I have lived without civilized society. I am alone with my thoughts and I would like to have you know them, speaking with me not as the 'bloody mad Baron,' as my enemies call me, nor as the 'severe grandfather,' which my officers and soldiers call me, but as an ordinary man who has sought much and has suffered even more."

The Baron reflected for some minutes and then continued:

"I have thought about the further trip of your group and I shall arrange everything for you, but I ask you to remain here these nine days."

What was I to do? I agreed. The Baron shook my hand warmly and ordered tea.

CHAPTER XXXVI

A SON OF CRUSADERS AND PRIVATEERS

"TELL me about yourself and your trip," he urged. In response I related all that I thought would interest him and he appeared quite excited over my tale.

"Now I shall tell you about myself, who and what I am! My name is surrounded with such hate and fear that no one can judge what is the truth and what is false, what is history and what myth. Some time you will write about it, remembering your trip through Mongolia and your sojourn at the *yurta* of the 'bloody General.' "

He shut his eyes, smoking as he spoke, and tumbling out his sentences without finishing them as though some one would prevent him from phrasing them.

"The family of Ungern von Sternberg is an old family, a mixture of Germans with Hungarians—Huns from the time of Attila. My warlike ancestors took part in all the European struggles. They participated in the Crusades and one Ungern was killed under the walls of Jerusalem, fighting under Richard Cœur de Lion. Even the tragic Crusade of the Children was marked by the death of Ralph Ungern, eleven years old. When the boldest warriors of the country were despatched to the eastern border of the German Empire against the Slavs in the twelfth century, my ancestor Arthur was among them, Baron Halsa Ungern Sternberg. Here these bor-

der knights formed the order of Monk Knights or Teutons, which with fire and sword spread Christianity among
the pagan Lithuanians, Esthonians, Latvians and Slavs.
Since then the Teuton Order of Knights has always had
among its members representatives of our family. When
the Teuton Order perished in the Grünwald under the
swords of the Polish and Lithuanian troops, two Barons
Ungern von Sternberg were killed there. Our family
was warlike and given to mysticism and asceticism.

"During the sixteenth and seventeenth centuries several
Barons von Ungern had their castles in the lands of
Latvia and Esthoria. Many legends and tales lived after
them. Heinrich Ungern von Sternberg, called 'Ax,' was
a wandering knight. The tournaments of France, England, Spain and Italy knew his name and lance, which
filled the hearts of his opponents with fear. He fell at
Cadiz 'neath the sword of a knight who cleft both his
helmet and his skull. Baron Ralph Ungern was a brigand
knight between Riga and Reval. Baron Peter Ungern
had his castle on the island of Dago in the Baltic Sea,
where as a privateer he ruled the merchantmen of his day.

"In the beginning of the eighteenth century there was
also a well-known Baron Wilhelm Ungern, who was referred to as the 'brother of Satan' because he was an
alchemist. My grandfather was a privateer in the Indian
Ocean, taking his tribute from the English traders whose
warships could not catch him for several years. At last
he was captured and handed to the Russian Consul, who
transported him to Russia where he was sentenced to
deportation to the Transbaikal. I am also a naval officer
but the Russo-Japanese War forced me to leave my regular profession to join and fight with the Zabaikal Cos-

sacks. I have spent all my life in war or in the study and learning of Buddhism. My grandfather brought Buddhism to us from India and my father and I accepted and professed it. In Transbaikalia I tried to form the order of Military Buddhists for an uncompromising fight against the depravity of revolution."

He fell into silence and began drinking cup after cup of tea as strong and black as coffee.

"Depravity of revolution!... Has anyone ever thought of it besides the French philosopher, Bergson, and the most learned Tashi Lama in Tibet?"

The grandson of the privateer, quoting scientific theories, works, the names of scientists and writers, the Holy Bible and Buddhist books, mixing together French, German, Russian and English, continued:

"In the Buddhistic and ancient Christian books we read stern predictions about the time when the war between the good and evil spirits must begin. Then there must come the unknown 'Curse' which will conquer the world, blot out culture, kill morality and destroy all the people. Its weapon is revolution. During every revolution the previously experienced intellect-creator will be replaced by the new rough force of the destroyer. He will place and hold in the first rank the lower instincts and desires. Man will be farther removed from the divine and the spiritual. The Great War proved that humanity must progress upward toward higher ideals; but then appeared that Curse which was seen and felt by Christ, the Apostle John, Buddha, the first Christian martyrs, Dante, Leonardo da Vinci, Goethe and Dostoyevsky. It appeared, turned back the wheel of progress and blocked our road to the Divinity. Revolution is

an infectious disease and Europe making the treaty with
Moscow deceived itself and the other parts of the world.
The Great Spirit put at the threshold of our lives Karma,
who knows neither anger nor pardon. He will reckon
the account, whose total will be famine, destruction, the
death of culture, of glory, of honor and of spirit, the
death of states and the death of peoples. I see already
this horror, this dark, mad destruction of humanity."

The door of the *yurta* suddenly swung open and an
adjutant snapped into a position of attention and salute.

"Why do you enter a room by force?" the General
exclaimed in anger.

"Your Excellency, our outpost on the border has
caught a Bolshevik reconnaissance party and brought
them here."

The Baron arose. His eyes sparkled and his face contracted with spasms.

"Bring them in front of my *yurta!*" he ordered.

All was forgotten—the inspired speech, the penetrating voice—all were sunk in the austere order of the
severe commander. The Baron put on his cap, caught up
the bamboo *tashur* which he always carried with him and
rushed from the *yurta*. I followed him out. There
in front of the *yurta* stood six Red soldiers surrounded
by the Cossacks.

The Baron stopped and glared sharply at them for
several minutes. In his face one could see the strong
play of his thoughts. Afterwards he turned away from
them, sat down on the doorstep of the Chinese house
and for a long time was buried in thought. Then he
rose, walked over to them and, with an evident show of
decisiveness in his movements, touched all the prisoners

on the shoulder with his *tashur* and said: "You to the left and you to the right!" as he divided the squad into two sections, four on the right and two on the left.

"Search those two! They must be commissars!" commanded the Baron and, turning to the other four, asked: "Are you peasants mobilized by the Bolsheviki?"

"Just so, Your Excellency!" cried the frightened soldiers.

"Go to the Commandant and tell him that I have ordered you to be enlisted in my troops!"

On the two to the left they found passports of Commissars of the Communist Political Department. The General knitted his brows and slowly pronounced the following:

"Beat them to death with sticks!"

He turned and entered the *yurta*. After this our conversation did not flow readily and so I left the Baron to himself.

After dinner in the Russian firm where I was staying some of Ungern's officers came in. We were chatting animatedly when suddenly we heard the horn of an automobile, which instantly threw the officers into silence.

"The General is passing somewhere near," one of them remarked in a strangely altered voice.

Our interrupted conversation was soon resumed but not for long. The clerk of the firm came running into the room and exclaimed: "The Baron!"

He entered the door but stopped on the threshold. The lamps had not yet been lighted and it was getting dark inside, but the Baron instantly recognized us all, approached and kissed the hand of the hostess, greeted everyone very cordially and, accepting the cup of tea offered him, drew up to the table to drink. Soon he spoke:

"I want to steal your guest," he said to the hostess and then, turning to me, asked: "Do you want to go for a motor ride? I shall show you the city and the environs."

Donning my coat, I followed my established custom and slipped my revolver into it, at which the Baron laughed.

"Leave that trash behind! Here you are in safety. Besides you must remember the prediction of Narabanchi Hutuktu that Fortune will ever be with you."

"All right," I answered, also with a laugh. "I remember very well this prediction. Only I do not know what the Hutuktu thinks 'Fortune' means for me. Maybe it is death like the rest after my hard, long trip, and I must confess that I prefer to travel farther and am not ready to die."

We went out to the gate where the big Fiat stood with its intruding great lights. The chauffeur officer sat at the wheel like a statue and remained at salute all the time we were entering and seating ourselves.

"To the wireless station!" commanded the Baron.

We veritably leapt forward. The city swarmed, as earlier, with the Oriental throng, but its appearance now was even more strange and miraculous. In among the noisy crowd Mongol, Buriat and Tibetan riders threaded swiftly; caravans of camels solemnly raised their heads as we passed; the wooden wheels of the Mongol carts screamed in pain; and all was illumined by splendid great arc lights from the electric station which Baron Ungern had ordered erected immediately after the cap-

ture of Urga, together with a telephone system and
wireless station. He also ordered his men to clean and
disinfect the city which had probably not felt the broom
since the days of Jenghiz Khan. He arranged an auto-
bus traffic between different parts of the city; built
bridges over the Tola and Orkhon; published a news-
paper; arranged a veterinary laboratory and hospitals;
re-opened the schools; protected commerce, mercilessly
hanging Russian and Mongolian soldiers for pillaging
Chinese firms.

In one of these cases his Commandant arrested two
Cossacks and a Mongol soldier who had stolen brandy
from one of the Chinese shops and brought them before
him. He immediately bundled them all into his car,
drove off to the shop, delivered the brandy back to the
proprietor and as promptly ordered the Mongol to hang
one of the Russians to the big gate of the compound.
With this one swung he commanded: "Now hang the
other!" and this had only just been accomplished when
he turned to the Commandant and ordered him to hang
the Mongol beside the other two. That seemed expedi-
tious and just enough until the Chinese proprietor came
in dire distress to the Baron and plead with him:

"General Baron! General Baron! Please take those
men down from my gateway, for no one will enter my
shop!"

After the commercial quarter was flashed past our
eyes, we entered the Russian settlement across a small
river. Several Russian soldiers and four very spruce-
looking Mongolian women stood on the bridge as we
passed. The soldiers snapped to salute like immobile
statues and fixed their eyes on the severe face of their

Commander. The women first began to run and shift about and then, infected by the discipline and order of events, swung their hands up to salute and stood as immobile as their northern swains. The Baron looked at me and laughed:

"You see the discipline! Even the Mongolian women salute me."

Soon we were out on the plain with the car going like an arrow, with the wind whistling and tossing the folds of our coats and caps. But Baron Ungern, sitting with closed eyes, repeated: "Faster! Faster!" For a long time we were both silent.

"And yesterday I beat my adjutant for rushing into my *yurta* and interrupting my story," he said.

"You can finish it now," I answered.

"And are you not bored by it? Well, there isn't much left and this happens to be the most interesting. I was telling you that I wanted to found an order of military Buddhists in Russia. For what? For the protection of the processes of evolution of humanity and for the struggle against revolution, because I am certain that evolution leads to the Divinity and revolution to bestiality. But I worked in Russia! In Russia, where the peasants are rough, untutored, wild and constantly angry, hating everybody and everything without understanding why. They are suspicious and materialistic, having no sacred ideals. Russian intelligents live among imaginary ideals without realities. They have a strong capacity for criticising everything but they lack creative power. Also they have no will power, only the capacity for talking and talking. With the peasants, they cannot like anything or anybody. Their love and feelings are imaginary.

Their thoughts and sentiments pass without trace like futile words. My companions, therefore, soon began to violate the regulations of the Order. Then I introduced the condition of celibacy, the entire negation of woman, of the comforts of life, of superfluities, according to the teachings of the Yellow Faith; and, in order that the Russian might be able to live down his physical nature, I introduced the limitless use of alcohol, hasheesh and opium. Now for alcohol I hang my officers and soldiers; then we drank to the 'white fever,' delirium tremens. I could not organize the Order but I gathered round me and developed three hundred men wholly bold and entirely ferocious. Afterward they were heroes in the war with Germany and later in the fight against the Bolsheviki, but now only a few remain."

"The wireless, Excellency!" reported the chauffeur.

"Turn in there!" ordered the General.

On the top of a flat hill stood the big, powerful radio station which had been partially destroyed by the retreating Chinese but reconstructed by the engineers of Baron Ungern. The General perused the telegrams and handed them to me. They were from Moscow, Chita, Vladivostok and Peking. On a separate yellow sheet were the code messages, which the Baron slipped into his pocket as he said to me:

"They are from my agents, who are stationed in Chita, Irkutsk, Harbin and Vladivostok. They are all Jews, very skilled and very bold men, friends of mine all. I have also one Jewish officer, Vulfovitch, who commands my right flank. He is as ferocious as Satan but clever and brave. . . . Now we shall fly into space."

Once more we rushed away, sinking into the darkness

of night. It was a wild ride. The car bounded over small stones and ditches, even taking narrow streamlets, as the skilled chauffeur only seemed to guide it round the larger rocks. On the plain, as we sped by, I noticed several times small bright flashes of fire which lasted but for a second and then were extinguished.

"The eyes of wolves," smiled my companion. "We have fed them to satiety from the flesh of ourselves and our enemies!" he quietly interpolated, as he turned to continue his confession of faith.

"During the War we saw the gradual corruption of the Russian army and foresaw the treachery of Russia to the Allies as well as the approaching danger of revolution. To counteract this latter a plan was formed to join together all the Mongolian peoples which had not forgotten their ancient faiths and customs into one Asiatic State, consisting of autonomous tribal units, under the moral and legislative leadership of China, the country of loftiest and most ancient culture. Into this State must come the Chinese, Mongols, Tibetans, Afghans, the Mongol tribes of Turkestan, Tartars, Buriats, Kirghiz and Kalmucks. This State must be strong, physically and morally, and must erect a barrier against revolution and carefully preserve its own spirit, philosophy and individual policy. If humanity, mad and corrupted, continues to threaten the Divine Spirit in mankind, to spread blood and to obstruct moral development, the Asiatic State must terminate this movement decisively and establish a permanent, firm peace. This propaganda even during the War made splendid progress among the Turkomans, Kirghiz, Buriats and Mongols. . . . Stop!" suddenly shouted the Baron.

The car pulled up with a jerk. The General jumped out and called me to follow. We started walking over the prairie and the Baron kept bending down all the time as though he were looking for something on the ground.

"Ah!" he murmured at last, "He has gone away. . . ."

I looked at him in amazement.

"A rich Mongol formerly had his *yurta* here. He was the outfitter for the Russian merchant, Noskoff. Noskoff was a ferocious man as shown by the name the Mongols gave him—'Satan.' He used to have his Mongol debtors beaten or imprisoned through the instrumentality of the Chinese authorities. He ruined this Mongol, who lost everything and escaped to a place thirty miles away; but Noskoff found him there, took all that he had left of cattle and horses and left the Mongol and his family to die of hunger. When I captured Urga, this Mongol appeared and brought with him thirty other Mongol families similarly ruined by Noskoff. They demanded his death. . . . So I hung 'Satan' . . ."

Anew the motor car was rushing along, sweeping a great circle on the prairie, and anew Baron Ungern with his sharp, nervous voice carried his thoughts round the whole circumference of Asian life.

"Russia turned traitor to France, England and America, signed the Brest-Litovsk Treaty and ushered in a reign of chaos. We then decided to mobilize Asia against Germany. Our envoys penetrated Mongolia, Tibet, Turkestan and China. At this time the Bolsheviki began to kill all the Russian officers and we were forced to open civil war against them, giving up our Pan-Asiatic plans; but we hope later to awake all Asia and with their help to bring peace and God back to earth. I want to feel that I have helped this idea by the liberation of Mongolia."

He became silent and thought for a moment.

"But some of my associates in the movement do not like me because of my atrocities and severity," he remarked in a sad voice. "They cannot understand as yet that we are not fighting a political party but a sect of murderers of all contemporary spiritual culture. Why do the Italians execute the 'Black Hand' gang? Why are the Americans electrocuting anarchistic bomb throwers? and I am not allowed to rid the world of those who would kill the soul of the people? I, a Teuton, descendant of crusaders and privateers, I recognize only death for murderers! . . . Return!" he commanded the chauffeur.

An hour and a half later we saw the electric lights of Urga.

CHAPTER XXXVII

THE CAMP OF MARTYRS

NEAR the entrance to the town, a motor car stood before a small house.

"What does that mean?" exclaimed the Baron. "Go over there!"

Our car drew up beside the other. The house door opened sharply, several officers rushed out and tried to hide.

"Stand!" commanded the General. "Go back inside."

They obeyed and he entered after them, leaning on his *tashur*. As the door remained open, I could see and hear everything.

"Woe to them!" whispered the chauffeur. "Our officers knew that the Baron had gone out of the town with me, which means always a long journey, and must have decided to have a good time. He will order them beaten to death with sticks."

I could see the end of the table covered with bottles and tinned things. At the side two young women were seated, who sprang up at the appearance of the General. I could hear the hoarse voice of Baron Ungern pronouncing sharp, short, stern phrases.

"Your native land is perishing. . . . The shame of it is upon all you Russians . . . and you cannot understand it . . . nor feel it. . . . You need wine and women. . . . Scoundrels! Brutes! . . . One hundred fifty *tashur* for every man of you."

The voice fell to a whisper.

"And you, Mesdames, do you not realize the ruin of your people? No? For you it is of no moment. And have you no feeling for your husbands at the front who may even now be killed? You are not women. . . . I honor woman, who feels more deeply and strongly than man; but you are not women! . . . Listen to me, Mesdames. Once more and I will hang you. . . ."

He came back to the car and himself sounded the horn several times. Immediately Mongol horsemen galloped up.

"Take these men to the Commandant. I will send my orders later."

On the way to the Baron's *yurta* we were silent. He was excited and breathed heavily, lighting cigarette after cigarette and throwing them aside after but a single puff or two.

"Take supper with me," he proposed.

He also invited his Chief of Staff, a very retiring, oppressed but splendidly educated man. The servants spread a Chinese hot course for us followed by cold meat and fruit compote from California with the inevitable tea. We ate with chopsticks. The Baron was greatly distraught.

Very cautiously I began speaking of the offending officers and tried to justify their actions by the extremely trying circumstances under which they were living.

"They are rotten through and through, demoralized, sunk into the depths," murmured the General.

The Chief of Staff helped me out and at last the Baron

directed him to telephone the Commandant to release these gentlemen.

The following day I spent with my friends, walking a great deal about the streets and watching their busy life. The great energy of the Baron demanded constant nervous activity from himself and every one round him. He was everywhere, seeing everything but never interfering with the work of his subordinate administrators. Every one was at work.

In the evening I was invited by the Chief of Staff to his quarters, where I met many intelligent officers. I related again the story of my trip and we were all chatting along animatedly when suddenly Colonel Sepailoff entered, singing to himself. All the others at once became silent and one by one under various pretexts they slipped out. He handed our host some papers and, turning to us, said:

"I shall send you for supper a splendid fish pie and some hot tomato soup."

As he left, my host clasped his head in desperation and said:

"With such scum of the earth are we now forced after this revolution to work!"

A few minutes later a soldier from Sepailoff brought us a tureen full of soup and the fish pie. As the soldier bent over the table to set the dishes down, the Chief motioned me with his eyes and slipped to me the words: "Notice his face."

When the man went out, my host sat attentively listening until the sounds of the man's steps ceased.

"He is Sepailoff's executioner who hangs and strangles the unfortunate condemned ones."

Then, to my amazement, he began to pour out the soup on the ground beside the brazier and, going out of the *yurta,* threw the pie over the fence.

"It is Sepailoff's feast and, though it may be very tasty, it may also be poison.   In Sepailoff's house it is dangerous to eat or drink anything."

Distinctly oppressed by these doings, I returned to my house.   My host was not yet asleep and met me with a frightened look.   My friends were also there.

"God be thanked!" they all exclaimed.   "Has nothing happened to you?"

"What is the matter?" I asked.

"You see," began the host, "after your departure a soldier came from Sepailoff and took your luggage, saying that you had sent him for it; but we knew what it meant—that they would first search it and afterwards. . . ."

I at once understood the danger.   Sepailoff could place anything he wanted in my luggage and afterwards accuse me.   My old friend, the agronome, and I started at once for Sepailoff's, where I left him at the door while I went in and was met by the same soldier who had brought the supper to us.   Sepailoff received me immediately.   In answer to my protest he said that it was a mistake and, asking me to wait for a moment, went out.   I waited five, ten, fifteen minutes but nobody came. I knocked on the door but no one answered me.   Then I decided to go to Baron Ungern and started for the exit.   The door was locked.   Then I tried the other door and found that also locked.   I had been trapped! I wanted at once to whistle to my friend but just then noticed a telephone on the wall and called up Baron

Ungern. In a few minutes he appeared together with Sepailoff.

"What is this?" he asked Sepailoff in a severe, threatening voice; and, without waiting for an answer, struck him a blow with his *tashur* that sent him to the floor.

We went out and the General ordered my luggage produced. Then he brought me to his own *yurta*.

"Live here, now," he said. "I am very glad of this accident," he remarked with a smile, "for now I can say all that I want to."

This drew from me the question:

"May I describe all that I have heard and seen here?"

He thought a moment before replying: "Give me your notebook."

I handed him the album with my sketches of the trip and he wrote therein: "After my death, Baron Ungern."

"But I am older than you and I shall die before you," I remarked.

He shut his eyes, bowed his head and whispered:

"Oh, no! One hundred thirty days yet and it is finished; then . . . Nirvana! How wearied I am with sorrow, woe and hate!"

We were silent for a long time. I felt that I had now a mortal enemy in Colonel Sepailoff and that I should get out of Urga at the earliest possible moment. It was two o'clock at night. Suddenly Baron Ungern stood up.

"Let us go to the great, good Buddha," he said with a countenance held in deep thought and with eyes aflame, his whole face contracted by a mournful, bitter smile. He ordered the car brought.

Thus lived this camp of martyrs, refugees pursued by

events to their tryst with Death, driven on by the hate and contempt of this offspring of Teutons and privateers! And he, martyring them, knew neither day nor night of peace. Fired by impelling, poisonous thoughts, he tormented himself with the pains of a Titan, knowing that every day in this shortening chain of one hundred thirty links brought him nearer to the precipice called "Death."

CHAPTER XXXVIII

BEFORE THE FACE OF BUDDHA

AS we came to the monastery we left the automobile and dipped into the labyrinth of narrow alleyways until at last we were before the greatest temple of Urga with the Tibetan walls and windows and its pretentious Chinese roof. A single lantern burned at the entrance. The heavy gate with the bronze and iron trimmings was shut. When the General struck the big brass gong hanging by the gate, frightened monks began running up from all directions and, seeing the "General Baron," fell to the earth in fear of raising their heads.

"Get up," said the Baron, "and let us into the Temple!"

The inside was like that of all Lama temples, the same multi-colored flags with the prayers, symbolic signs and the images of holy saints; the big bands of silk cloth hanging from the ceiling; the images of the gods and goddesses. On both sides of the approach to the altar were the low red benches for the Lamas and choir. On the altar small lamps threw their rays on the gold and silver vessels and candlesticks. Behind it hung a heavy yellow silk curtain with Tibetan inscriptions. The Lamas drew the curtain aside. Out of the dim light from the flickering lamps gradually appeared the great gilded statue of Buddha seated in the Golden Lotus. The face of the god was indifferent and calm with only a soft gleam of light animating it.   On either side he was guarded by many thousands of lesser Buddhas brought by the faithful as offerings in prayer. The Baron struck the gong to attract Great Buddha's attention to his prayer and threw a handful of coins into the large bronze bowl.   And then this scion of crusaders who had read all the philosophers of the West, closed his eyes, placed his hands together before his face and prayed. I noticed a black rosary on his left wrist. He prayed about ten minutes. Afterwards he led me to the other end of the monastery and, during our passage, said to me:

"I do not like this temple. It is new, erected by the Lamas when the Living Buddha became blind. I do not find on the face of the golden Buddha either tears, hopes, distress or thanks of the people. They have not yet had time to leave these traces on the face of the god. We shall go now to the old Shrine of Prophecies."

This was a small building, blackened with age and resembling a tower with a plain round roof. The doors stood open. At both sides of the door were prayer wheels ready to be spun; over it a slab of copper with the signs of the zodiac. Inside two monks, who were intoning the sacred *sutras*, did not lift their eyes as we entered. The General approached them and said:

"Cast the dice for the number of my days!"

The priests brought two bowls with many dice therein and rolled them out on their low table. The Baron looked and reckoned with them the sum before he spoke:

"One hundred thirty! Again one hundred thirty!"

Approaching the altar carrying an ancient stone statue of Buddha brought all the way from India, he again prayed. As day dawned, we wandered out through the

monastery, visited all the temples and shrines, the museum
of the medical school, the astrological tower and then the
court where the *Bandi* and young Lamas have their daily
morning wrestling exercises. In other places the Lamas
were practising with the bow and arrow. Some of the
higher Lamas feasted us with hot mutton, tea and wild
onions. After we returned to the *yurta* I tried to sleep
but in vain. Too many different questions were troubling
me. "Where am I? In what epoch am I living?" I
knew not but I dimly felt the unseen touch of some great
idea, some enormous plan, some indescribable human woe.

After our noon meal the General said he wanted to
introduce me to the Living Buddha. It is so difficult
to secure audience with the Living Buddha that I was
very glad to have this opportunity offered me. Our auto
soon drew up at the gate of the red and white striped
wall surrounding the palace of the god. Two hundred
Lamas in yellow and red robes rushed to greet the arriving *"Chiang Chün,"* General, with the low-toned, respect-
ful whisper "Khan! God of War!" As a regiment of
formal ushers they led us to a spacious great hall softened
by its semi-darkness. Heavy carved doors opened to the
interior parts of the palace. In the depths of the hall
stood a dais with the throne covered with yellow silk
cushions. The back of the throne was red inside a gold
framing; at either side stood yellow silk screens set in
highly ornamented frames of black Chinese wood; while
against the walls at either side of the throne stood glass
cases filled with varied objects from China, Japan, India
and Russia. I noticed also among them a pair of exquisite
Marquis and Marquises in the fine porcelain of Sèvres.
Before the throne stood a long, low table at which eight

noble Mongols were seated, their chairman, a highly esteemed old man with a clever, energetic face and with
large penetrating eyes.   His appearance reminded me
of the authentic wooden images of the Buddhist holymen
with eyes of precious stones which I saw at the Tokyo
Imperial Museum in the department devoted to Buddhism, where the Japanese show the ancient statues of
Amida, Daunichi-Buddha, the Goddess Kwannon and the
jolly old Hotei.

   This man was the Hutuktu Jahantsi, Chairman of the
Mongolian Council of Ministers, and honored and revered far beyond the bournes of Mongolia.   The others
were the Ministers—Khans and the Highest Princes of
Khalkha.   Jahantsi Hutuktu invited Baron Ungern to
the place at his side, while they brought in a European
chair for me.   Baron Ungern announced to the Council
of Ministers through an interpreter that he would leave
Mongolia in a few days and urged them to protect the
freedom won for the lands inhabited by the successors
of Jenghiz Khan, whose soul still lives and calls upon
the Mongols to become anew a powerful people and re-
unite again into one great Mid-Asiatic State all the Asian
kingdoms he had ruled.

   The General rose and all the others followed him.   He
took leave of each one separately and sternly.   Only
before Jahantsi Lama he bent low while the Hutuktu
placed his hands on the Baron's head and blessed him.
From the Council Chamber we passed at once to the
Russian style house which is the personal dwelling of the
Living Buddha.   The house was wholly surrounded by
a crowd of red and yellow Lamas; servants, councilors
of Bogdo, officials, fortune tellers, doctors and favorites.

From the front entrance stretched a long red rope whose outer end was thrown over the wall beside the gate. Crowds of pilgrims crawling up on their knees touch this end of the rope outside the gate and hand the monk a silken *hatyk* or a bit of silver. This touching of the rope whose inner end is in the hand of the Bogdo establishes direct communication with the holy, incarnated Living God. A current of blessing is supposed to flow through this cable of camel's wool and horse hair. Any Mongol who has touched the mystic rope receives and wears about his neck a red band as the sign of his accomplished pilgrimage.

I had heard very much about the Bogdo Khan before this opportunity to see him. I had heard of his love of alcohol, which had brought on blindness, about his leaning toward exterior western culture and about his wife drinking deep with him and receiving in his name numerous delegations and envoys.

In the room which the Bogdo used as his private study, where two Lama secretaries watched day and night over the chest that contained his great seals, there was the severest simplicity. On a low, plain, Chinese lacquered table lay his writing implements, a case of seals given by the Chinese Government and by the Dalai Lama and wrapped in a cloth of yellow silk. Nearby was a low easy chair, a bronze brazier with an iron stovepipe leading up from it; on the walls were the signs of the swastika, Tibetan and Mongolian inscriptions; behind the easy chair a small altar with a golden statue of Buddha before which two tallow lamps were burning; the floor was covered with a thick yellow carpet.

When we entered, only the two Lama secretaries were

there, for the Living Buddha was in the small private shrine in an adjoining chamber, where no one is allowed to enter save the Bogdo Khan himself and one Lama, *Kanpo-Gelong,* who cares for the temple arrangements and assists the Living Buddha during his prayers of solitude. The secretary told us that the Bogdo had been greatly excited this morning. At noon he had entered his shrine. For a long time the voice of the head of the Yellow Faith was heard in earnest prayer and after his another unknown voice came clearly forth. In the shrine had taken place a conversation between the Buddha on earth and the Buddha of heaven—thus the Lamas phrased it to us.

"Let us wait a little," the Baron proposed. "Perhaps he will soon come out."

As we waited the General began telling me about Jahantsi Lama, saying that, when Jahantsi is calm, he is an ordinary man but, when he is disturbed and thinks very deeply, a nimbus appears about his head.

After half an hour the Lama secretaries suddenly showed signs of deep fear and began listening closely by the entrance to the shrine. Shortly they fell on their faces on the ground. The door slowly opened and there entered the Emperor of Mongolia, the Living Buddha, His Holiness Bogdo Djebtsung Damba Hutuktu, Khan of Outer Mongolia. He was a stout old man with a heavy shaven face resembling those of the Cardinals of Rome. He was dressed in the yellow silken Mongolian coat with a black binding. The eyes of the blind man stood widely open. Fear and amazement were pictured in them. He lowered himself heavily into the easy chair and whispered: "Write!"

A secretary immediately took paper and a Chinese pen as the Bogdo began to dictate his vision, very complicated and far from clear. He finished with the following words:

"This I, Bogdo Hutuktu Khan, saw, speaking with the great wise Buddha, surrounded by the good and evil spirits. Wise Lamas, Hutuktus, Kanpos, Marambas and Holy Gheghens, give the answer to my vision!"

As he finished, he wiped the perspiration from his head and asked who were present.

"Khan *Chiang Chün* Baron Ungern and a stranger," one of the secretaries answered on his knees.

The General presented me to the Bogdo, who bowed his head as a sign of greeting. They began speaking together in low tones. Through the open door I saw a part of the shrine. I made out a big table with a heap of books on it, some open and others lying on the floor below; a brazier with the red charcoal in it; a basket containing the shoulder blades and entrails of sheep for telling fortunes. Soon the Baron rose and bowed before the Bogdo. The Tibetan placed his hands on the Baron's head and whispered a prayer. Then he took from his own neck a heavy *ikon* and hung it around that of the Baron.

"You will not die but you will be incarnated in the highest form of being. Remember that, Incarnated God of War, Khan of grateful Mongolia!" I understood that the Living Buddha blessed the "Bloody General" before death.

During the next two days I had the opportunity to visit the Living Buddha three times together with a friend of the Bogdo, the Buriat Prince Djam Bolon. I shall describe these visits in Part IV.

Baron Ungern organized the trip for me and my party to the shore of the Pacific. We were to go on camels to northern Manchuria, because there it was easy to avoid cavilling with the Chinese authorities so badly oriented in the international relationship with Poland. Having sent a letter from Uliassutai to the French Legation at Peking and bearing with me a letter from the Chinese Chamber of Commerce, expressing thanks for the saving of Uliassutai from a *pogrom,* I intended to make for the nearest station on the Chinese Eastern Railway and from there proceed to Peking. The Danish merchant E. V. Olufsen was to have traveled out with me and also a learned Lama Turgut, who was headed for China.

Never shall I forget the night of May 19th to 20th of 1921! After dinner Baron Ungern proposed that we go to the *yurta* of Djam Bolon, whose acquaintance I had made on the first day after my arrival in Urga. His *yurta* was placed on a raised wooden platform in a compound located behind the Russian settlement. Two Buriat officers met us and took us in. Djam Bolon was a man of middle age, tall and thin with an unusually long face. Before the Great War he had been a simple shepherd but had fought together with Baron Ungern on the German front and afterwards against the Bolsheviki. He was a Grand Duke of the Buriats, the successor of former Buriat kings who had been dethroned by the Russian Government after their attempt to establish the Independence of the Buriat people. The servants brought us dishes with nuts, raisins, dates and cheese and served us tea.

"This is the last night, Djam Bolon!" said Baron Ungern. "You promised me . . ."

"I remember," answered the Buriat, "all is ready."

For a long time I listened to their reminiscences about former battles and friends who had been lost. The clock pointed to midnight when Djam Bolon got up and went out of the *yurta*.

"I want to have my fortune told once more," said Baron Ungern, as though he were justifying himself. "For the good of our cause it is too early for me to die. . . ."

Djam Bolon came back with a little woman of middle years, who squatted down eastern style before the brazier, bowed low and began to stare at Baron Ungern. Her face was whiter, narrower and thinner than that of a Mongol woman. Her eyes were black and sharp. Her dress resembled that of a gypsy woman. Afterwards I learned that she was a famous fortune teller and prophet among the Buriats, the daughter of a gypsy woman and a Buriat. She drew a small bag very slowly from her girdle, took from it some small bird bones and a handful of dry grass. She began whispering at intervals unintelligible words, as she threw occasional handfuls of the grass into the fire, which gradually filled the tent with a soft fragrance. I felt a distinct palpitation of my heart and a swimming in my head. After the fortune teller had burned all her grass, she placed the bird bones on the charcoal and turned them over again and again with a small pair of bronze pincers. As the bones blackened, she began to examine them and then suddenly her face took on an expression of fear and pain. She nervously tore off the kerchief which bound her head and, contracted with convulsions, began snapping out short, sharp phrases.

"I see . . . I see the God of War. . . . His life runs out . . . horribly. . . . After it a shadow . . . black like the night. . . . Shadow. . . . One hundred thirty steps remain. . . . Beyond darkness. . . . Nothing . . . I see nothing. . . . The God of War has disappeared. . . ."

Baron Ungern dropped his head. The woman fell over on her back with her arms stretched out. She had fainted, but it seemed to me that I noticed once a bright pupil of one of her eyes showing from under the closed lashes. Two Buriats carried out the lifeless form, after which a long silence reigned in the *yurta* of the Buriat Prince. Baron Ungern finally got up and began to walk around the brazier, whispering to himself. Afterwards he stopped and began speaking rapidly:

"I shall die! I shall die! . . . but no matter, no matter. . . . The cause has been launched and will not die. . . . I know the roads this cause will travel. The tribes of Jenghiz Khan's successors are awakened. Nobody shall extinguish the fire in the heart of the Mongols! In Asia there will be a great State from the Pacific and Indian Oceans to the shore of the Volga. The wise religion of Buddha shall run to the north and the west. It will be the victory of the spirit. A conqueror and leader will appear stronger and more stalwart than Jenghiz Khan and Ugadai. He will be more clever and more merciful than Sultan Baber and he will keep power in his hands until the happy day when, from his subterranean capital, shall emerge the King of the World. Why, why shall I not be in the first ranks of the warriors of Buddhism?

Why has Karma decided so? But so it must be! And Russia must first wash herself from the insult of revolution, purifying herself with blood and death; and all people accepting Communism must perish with their families in order that all their offspring may be rooted out!"

The Baron raised his hand above his head and shook it, as though he were giving his orders and bequests to some invisible person.

Day was dawning.

"My time has come!" said the General. "In a little while I shall leave Urga."

He quickly and firmly shook hands with us and said:

"Good-bye for all time! I shall die a horrible death but the world has never seen such a terror and such a sea of blood as it shall now see. . . ."

The door of the *yurta* slammed shut and he was gone. I never saw him again.

"I must go also, for I am likewise leaving Urga today."

"I know it," answered the Prince, "the Baron has left you with me for some purpose. I will give you a fourth companion, the Mongol Minister of War. You will accompany him to your *yurta*. It is necessary for you. . . ."

Djam Bolon pronounced this last with an accent on every word. I did not question him about it, as I was accustomed to the mystery of this country of the mysteries of good and evil spirits.

CHAPTER XXXIX

"THE MAN WITH A HEAD LIKE A SADDLE"

AFTER drinking tea at Djam Bolon's *yurta* I rode back to my quarters and packed my few belongings. The Lama Turgut was already there.

"The Minister of War will travel with us," he whispered. "It is necessary."

"All right," I answered, and rode off to Olufsen to summon him. But Olufsen unexpectedly announced that he was forced to spend some few days more in Urga —a fatal decision for him, for a month later he was reported killed by Sepailoff who remained as Commandant of the city after Baron Ungern's departure. The War Minister, a stout, young Mongol, joined our caravan. When we had gone about six miles from the city, we saw an automobile coming up behind us. The Lama shrunk up inside his coat and looked at me with fear. I felt the now familiar atmosphere of danger and so opened my holster and threw over the safety catch of my revolver. Soon the motor stopped alongside our caravan. In it sat Sepailoff with a smiling face and beside him his two executioners, Chestiakoff and Jdanoff. Sepailoff greeted us very warmly and asked:

"You are changing your horses in Khazahuduk? Does

the road cross that pass ahead? I don't know the way and must overtake an envoy who went there."

The Minister of War answered that we would be in Khazahuduk that evening and gave Sepailoff directions as to the road. The motor rushed away and, when it had topped the pass, he ordered one of the Mongols to gallop forward to see whether it had not stopped somewhere near the other side. The Mongol whipped his steed and sped away. We followed slowly.

"What is the matter?" I asked. "Please explain!"

The Minister told me that Djam Bolon yesterday received information that Sepailoff planned to overtake me on the way and kill me. Sepailoff suspected that I had stirred up the Baron against him. Djam Bolon reported the matter to the Baron, who organized this column for my safety. The returning Mongol reported that the motor car had gone on out of sight.

"Now," said the Minister, "we shall take quite another route so that the Colonel will wait in vain for us at Khazahuduk."

We turned north at Undur Dobo and at night were in the camp of a local prince. Here we took leave of our Minister, received splendid fresh horses and quickly continued our trip to the east, leaving behind us "the man with the head like a saddle" against whom I had been warned by the old fortune teller in the vicinity of Van Kure.

After twelve days without further adventures we reached the first railway station on the Chinese Eastern Railway, from where I traveled in unbelievable luxury to Peking.

*　　*　　*　　*　　*　　*

Surrounded by the comforts and conveniences of the splendid hotel at Peking, while shedding all the attributes of traveler, hunter and warrior, I could not, however, throw off the spell of those nine days spent in Urga, where I had daily met Baron Ungern, "Incarnated God of War." The newspapers carrying accounts of the bloody march of the Baron through Transbaikalia brought the pictures ever fresh to my mind. Even now, although more than seven months have elapsed, I cannot forget those nights of madness, inspiration and hate.

The predictions are fulfilled. Approximately one hundred thirty days afterwards Baron Ungern was captured by the Bolsheviki through the treachery of his officers and, it is reported, was executed at the end of September.

Baron R. F. Ungern von Sternberg. . . . Like a bloody storm of avenging Karma he spread over Central Asia. What did he leave behind him? The severe order to his soldiers closing with the words of the Revelations of St. John:

"Let no one check the revenge against the corrupter and slayer of the soul of the Russian people. Revolution must be eradicated from the World. Against it the Revelations of St. John have warned us thus: 'And the woman was arrayed in purple and scarlet, and decked with gold and precious stones and pearls, having in her hand a golden cup full of abominations, even the unclean things of her fornication, and upon her forehead a name written, MYSTERY, BABYLON THE GREAT, THE MOTHER OF THE HARLOTS AND OF THE ABOMINATIONS OF THE EARTH. And I saw the woman drunken with the blood of the saints, and with the blood of the martyrs of Jesus.'"

It is a human document, a document of Russian and, perhaps, of world tragedy.

But there remained another and more important trace.

In the Mongol *yurtas* and at the fires of Buriat, Mongol, Djungar, Kirkhiz, Kalmuck and Tibetan shepherds still speak the legend born of this son of crusaders and privateers:

"From the north a white warrior came and called on the Mongols to break their chains of slavery, which fell upon our freed soil. This white warrior was the Incarnated Jenghiz Khan and he predicted the coming of the greatest of all Mongols who will spread the fair faith of Buddha and the glory and power of the offspring of Jenghiz, Ugadai and Kublai Khan. So it shall be!"

Asia is awakened and her sons utter bold words.

It were well for the peace of the world if they go forth as disciples of the wise creators, Ugadai and Sultan Baber, rather than under the spell of the "bad demons" of the destructive Tamerlane.

Part IV

THE LIVING BUDDHA

Part IV

THE LIVING BUDDHA

CHAPTER XL

IN THE BLISSFUL GARDEN OF A THOUSAND JOYS

IN Mongolia, the country of miracles and mysteries, lives the custodian of all the mysterious and unknown, the Living Buddha, His Holiness Djebtsung Damba Hutuktu Khan or Bogdo Gheghen, Pontiff of Ta Kure. He is the incarnation of the never-dying Buddha, the representative of the unbroken, mysteriously continued line of spiritual emperors ruling since 1670, concealing in themselves the ever refining spirit of Buddha Amitabha joined with Chan-ra-zi or the "Compassionate Spirit of the Mountains." In him is everything, even the Sun Myth and the fascination of the mysterious peaks of the Himalayas, tales of the Indian pagoda, the stern majesty of the Mongolian Conquerors—Emperors of All Asia— and the ancient, hazy legends of the Chinese sages; immersion in the thoughts of the Brahmans; the severities of life of the monks of the "Virtuous Order"; the vengeance of the eternally wandering warriors, the Olets, with their Khans, Batur Hun Taigi and Gushi; the proud

bequests of Jenghiz and Kublai Khan; the clerical re-
actionary psychology of the Lamas; the mystery of
Tibetan kings beginning from Srong-Tsang Gampo; and
the mercilessness of the Yellow Sect of Paspa. All the
hazy history of Asia, of Mongolia, Pamir, Himalayas,
Mesopotamia, Persia and China, surrounds the Living
God of Urga. It is little wonder that his name is honored along the Volga, in Siberia, Arabia, between the
Tigris and Euphrates, in Indo-China and on the shores
of the Arctic Ocean.

During my stay in Urga I visited the abode of the
Living Buddha several times, spoke with him and observed his life. His favorite learned Marambas gave me
long accounts of him. I saw him reading horoscopes, I
heard his predictions, I looked over his archives of ancient
books and the manuscripts containing the lives and predictions of all the Bogdo Khans. The Lamas were very
frank and open with me, because the letter of the Hutuktu of Narabanchi won for me their confidence.

The personality of the Living Buddha is double, just
as everything in Lamaism is double. Clever, penetrating,
energetic, he at the same time indulges in the drunkenness which has brought on blindness. When he became
blind, the Lamas were thrown into a state of desperation. Some of them maintained that Bogdo Khan must
be poisoned and another Incarnate Buddha set in his
place; while the others pointed out the great merits of
the Pontiff in the eyes of Mongolians and the followers
of the Yellow Faith. They finally decided to propitiate
the gods by building a great temple with a gigantic statue
of Buddha. However, this did not help the Bogdo's sight
but the whole incident gave him the opportunity of hurry-

ing on to their higher life those among the Lamas who had shown too much radicalism in their proposed method of solving his problem.

He never ceases to ponder upon the cause of the church and of Mongolia and at the same time likes to indulge himself with useless trifles. He amuses himself with artillery. A retired Russian officer presented him with two old guns, for which the donor received the title of Tumbaiir Hun, that is, "Prince Dear-to-my-Heart." On holidays these cannon were fired to the great amusement of the blind man. Motor cars, gramophones, telephones, crystals, porcelains, pictures, perfumes, musical instruments, rare animals and birds; elephants, Himalayan bears, monkeys, Indian snakes and parrots—all these were in the palace of "the god" but all were soon cast aside and forgotten.

To Urga come pilgrims and presents from all the Lamaite and Buddhist world. Once the treasurer of the palace, the Honorable Balma Dorji, took me into the great hall where the presents were kept. It was a most unique museum of precious articles. Here were gathered together rare objects unknown to the museums of Europe. The treasurer, as he opened a case with a silver lock, said to me:

"These are pure gold nuggets from Bei Kem; here are black sables from Kemchick; these the miraculous deer horns; this a box sent by the Orochons and filled with precious ginseng roots and fragrant musk; this a bit of amber from the coast of the 'frozen sea' and it weighs 124 *lans* (about ten pounds); these are precious stones from India, fragrant *zebet* and carved ivory from China."

He showed the exhibits and talked of them for a long time and evidently enjoyed the telling. And really it was wonderful! Before my eyes lay the bundles of rare furs; white beaver, black sables, white, blue and black fox and black panthers; small beautifully carved tortoise shell boxes containing *hatyks* ten or fifteen yards long, woven from Indian silk as fine as the webs of the spider; small bags made of golden thread filled with pearls, the presents of Indian Rajahs; precious rings with sapphires and rubies from China and India; big pieces of jade, rough diamonds; ivory tusks ornamented with gold, pearls and precious stones; bright clothes sewn with gold and silver thread; walrus tusks carved in bas-relief by the primitive artists on the shores of the Behring Sea; and much more that one cannot recall or recount. In a separate room stood the cases with the statues of Buddha, made of gold, silver, bronze, ivory, coral, mother of pearl and from a rare colored and fragrant species of wood.

"You know when conquerors come into a country where the gods are honored, they break the images and throw them down. So it was more than three hundred years ago when the Kalmucks went into Tibet and the same was repeated in Peking when the European troops looted the place in 1900. But do you know why this is done? Take one of the statues and examine it."

I picked up one nearest the edge, a wooden Buddha, and began examining it. Inside something was loose and rattled.

"Do you hear it?" the Lama asked. "These are precious stones and bits of gold, the entrails of the god. This is the reason why the conquerors at once break up the statues of the gods. Many famous precious stones have appeared from the interior of the statues of the gods in India, Babylon and China."

Some rooms were devoted to the library, where manuscripts and volumes of different epochs in different languages and with many diverse themes fill the shelves. Some of them are mouldering or pulverizing away and the Lamas cover these now with a solution which partially solidifies like a jelly to protect what remains from the ravages of the air. There also we saw tablets of clay with the cuneiform inscriptions, evidently from Babylonia; Chinese, Indian and Tibetan books shelved beside those of Mongolia; tomes of the ancient pure Buddhism; books of the "Red Caps" or corrupt Buddhism; books of the "Yellow" or Lamaite Buddhism; books of traditions, legends and parables. Groups of Lamas were perusing, studying and copying these books, preserving and spreading the ancient wisdom for their successors.

One department is devoted to the mysterious books on magic, the historical lives and works of all the thirty-one Living Buddhas, with the bulls of the Dalai Lama, of the Pontiff from Tashi Lumpo, of the Hutuktu of Utai in China, of the Pandita Gheghen of Dolo Nor in Inner Mongolia and of the Hundred Chinese Wise Men. Only the Bogdo Hutuktu and Maramba Ta-Rimpo-Cha can enter this room of mysterious lore. The keys to it rest with the seals of the Living Buddha and the ruby ring of Jenghiz Khan ornamented with the sign of the swastika in the chest in the private study of the Bogdo.

The person of His Holiness is surrounded by five thousand Lamas. They are divided into many ranks from simple servants to the "Councillors of God," of which latter the Government consists. Among these

Councillors are all the four Khans of Mongolia and the five highest Princes.

Of all the Lamas there are three classes of peculiar interest, about which the Living Buddha himself told me when I visited him with Djam Bolon.

"The God" sorrowfully mourned over the demoralized and sumptuous life led by the Lamas which decreased rapidly the number of fortune tellers and clairvoyants among their ranks, saying of it:

"If the Jahantsi and Narabanchi monasteries had not preserved their strict régime and rules, Ta Kure would have been left without prophets and fortune tellers. Barun Abaga Nar, Dorchiul-Jurdok and the other holy Lamas who had the power of seeing that which is hidden from the sight of the common people have gone with the blessing of the gods."

This class of Lamas is a very important one, because every important personage visiting the monasteries at Urga is shown to the Lama *Tzuren* or fortune teller without the knowledge of the visitor for the study of his destiny and fate, which are then communicated to the Bogdo Hutuktu, so that with these facts in his possession the Bogdo knows in what way to treat his guest and what policy to follow toward him. The *Tzurens* are mostly old men, skinny, exhausted and severe ascetics. But I have met some who were young, almost boys. They were the Hubilgan, "incarnate gods," the future Hutuktus and Gheghens of the various Mongolian monasteries.

The second class is the doctors or "Ta Lama." They observe the actions of plants and certain products from animals upon people, preserve Tibetan medicines and cures, and study anatomy very carefully but without making use of vivisection and the scalpel. They are skilful bone setters, masseurs and great connoisseurs of hypnotism and animal magnetism.

The third class is the highest rank of doctors, consisting chiefly of Tibetans and Kalmucks—poisoners. They may be said to be "doctors of political medicine." They live by themselves, apart from any associates, and are the great silent weapon in the hands of the Living Buddha. I was informed that a large portion of them are dumb. I saw one such doctor,—the very person who poisoned the Chinese physician sent by the Chinese Emperor from Peking to "liquidate" the Living Buddha,—a small white old fellow with a deeply wrinkled face, a curl of white hairs on his chin and with vivacious eyes that were ever shifting inquiringly about him. Whenever he comes to a monastery, the local "god" ceases to eat and drink in fear of the activities of this Mongolian Locusta. But even this cannot save the condemned, for a poisoned cap or shirt or boots, or a rosary, a bridle, books or religious articles soaked in a poisonous solution will surely accomplish the object of the Bogdo-Khan.

The deepest esteem and religious faithfulness surround the blind Pontiff. Before him all fall on their faces. Khans and Hutuktus approach him on their knees. Everything about him is dark, full of Oriental antiquity. The drunken blind man, listening to the banal arias of the gramophone or shaking his servants with an electric current from his dynamo, the ferocious old fellow poisoning his political enemies, the Lama keeping his people in darkness and deceiving them with his prophecies and fortune telling,—he is, however, not an entirely ordinary man.

One day we sat in the room of the Bogdo and Prince Djam Bolon translated to him my story of the Great War. The old fellow was listening very carefully but suddenly opened his eyes widely and began to give attention to some sounds coming in from outside the room. His face became reverent, supplicant and frightened.

"The Gods call me," he whispered and slowly moved into his private shrine, where he prayed loudly about two hours, kneeling immobile as a statue. His prayer consists of conversation with the invisible gods, to whose questions he himself gave the answers. He came out of the shrine pale and exhausted but pleased and happy. It was his personal prayer. During the regular temple service he did not participate in the prayers, for then he is "God." Sitting on his throne, he is carried and placed on the altar and there prayed to by the Lamas and the people. He only receives the prayers, hopes, tears, woe and desperation of the people, immobilely gazing into space with his sharp and bright but blind eyes. At various times in the service the Lamas robe him in different vestments, combinations of yellow and red, and change his caps. The service always finishes at the solemn moment when the Living Buddha with the tiara on his head pronounces the pontifical blessing upon the congregation, turning his face to all four cardinal points of the compass and finally stretching out his hands toward the northwest, that is, to Europe, whither in the belief of the Yellow Faith must travel the teachings of the wise Buddha.

After earnest prayers or long temple services the Pontiff seems very deeply shaken and often calls his secretaries and dictates his visions and prophecies, always very complicated and unaccompanied by his deductions.

Sometimes with the words "Their souls are communicating," he puts on his white robes and goes to pray in his shrine. Then all the gates of the palace are shut and all the Lamas are sunk in solemn, mystic fear; all are praying, telling their rosaries and whispering the orison: *"Om! Mani padme Hung!"* or turning the prayer wheels with their prayers or exorcisings; the fortune tellers read their horoscopes; the clairvoyants write out their visions; while Marambas search the ancient books for explanations of the words of the Living Buddha.

CHAPTER XLI

THE DUST OF CENTURIES

HAVE you ever seen the dusty cobwebs and the mould in the cellars of some ancient castle in Italy, France or England? This is the dust of centuries. Perhaps it touched the faces, helmets and swords of a Roman Augustus, St. Louis, the Inquisitor, Galileo or King Richard. Your heart is involuntarily contracted and you feel a respect for these witnesses of elapsed ages. This same impression came to me in Ta Kure, perhaps more deep, more realistic. Here life flows on almost as it flowed eight centuries ago; here man lives only in the past; and the contemporary only complicates and prevents the normal life.

"Today is a great day," the Living Buddha once said to me, "the day of the victory of Buddhism over all other religions. It was a long time ago—on this day Kublai Khan called to him the Lamas of all religions and ordered them to state to him how and what they believed. They praised their Gods and their Hutuktus. Discussions and quarrels began. Only one Lama remained silent. At last he mockingly smiled and said:

" 'Great Emperor! Order each to prove the power of his Gods by the performance of a miracle and afterwards judge and choose.'

"Kublai Khan so ordered all the Lamas to show him a miracle but all were silent, confused and powerless before him.

" 'Now,' said the Emperor, addressing the Lama who had tendered this suggestion, 'now you must prove the power of your Gods!'

"The Lama looked long and silently at the Emperor, turned and gazed at the whole assembly and then quietly stretched out his hand toward them. At this instant the golden goblet of the Emperor raised itself from the table and tipped before the lips of the Khan without a visible hand supporting it. The Emperor felt the delight of a fragrant wine. All were struck with astonishment and the Emperor spoke:

" 'I elect to pray to your Gods and to them all people subject to me must pray. What is your faith? Who are you and from where do you come?'

" 'My faith is the teaching of the wise Buddha. I am Pandita Lama, Turjo Gamba, from the distant and glorious monastery of Sakkia in Tibet, where dwells incarnate in a human body the Spirit of Buddha, his Wisdom and his Power. Remember, Emperor, that the peoples who hold our faith shall possess all the Western Universe and during eight hundred and eleven years shall spread their faith throughout the whole world.'

"Thus it happened on this same day many centuries ago! Lama Turjo Gamba did not return to Tibet but lived here in Ta Kure, where there was then only a small temple. From here he traveled to the Emperor at Karakorum and afterwards with him to the capital of China to fortify him in the Faith, to predict the fate of state affairs and to enlighten him according to the will of God."

The Living Buddha was silent for a time, whispered a prayer and then continued:

"Urga, the ancient nest of Buddhism. . . . With Jenghiz Khan on his European conquest went out the Olets or Kalmucks. They remained there almost four hundred years, living on the plains of Russia. Then they returned to Mongolia because the Yellow Lamas called them to fight against the Kings of Tibet, Lamas of the 'red caps,' who were oppressing the people. The Kalmucks helped the Yellow Faith but they realized that Lhasa was too distant from the whole world and could not spread our Faith throughout the earth. Consequently the Kalmuck Gushi Khan brought up from Tibet a holy Lama, Undur Gheghen, who had visited the 'King of the World.' From that day the Bogdo Gheghen has continuously lived in Urga, a protector of the freedom of Mongolia and of the Chinese Emperors of Mongolian origin. Undur Gheghen was the first Living Buddha in the land of the Mongols. He left to us, his successors, the ring of Jenghiz Khan, which was sent by Kublai Khan to Dalai Lama in return for the miracle shown by the Lama Turjo Gamba; also the top of the skull of a black, mysterious miracle worker from India, using which as a bowl, Strongtsan, King of Tibet, drank during the temple ceremonies one thousand six hundred years ago; as well as an ancient stone statue of Buddha brought from Delhi by the founder of the Yellow Faith, Paspa."

The Bogdo clapped his hands and one of the secretaries took from a red kerchief a big silver key with which he unlocked the chest with the seals. The Living Buddha slipped his hand into the chest and drew forth a small box of carved ivory, from which he took out and showed to me a large gold ring set with a magnificent ruby carved with the sign of the swastika.

"This ring was always worn on the right hand of the Khans Jenghiz and Kublai," said the Bogdo.

When the secretary had closed the chest, the Bogdo ordered him to summon his favorite Maramba, whom he directed to read some pages from an ancient book lying on the table. The Lama began to read monotonously.

"When Gushi Khan, the Chief of all the Olets or Kalmucks, finished the war with the 'Red Caps' in Tibet, he carried out with him the miraculous 'black stone' sent to the Dalai Lama by the 'King of the World.' Gushi Khan wanted to create in Western Mongolia the capital of the Yellow Faith; but the Olets at that time were at war with the Manchu Emperors for the throne of China and suffered one defeat after another. The last Khan of the Olets, Amursana, ran away into Russia but before his escape sent to Urga the sacred 'black stone.' While it remained in Urga so that the Living Buddha could bless the people with it, disease and misfortune never touched the Mongolians and their cattle. About one hundred years ago, however, some one stole the sacred stone and since then Buddhists have vainly sought it throughout the whole world. With its disappearance the Mongol people began gradually to die."

"Enough!" ordered Bogdo Gheghen. "Our neighbors hold us in contempt. They forget that we were their sovereigns but we preserve our holy traditions and we know that the day of triumph of the Mongolian tribes and the Yellow Faith will come. We have the Protectors of the Faith, the Buriats. They are the truest guardians of the bequests of Jenghiz Khan."

So spoke the Living Buddha and so have spoken the ancient books!

CHAPTER XLII

THE BOOKS OF MIRACLES

PRINCE DJAM BOLON asked a Maramba to show us the library of the Living Buddha. It is a big room occupied by scores of writers who prepare the works dealing with the miracles of all the Living Buddhas, beginning with Undur Gheghen and ending with those of the Gheghens and Hutuktus of the different Mongol monasteries. These books are afterwards distributed through all the Lama Monasteries, temples and schools of Bandi. A Maramba read two selections:

". . . The beatific Bogdo Gheghen breathed on a mirror. Immediately as through a haze there appeared the picture of a valley in which many thousands of thousands of warriors fought one against another. . . ."

"The wise and favored-of-the-gods Living Buddha burned incense in a brazier and prayed to the Gods to reveal the lot of the Princes. In the blue smoke all saw a dark prison and the pallid, tortured bodies of the dead Princes. . . ."

A special book, already done into thousands of copies, dwelt upon the miracles of the present Living Buddha. Prince Djam Bolon described to me some of the contents of this volume.

"There exists an ancient wooden Buddha with open eyes. He was brought here from India and Bogdo

Gheghen placed him on the altar and began to pray.
When he returned from the shrine, he ordered the statue
of Buddha brought out. All were struck with amazement,
for the eyes of the God were shut and tears were falling
from them; from the wooden body green sprouts appeared; and the Bogdo said:

"'Woe and joy are awaiting me. I shall become blind
but Mongolia will be free.'

"The prophecy is fulfilled. At another time, on a day
when the Living Buddha was very much excited, he
ordered a basin of water brought and set before the altar.
He called the Lamas and began to pray. Suddenly the
altar candles and lamps lighted themselves and the water
in the basin became iridescent."

Afterwards the Prince described to me how the Bogdo
Khan tells fortunes with fresh blood, upon whose surface
appear words and pictures; with the entrails of sheep
and goats, according to whose distribution the Bogdo
reads the fate of the Princes and knows their thoughts;
with stones and bones from which the Living Buddha
with great accuracy reads the lot of all men; and by the
stars, in accordance with whose positions the Bogdo pre-
pares amulets against bullets and disease.

"The former Bogdo Khans told fortunes only by the
use of the 'black stone,'" said the Maramba. "On the
surface of the stone appeared Tibetan inscriptions which
the Bogdo read and thus learned the lot of whole nations."

When the Maramba spoke of the black stone with the
Tibetan legends appearing on it, I at once recalled that
it was possible. In southeastern Urianhai, in Ulan
Taiga, I came across a place where black slate was de-
composing. All the pieces of this slate were covered with

a special white lichen, which formed very complicated designs, reminding me of a Venetian lace pattern or whole pages of mysterious runes. When the slate was wet, these designs disappeared; and then, as they were dried, the patterns came out again.

Nobody has the right or dares to ask the Living Buddha to tell his fortune. He predicts only when he feels the inspiration or when a special delegate comes to him bearing a request for it from the Dalai Lama or the Tashi Lama. When the Russian Czar, Alexander I, fell under the influence of Baroness Kzudener and of her extreme mysticism, he despatched a special envoy to the Living Buddha to ask about his destiny. The then Bogdo Khan, quite a young man, told his fortune according to the "black stone" and predicted that the White Czar would finish his life in very painful wanderings unknown to all and everywhere pursued. In Russia today there exists a popular belief that Alexander I spent the last days of his life as a wanderer throughout Russia and Siberia under the pseudonym of Feodor Kusmitch, helping and consoling prisoners, beggars and other suffering people, often pursued and imprisoned by the police and finally dying at Tomsk in Siberia, where even until now they have preserved the house where he spent his last days and have kept his grave sacred, a place of pilgrimages and miracles. The former dynasty of Romanoff was deeply interested in the biography of Feodor Kusmitch and this interest fixed the opinion that Kusmitch was really the Czar Alexander I, who had voluntarily taken upon himself this severe penance.

CHAPTER XLIII

THE BIRTH OF THE LIVING BUDDHA

THE Living Buddha does not die. His soul sometimes passes into that of a child born on the day of his death and sometimes transfers itself to another being during the life of the Buddha. This new mortal dwelling of the sacred spirit of the Buddha almost always appears in the *yurta* of some poor Tibetan or Mongol family. There is a reason of policy for this. If the Buddha appears in the family of a rich prince, it could result in the elevation of a family that would not yield obedience to the clergy (and such has happened in the past), while on the other hand any poor, unknown family that becomes the heritor of the throne of Jenghiz Khan acquires riches and is readily submissive to the Lamas. Only three or four Living Buddhas were of purely Mongolian origin; the remainder were Tibetans.

One of the Councillors of the Living Buddha, Lama-Khan Jassaktu, told me the following:

"In the monasteries at Lhasa and Tashi Lumpo they are kept constantly informed through letters from Urga about the health of the Living Buddha. When his human body becomes old and the Spirit of Buddha strives to extricate itself, special solemn services begin in the Tibetan temples together with the telling of fortunes by astrology. These rites indicate the specially pious Lamas who must discover where the Spirit of the Buddha will be re-incarnated. For this purpose they travel throughout the whole land and observe. Often God himself gives them signs and indications. Sometimes the white wolf appears near the *yurta* of a poor shepherd or a lamb with two heads is born or a meteor falls from the sky. Some Lamas take fish from the sacred lake Tangri Nor and read on the scales thereof the name of the new Bogdo Khan; others pick out stones whose cracks indicate to them where they must search and whom they must find; while others secrete themselves in narrow mountain ravines to listen to the voices of the spirits of the mountains, pronouncing the name of the new choice of the Gods. When he is found, all the possible information about his family is secretly collected and presented to the Most Learned Tashi Lama, having the name of Erdeni, "The Great Gem of Learning," who, according to the runes of Rama, verifies the selection. If he is in agreement with it, he sends a secret letter to the Dalai Lama, who holds a special sacrifice in the Temple of the "Spirit of the Mountains" and confirms the election by putting his great seal on this letter of the Tashi Lama.

If the old Living Buddha be still alive, the name of his successor is kept a deep secret; if the Spirit of Buddha has already gone out from the body of Bogdo Khan, a special legation appears from Tibet with the new Living Buddha. The same process accompanies the election of the Gheghen and Hutuktus in all the Lamaite monasteries in Mongolia; but confirmation of the election resides with the Living Buddha and is only announced to Lhasa after the event.

CHAPTER XLIV

A PAGE IN THE HISTORY OF THE PRESENT LIVING BUDDHA

THE present Bogdo Khan of Outer Mongolia is a Tibetan. He sprang from a poor family living in the neighborhood of Sakkia Kure in western Tibet. From earliest youth he had a stormy, quite unaesthetic nature. He was fired with the idea of the independence and glorification of Mongolia and the successors of Jenghiz Khan. This gave him at once a great influence among the Lamas, Princes and Khans of Mongolia and also with the Russian Government which always tried to attract him to their side. He did not fear to arraign himself against the Manchu dynasty in China and always had the help of Russia, Tibet, the Buriats and Kirghiz, furnishing him with money, weapons, warriors and diplomatic aid. The Chinese Emperors avoided open war with the Living God, because it might arouse the protests of the Chinese Buddhists. At one time they sent to the Bogdo Khan a skilful doctor-poisoner. The Living Buddha, however, at once understood the meaning of this medical attention and, knowing the power of Asiatic poisons, decided to make a journey through the Mongol monasteries and through Tibet. As his substitute he left a Hubilgan who made friends with the Chinese doctor and inquired from him the purposes and details of his arrival. Very soon the Chinese died from some unknown cause and the Living Buddha returned to his comfortable capital.

On another occasion danger threatened the Living God. It was when Lhasa decided that the Bogdo Khan was carrying out a policy too independent of Tibet. The Dalai Lama began negotiations with several Khans and Princes with the Sain Noion Khan and Jassaktu Khan leading the movement and persuaded them to accelerate the immigration of the Spirit of Buddha into another human form. They came to Urga where the Bogdo Khan met them with honors and rejoicings. A great feast was made for them and the conspirators already felt themselves the accomplishers of the orders of the Dalai Lama. However, at the end of the feast, they had different feelings and died with them during the night. The Living Buddha ordered their bodies sent with full honors to their families.

The Bogdo Khan knows every thought, every movement of the Princes and Khans, the slightest conspiracy against himself, and the offender is usually kindly invited to Urga, from where he does not return alive.

The Chinese Government decided to terminate the line of the Living Buddhas. Ceasing to fight with the Pontiff of Urga, the Government contrived the following scheme for accomplishing its ends.

Peking invited the Pandita Gheghen from Dolo Nor and the head of the Chinese Lamaites, the Hutuktu of Utai, both of whom do not recognize the supremacy of the Living Buddha, to come to the capital. They decided, after consulting the old Buddhistic books, that the present Bogdo Khan was to be the last Living Buddha, because that part of the Spirit of Buddha which dwells in the

Bogdo Khans can abide only thirty-one times in the human body. Bogdo Khan is the thirty-first Incarnated Buddha from the time of Undur Gheghen and with him, therefore, the dynasty of the Urga Pontiffs must cease. However, on hearing this the Bogdo Khan himself did some research work and found in the old Tibetan manuscripts that one of the Tibetan Pontiffs was married and his son was a natural Incarnated Buddha. So the Bogdo Khan married and now has a son, a very capable and energetic young man, and thus the religious throne of Jenghiz Khan will not be left empty. The dynasty of the Chinese emperors disappeared from the stage of political events but the Living Buddha continues to be a center for the Pan-Asiatic idea.

The new Chinese Government in 1920 held the Living Buddha under arrest in his palace but at the beginning of 1921 Baron Ungern crossed the sacred Bogdo-Ol and approached the palace from the rear. Tibetan riders shot the Chinese sentries with bow and arrow and afterwards the Mongols penetrated into the palace and stole their "God," who immediately stirred up all Mongolia and awakened the hopes of the Asiatic peoples and tribes.

In the great palace of the Bogdo a Lama showed me a special casket covered with a precious carpet, wherein they keep the bulls of the Dalai and Tashi Lamas, the decrees of the Russian and Chinese Emperors and the Treaties between Mongolia, Russia, China and Tibet. In this same casket is the copper plate bearing the mysterious sign of the "King of the World" and the chronicle of the last vision of the Living Buddha.

CHAPTER XLV

THE VISION OF THE LIVING BUDDHA OF
MAY 17, 1921

"I PRAYED and saw that which is hidden from the eyes of the people. A vast plain was spread before me surrounded by distant mountains. An old Lama carried a basket filled with heavy stones. He hardly moved. From the north a rider appeared in white robes and mounted on a white horse. He approached the Lama and said to him:

" 'Give me your basket. I shall help you to carry them to the Kure.'

"The Lama handed his heavy burden up to him but the rider could not raise it to his saddle so that the old Lama had to place it back on his shoulder and continue on his way, bent under its heavy weight. Then from the north came another rider in black robes and on a black horse, who also approached the Lama and said:

" 'Stupid! Why do you carry these stones when they are everywhere about the ground?'

"With these words he pushed the Lama over with the breast of his horse and scattered the stones about the ground. When the stones touched the earth, they became diamonds. All three rushed to raise them but not one of them could break them loose from the ground. Then the old Lama exclaimed:

" 'Oh Gods! All my life I have carried this heavy burden and now, when there was left so little to go, I have lost it. Help me, great, good Gods!'

"Suddenly a tottering old man appeared. He collected all the diamonds into the basket without trouble, cleaned the dust from them, raised the burden to his shoulder and started out, speaking with the Lama:

" 'Rest a while, I have just carried my burden to the goal and I am glad to help you with yours.'

"They went on and were soon out of sight, while the riders began to fight. They fought one whole day and then the whole night and, when the sun rose over the plain, neither was there, either alive or dead, and no trace of either remained. This I saw, Bogdo Hutuktu Khan, speaking with the Great and Wise Buddha, surrounded by the good and bad demons! Wise Lamas, Hutuktus, Kampos, Marambas and Holy Gheghens, give the answer to my vision!"

This was written in my presence on May 17th, 1921, from the words of the Living Buddha just as he came out of his private shrine to his study. I do not know what the Hutuktu and Gheghens, the fortune tellers, sorcerers and clairvoyants replied to him; but does not the answer seem clear, if one realizes the present situation in Asia?

Awakened Asia is full of enigmas but it is also full of answers to the questions set by the destiny of humankind. This great continent of mysterious Pontiffs, Living Gods, Mahatmas and readers of the terrible book of Karma is awakening and the ocean of hundreds of millions of human lives is lashed with monstrous waves.

Part V

MYSTERY OF MYSTERIES—THE KING OF THE WORLD

Part V

MYSTERY OF MYSTERIES—THE KING OF THE WORLD

CHAPTER XLVI

THE SUBTERRANEAN KINGDOM

"STOP!" whispered my old Mongol guide, as we were one day crossing the plain near Tzagan Luk. "Stop!"

He slipped from his camel which lay down without his bidding. The Mongol raised his hands in prayer before his face and began to repeat the sacred phrase: "*Om! Mani padme Hung!*" The other Mongols immediately stopped their camels and began to pray.

"What has happened?" I thought, as I gazed round over the tender green grass, up to the cloudless sky and out toward the dreamy soft rays of the evening sun.

The Mongols prayed for some time, whispered among themselves and, after tightening up the packs on the camels, moved on.

"Did you see," asked the Mongol, "how our camels moved their ears in fear? How the herd of horses on

the plain stood fixed in attention and how the herds of
sheep and cattle lay crouched close to the ground? Did
you notice that the birds did not fly, the marmots did
not run and the dogs did not bark? The air trembled
softly and bore from afar the music of a song which
penetrated to the hearts of men, animals and birds alike.
Earth and sky ceased breathing. The wind did not blow
and the sun did not move. At such a moment the wolf
that is stealing up on the sheep arrests his stealthy crawl;
the frightened herd of antelopes suddenly checks its wild
course; the knife of the shepherd cutting the sheep's
throat falls from his hand; the rapacious ermine ceases to
stalk the unsuspecting *salga*. All living beings in fear
are involuntarily thrown into prayer and waiting for their
fate. So it was just now. Thus it has always been whenever the King of the World in his subterranean palace
prays and searches out the destiny of all peoples on the
earth."

In this wise the old Mongol, a simple, coarse shepherd
and hunter, spoke to me.

Mongolia with her nude and terrible mountains, her
limitless plains, covered with the widely strewn bones of
the forefathers, gave birth to Mystery. Her people,
frightened by the stormy passions of Nature or lulled by
her deathlike peace, feel her mystery. Her "Red" and
"Yellow Lamas" preserve and poetize her mystery. The
Pontiffs of Lhasa and Urga know and possess her
mystery.

On my journey into Central Asia I came to know for
the first time about "the Mystery of Mysteries," which
I can call by no other name. At the outset I did not pay
much attention to it and did not attach to it such im-

portance as I afterwards realized belonged to it, when I had analyzed and connoted many sporadic, hazy and often controversial bits of evidence.

The old people on the shore of the River Amyl related to me an ancient legend to the effect that a certain Mongolian tribe in their escape from the demands of Jenghiz Khan hid themselves in a subterranean country. Afterwards a Soyot from near the Lake of Nogan Kul showed me the smoking gate that serves as the entrance to the "Kingdom of Agharti." Through this gate a hunter formerly entered into the Kingdom and, after his return, began to relate what he had seen there. The Lamas cut out his tongue in order to prevent him from telling about the Mystery of Mysteries. When he arrived at old age, he came back to the entrance of this cave and disappeared into the subterranean kingdom, the memory of which had ornamented and lightened his nomad heart.

I received more realistic information about this from Hutuktu Jelyb Djamsrap in Narabanchi Kure. He told me the story of the semi-realistic arrival of the powerful King of the World from the subterranean kingdom, of his appearance, of his miracles and of his prophecies; and only then did I begin to understand that in that legend, hypnosis or mass vision, whichever it may be, is hidden not only mystery but a realistic and powerful force capable of influencing the course of the political life of Asia. From that moment I began making some investigations.

The favorite Gelong Lama of Prince Chultun Beyli and the Prince himself gave me an account of the subterranean kingdom.

"Everything in the world," said the Gelong, "is con-

stantly in a state of change and transition—peoples,
science, religions, laws and customs. How many great
empires and brilliant cultures have perished! And that
alone which remains unchanged is Evil, the tool of Bad
Spirits. More than sixty thousand years ago a Holyman
disappeared with a whole tribe of people under the
ground and never appeared again on the surface of the
earth. Many people, however, have since visited this
kingdom, Sakkia Mouni, Undur Gheghen, Paspa, Khan
Baber and others. No one knows where this place is.
One says Afghanistan, others India. All the people there
are protected against Evil and crimes do not exist within
its bournes. Science has there developed calmly and
nothing is threatened with destruction. The subterranean people have reached the highest knowledge. Now
it is a large kingdom, millions of men with the King of
the World as their ruler. He knows all the forces of
the world and reads all the souls of humankind and the
great book of their destiny. Invisibly he rules eight hundred million men on the surface of the earth and they
will accomplish his every order."

Prince Chultun Beyli added: "This kingdom is Agharti.
It extends throughout all the subterranean passages of
the whole world. I heard a learned Lama of China relating to Bogdo Khan that all the subterranean caves of
America are inhabited by the ancient people who have
disappeared underground. Traces of them are still found
on the surface of the land. These subterranean peoples
and spaces are governed by rulers owing allegiance to
the King of the World. In it there is not much of the
wonderful. You know that in the two greatest oceans
of the east and the west there were formerly two con-

tinents. They disappeared under the water but their people went into the subterranean kingdom. In underground caves there exists a peculiar light which affords growth to the grains and vegetables and long life without disease to the people. There are many different peoples and many different tribes. An old Buddhist Brahman in Nepal was carrying out the will of the Gods in making a visit to the ancient kingdom of Jenghiz,—Siam,— where he met a fisherman who ordered him to take a place in his boat and sail with him upon the sea. On the third day they reached an island where he met a people having two tongues which could speak separately in different languages. They showed to him peculiar, unfamiliar animals, tortoises with sixteen feet and one eye, huge snakes with a very tasty flesh and birds with teeth which caught fish for their masters in the sea. These people told him that they had come up out of the subterranean kingdom and described to him certain parts of the underground country."

The Lama Turgut traveling with me from Urga to Peking gave me further details.

"The capital of Agharti is surrounded with towns of high priests and scientists. It reminds one of Lhasa where the palace of the Dalai Lama, the Potala, is the top of a mountain covered with monasteries and temples. The throne of the King of the World is surrounded by millions of incarnated Gods. They are the Holy Panditas. The palace itself is encircled by the palaces of the Goro, who possess all the visible and invisible forces of the earth, of inferno and of the sky and who can do everything for the life and death of man. If our mad humankind should begin a war against them, they would be able to explode the whole surface of our planet and transform it into deserts. They can dry up the seas, transform lands into oceans and scatter the mountains into the sands of the deserts. By his order trees, grasses and bushes can be made to grow; old and feeble men can become young and stalwart; and the dead can be resurrected. In cars strange and unknown to us they rush through the narrow cleavages inside our planet. Some Indian Brahmans and Tibetan Dalai Lamas during their laborious struggles to the peaks of mountains which no other human feet had trod have found there inscriptions carved on the rocks, footprints in the snow and the tracks of wheels. The blissful Sakkia Mouni found on one mountain top tablets of stone carrying words which he only understood in his old age and afterwards penetrated into the Kingdom of Agharti, from which he brought back crumbs of the sacred learning preserved in his memory. There in palaces of wonderful crystal live the invisible rulers of all pious people, the King of the World or Brahytma, who can speak with God as I speak with you, and his two assistants; Mahytma, knowing the purposes of future events, and Mahynga, ruling the causes of these events."

"The Holy Panditas study the world and all its forces. Sometimes the most learned among them collect together and send envoys to that place where the human eyes have never penetrated. This is described by the Tashi Lama living eight hundred and fifty years ago. The highest Panditas place their hands on their eyes and at the base of the brain of younger ones and force them into a deep sleep, wash their bodies with an infusion of grass and make them immune to pain and harder than stones, wrap them in magic cloths, bind them and then pray to the Great God. The petrified youths lie with eyes and ears open and alert, seeing, hearing and remembering everything. Afterwards a Goro approaches and fastens a long, steady gaze upon them. Very slowly the bodies lift themselves from the earth and disappear. The Goro sits and stares with fixed eyes to the place whither he has sent them. Invisible threads join them to his will. Some of them course among the stars, observe their events, their unknown peoples, their life and their laws. They listen to their talk, read their books, understand their fortunes and woes, their holiness and sins, their piety and evil. Some are mingled with flame and see the creature of fire, quick and ferocious, eternally fighting, melting and hammering metals in the depths of planets, boiling the water for geysers and springs, melting the rocks and pushing out molten streams over the surface of the earth through the holes in the mountains. Others rush together with the ever elusive, infinitesimally small, transparent creatures of the air and penetrate into the mysteries of their existence and into the purposes of their life. Others slip into the depths of the seas and observe the kingdom of the wise creatures of the water, who transport and spread genial warmth all over the earth, ruling the winds, waves and storms. . . . In Erdeni Dzu formerly lived Pandita Hutuktu, who had come from Agharti. As he was dying, he told about the time when he lived according to the will of the Goro on a red star in the east, floated in the ice-covered ocean and flew among the stormy fires in the depths of the earth."

These are the tales which I heard in the Mongolian *yurtas* of Princes and in the Lamaite monasteries. These stories were all related in a solemn tone which forbade challenge and doubt.

Mystery. . . .

CHAPTER XLVII

THE KING OF THE WORLD BEFORE THE FACE OF GOD

DURING my stay in Urga I tried to find an explanation of this legend about the King of the World. Of course, the Living Buddha could tell me most of all and so I endeavored to get the story from him. In a conversation with him I mentioned the name of the King of the World. The old Pontiff sharply turned his head toward me and fixed upon me his immobile, blind eyes. Unwillingly I became silent. Our silence was a long one and after it the Pontiff continued the conversation in such a way that I understood he did not wish to accept the suggestion of my reference. On the faces of the others present I noticed expressions of astonishment and fear produced by my words, and especially was this true of the custodian of the library of the Bogdo Khan. One can readily understand that all this only made me the more anxious to press the pursuit.

As I was leaving the study of the Bogdo Hutuktu, I met the librarian who had stepped out ahead of me and asked him if he would show me the library of the Living Buddha and used a very simple, sly trick with him.

"Do you know, my dear Lama," I said, "once I rode in the plain at the hour when the King of the World spoke with God and I felt the impressive majesty of this moment."

To my astonishment the old Lama very quietly answered me: "It is not right that the Buddhist and our Yellow Faith should conceal it. The acknowledgment of the existence of the most holy and most powerful man, of the blissful kingdom, of the great temple of sacred science is such a consolation to our sinful hearts and our corrupt lives that to conceal it from humankind is a sin. . . . Well, listen," he continued, "throughout the whole year the King of the World guides the work of the Panditas and Goros of Agharti. Only at times he goes to the temple cave where the embalmed body of his predecessor lies in a black stone coffin. This cave is always dark, but when the King of the World enters it the walls are striped with fire and from the lid of the coffin appear tongues of flame. The eldest Goro stands before him with covered head and face and with hands folded across his chest. This Goro never removes the covering from his face, for his head is a nude skull with living eyes and a tongue that speaks. He is in communion with the souls of all who have gone before.

"The King of the World prays for a long time and afterwards approaches the coffin and stretches out his hand. The flames thereon burn brighter; the stripes of fire on the walls disappear and revive, interlace and form mysterious signs from the alphabet *vatannan*. From the coffin transparent bands of scarcely noticeable light begin to flow forth. These are the thoughts of his predecessor. Soon the King of the World stands surrounded by an auriole of this light and fiery letters write and write upon the walls the wishes and orders of God. At this moment the King of the World is in contact with the thoughts of all the men who influence the lot and life of all humankind: with Kings, Czars, Khans, warlike leaders, High Priests, scientists and other strong men. He realizes all their thoughts and plans. If these be pleasing before God, the King of the World will invisibly help them; if they are unpleasant in the sight of God, the King will bring them to destruction. This power is given to Agharti by the mysterious science of '*Om*,' with which we begin all our prayers. '*Om*' is the name of an ancient Holyman, the first Goro, who lived three hundred thirty thousand years ago. He was the first man to know God and who taught humankind to believe, hope and struggle with Evil. Then God gave him power over all forces ruling the visible world.

"After his conversation with his predecessor the King of the World assembles the 'Great Council of God,' judges the actions and thoughts of great men, helps them or destroys them. Mahytma and Mahynga find the place for these actions and thoughts in the causes ruling the world. Afterwards the King of the World enters the great temple and prays in solitude. Fire appears on the altar, gradually spreading to all the altars near, and through the burning flame gradually appears the face of God. The King of the World reverently announces to God the decisions and awards of the 'Council of God' and receives in turn the Divine orders of the Almighty. As he comes forth from the temple, the King of the World radiates with Divine Light."

CHAPTER XLVIII

REALITY OR RELIGIOUS FANTASY?

"**H**AS anybody seen the King of the World?" I asked.

"Oh, yes!" answered the Lama. "During the solemn holidays of the ancient Buddhism in Siam and India the King of the World appeared five times. He rode in a splendid car drawn by white elephants and ornamented with gold, precious stones and finest fabrics; he was robed in a white mantle and red tiara with strings of diamonds masking his face. He blessed the people with a golden apple with the figure of a Lamb above it. The blind received their sight, the dumb spoke, the deaf heard, the crippled freely moved and the dead arose, wherever the eyes of the King of the World rested. He also appeared five hundred and forty years ago in Erdeni Dzu, he was in the ancient Sakkai Monastery and in the Narabanchi Kure.

"One of our Living Buddhas and one of the Tashi Lamas received a message from him, written with unknown signs on golden tablets. No one could read these signs. The Tashi Lama entered the temple, placed the golden tablet on his head and began to pray. With this the thoughts of the King of the World penetrated his brain and, without having read the enigmatical signs, he understood and accomplished the message of the King."

"How many persons have ever been to Agharti?" I questioned him.

"Very many," answered the Lama, "but all these people have kept secret that which they saw there. When the Olets destroyed Lhasa, one of their detachments in the southwestern mountains penetrated to the outskirts of Agharti. Here they learned some of the lesser mysterious sciences and brought them to the surface of our earth. This is why the Olets and Kalmucks are artful sorcerers and prophets. Also from the eastern country some tribes of black people penetrated to Agharti and lived there many centuries. Afterwards they were thrust out from the kingdom and returned to the earth, bringing with them the mystery of predictions according to cards, grasses and the lines of the palm. They are the Gypsies. . . . Somewhere in the north of Asia a tribe exists which is now dying and which came from the cave of Agharti, skilled in calling back the spirits of the dead as they float through the air."

The Lama was silent and afterwards, as though answering my thoughts, continued.

"In Agharti the learned Panditas write on tablets of stone all the science of our planet and of the other worlds. The Chinese learned Buddhists know this. Their science is the highest and purest. Every century one hundred sages of China collect in a secret place on the shores of the sea, where from its depths come out one hundred eternally-living tortoises. On their shells the Chinese write all the developments of the divine science of the century."

As I write I am involuntarily reminded of a tale of an old Chinese bonze in the Temple of Heaven at Peking.

He told me that tortoises live more than three thousand years without food and air and that this is the reason why all the columns of the blue Temple of Heaven were set on live tortoises to preserve the wood from decay.

"Several times the Pontiffs of Lhasa and Urga have sent envoys to the King of the World," said the Lama librarian, "but they could not find him. Only a certain Tibetan leader after a battle with the Olets found the cave with the inscription: 'This is the gate to Agharti.' From the cave a fine appearing man came forth, presented him with a gold tablet bearing the mysterious signs and said:

" 'The King of the World will appear before all people when the time shall have arrived for him to lead all the good people of the world against all the bad; but this time has not yet come. The most evil among mankind have not yet been born.'

"*Chiang Chün* Baron Ungern sent the young Prince Pounzig to seek out the King of the World but he returned with a letter from the Dalai Lama from Lhasa. When the Baron sent him a second time, he did not come back."

CHAPTER XLIX

THE PROPHECY OF THE KING OF THE
WORLD IN 1890

THE Hutuktu of Narabanchi related the following
to me, when I visited him in his monastery in the
beginning of 1921:

"When the King of the World appeared before the
Lamas, favored of God, in this monastery thirty years
ago he made a prophecy for the coming half century.
It was as follows:

" 'More and more the people will forget their souls
and care about their bodies. The greatest sin and corruption will reign on the earth. People will become as
ferocious animals, thirsting for the blood and death of
their brothers. The 'Crescent' will grow dim and its followers will descend into beggary and ceaseless war. Its
conquerors will be stricken by the sun but will not progress upward and twice they will be visited with the
heaviest misfortune, which will end in insult before the
eye of the other peoples. The crowns of kings, great
and small, will fall . . . one, two, three, four, five, six,
seven, eight. . . . There will be a terrible battle among
all the peoples. The seas will become red . . . the earth
and the bottom of the seas will be strewn with bones . . .
kingdoms will be scattered . . . whole peoples will die
. . . hunger, disease, crimes unknown to the law, never
before seen in the world. The enemies of God and of

the Divine Spirit in man will come. Those who take
the hand of another shall also perish. The forgotten and
pursued shall rise and hold the attention of the whole
world. There will be fogs and storms. Bare mountains
shall suddenly be covered with forests. Earthquakes will
come. . . . Millions will change the fetters of slavery
and humiliation for hunger, disease and death. The
ancient roads will be covered with crowds wandering
from one place to another. The greatest and most beautiful cities shall perish in fire . . . one, two, three. . . .
Father shall rise against son, brother against brother and
mother against daughter. . . . Vice, crime and the destruction of body and soul shall follow. . . . Families
shall be scattered. . . . Truth and love shall disappear.
. . . From ten thousand men one shall remain; he shall be
nude and mad and without force and the knowledge to
build him a house and find his food. . . . He will howl
as the raging wolf, devour dead bodies, bite his own flesh
and challenge God to fight. . . . All the earth will be
emptied. God will turn away from it and over it there
will be only night and death. Then I shall send a people,
now unknown, which shall tear out the weeds of madness and vice with a strong hand and will lead those who
still remain faithful to the spirit of man in the fight
against Evil. They will found a new life on the earth
purified by the death of nations. In the fiftieth year
only three great kingdoms will appear, which will exist
happily seventy-one years. Afterwards there will be
eighteen years of war and destruction. Then the peoples
of Agharti will come up from their subterranean caverns
to the surface of the earth.' "

*   *   *   *   *   *

Afterwards, as I traveled farther through Eastern Mongolia and to Peking, I often thought:

"And what if . . .? What if whole peoples of different colors, faiths and tribes should begin their migration toward the West?"

And now, as I write these final lines, my eyes involuntarily turn to this limitless Heart of Asia over which the trails of my wanderings twine. Through whirling snow and driving clouds of sand of the Gobi they travel back to the face of the Narabanchi Hutuktu as, with quiet voice and a slender hand pointing to the horizon, he opened to me the doors of his innermost thoughts:

"Near Karakorum and on the shores of Ubsa Nor I see the huge, multi-colored camps, the herds of horses and cattle and the blue *yurtas* of the leaders. Above them I see the old banners of Jenghiz Khan, of the Kings of Tibet, Siam, Afghanistan and of Indian Princes; the sacred signs of all the Lamaite Pontiffs; the coats of arms of the Khans of the Olets; and the simple signs of the north Mongolian tribes. I do not hear the noise of the animated crowd. The singers do not sing the mournful songs of mountain, plain and desert. The young riders are not delighting themselves with the races on their fleet steeds. . . . There are innumerable crowds of old men, women and children and beyond in the north and west, as far as the eye can reach, the sky is red as a flame, there is the roar and crackling of fire and the ferocious sound of battle. Who is leading these warriors who there beneath the reddened sky are shedding their own and others' blood? Who is leading these crowds of unarmed old men and women? I see severe order, deep religious understanding of purposes, patience and tenacity . . . a new great migration of peoples, the last march of the Mongols. . . ."

Karma may have opened a new page of history!

And what if the King of the World be with them?

But this greatest Mystery of Mysteries keeps its own deep silence.

GLOSSARY

Agronome.—Russian for trained agriculturalist.

Amour sayn.—Good-bye.

Ataman.—Headman or chief of the Cossacks.

Bandi.—Pupil or student of theological school in the Buddhist faith.

Buriat.—The most civilized Mongol tribe, living in the valley of the Selenga in Transbaikalia.

Chahars.—A warlike Mongolian tribe living along the Great Wall of China in Inner Mongolia.

Chaidje.—A high Lamaite priest, but not an incarnate god.

Cheka.—The Bolshevik Counter-Revolutionary Committee, the most relentless establishment of the Bolsheviki, organized for the persecution of the enemies of the Communistic government in Russia.

Chiang Chün.—Chinese for " General "—Chief of all Chinese troops in Mongolia.

Dalai Lama.—The first and highest Pontiff of the Lamaite or " Yellow Faith," living at Lhasa in Tibet.

Djungar.—A West Mongolian tribe.

Dugun.—Chinese commercial and military post.

Dzuk.—Lie down!

Fang-tzu.—Chinese for " house."

Fatil.—A very rare and precious root much prized in Chinese and Tibetan medicines.

Felcher.—Assistant of a doctor (surgeon).

Gelong.—Lamaite priest having the right to offer sacrifices to God.

Getul.—The third rank in the Lamaite monks.

Goro.—The high priest of the King of the World.

Hatyk.—An oblong piece of blue (or yellow) silk cloth, presented to honored guests, chiefs, Lamas and gods. Also a kind of coin, worth from 25 to 50 cents.

Hong.—A Chinese mercantile establishment.

Hun.—The lowest rank of princes.

Hunghutze.—Chinese brigand.

Hushun.—A fenced enclosure, containing the houses, paddocks, stores, stables, etc., of Russian Cossacks in Mongolia.

Hutuktu.—The highest rank of Lamaite monks; the form of any incarnated god; holy.

Imouran.—A small rodent like a gopher.

Izubr.—The American elk.

Kabarga.—The musk antelope.

Kalmuck.—A Mongolian tribe, which migrated from Mongolia under Jenghiz Khan (where they were known as the Olets or Eleuths), and now live in the Urals and on the shores of the Volga in Russia.

Kanpo.—The abbot of a Lamaite monastery, a monk; also the first rank of " white " clergy (not monks).

Kanpo-Gelong.—The highest rank of Gelongs (q.v.); an honorary title.

Karma.—The Buddhist materialization of the idea of Fate, a parallel with the Greek and Roman Nemesis (Justice).

Khan.—A king.

Khayrus.—A kind of trout.

Khirghiz.—The great Mongol nation living between the river Irtish in western Siberia, Lake Balhash and the Volga in Russia.

Kuropatka.—A partridge.

Lama.—The common name for a Lamaite priest.

Lan.—A weight of silver or gold equivalent to about one-eleventh of a Russian pound, or 9/110ths of a pound avoirdupois.

Lanhon.—A round bottle of clay.

Maramba.—A doctor of theology.

Merin.—The civil chief of police in every district of the Soyot country in Urianhai.

" Om! Mani padme Hung! ".—" Om " has two meanings. It is the name of the first *Goro* and also means: " Hail! " In this connection: " Hail! Great Lama in the Lotus Flower! "

Mendé.—Soyot greeting—" Good Day."

Nagan-hushun.—A Chinese vegetable garden or enclosure in Mongolia.

Naida.—A form of fire used by Siberian woodsmen.

Noyon.—A Prince or Khan. In polite address: " Chief," " Excellency."

Obo.—The sacred and propitiatory signs in all the dangerous places in Urianhai and Mongolia.

Olets.—Vid: Kalmuck.

Om.—The name of the first *Goro* (q.v.) and also of the mysterious, magic science of the Subterranean State. It means, also: " Hail! "

Orochons.—A Mongolian tribe, living near the shores of the Amur River in Siberia.

Oulatchen.—The guard for the post horses; official guide.

Ourton.—A post station, where the travelers change horses and *oulatchens.*

Pandita.—The high rank of Buddhist monks.

Panti.—Deer horns in the velvet, highly prized as a Tibetan and Chinese medicine.

Pogrom.—A wholesale slaughter of unarmed people; a massacre.

Paspa.—The founder of the Yellow Sect, predominating now in the Lamaite faith.

Sait.—A Mongolian governor.

Salga.—A sand partridge.

Sayn.—" Good day! " " Good morning! " " Good evening! " All right; good.

Taiga.—A Siberian word for forest.

Taimen.—A species of big trout, reaching 120 pounds.

Ta Lama.—Literally: " the great priest," but it means now " a doctor of medicine."

Tashur.—A strong bamboo stick.

Turpan.—The red wild goose or Lama-goose.

Tzagan.—White.

Tzara.—A document, giving the right to receive horses and *oulatchens* at the post stations.

Tsirik.—Mongolian soldiers mobilized by levy.

Tzuren.—A doctor-poisoner.

Ulan.—Red.

Urga.—The name of the capital of Mongolia; (2) a kind of Mongolian lasso.

Vatannen.—The language of the Subterranean State of the King of the World.

Wapiti.—The American elk.

Yurta.—The common Mongolian tent or house, made of felt.

Zahachine.—A West Mongolian wandering tribe.

Zaberega.—The ice-mountains formed along the shores of a river in spring.

Zikkurat.—A high tower of Babylonish style.

INDEX

321

Featured Titles from Westphalia Press

Issues in Maritime Cyber Security Edited by Nicole K. Drumhiller, Fred S. Roberts, Joseph DiRenzo III and Fred S. Roberts

While there is literature about the maritime transportation system, and about cyber security, to date there is very little literature on this converging area. This pioneering book is beneficial to a variety of audiences looking at risk analysis, national security, cyber threats, or maritime policy.

The Rise of the Book Plate: An Exemplative of the Art by W. G. Bowdoin, Introduction by Henry Blackwel

Bookplates were made to denote ownership and hopefully steer the volume back to the rightful shelf if borrowed. They often contained highly stylized writing, drawings, coat of arms, badges or other images of interest to the owner.

The Great Indian Religions by G. T. Bettany

G. T. (George Thomas) Bettany (1850-1891) was born and educated in England, attending Gonville and Caius College in Cambridge University, studying medicine and the natural sciences. This book is his account of Brahmanism, Hinduism, Buddhism, and Zoroastrianism

Unworkable Conservatism: Small Government, Freemarkets, and Impracticality by Max J. Skidmore

Unworkable Conservatism looks at what passes these days for "conservative" principles—small government, low taxes, minimal regulation—and demonstrates that they are not feasible under modern conditions.

A Place in the Lodge: Dr. Rob Morris, Freemasonry and the Order of the Eastern Star by Nancy Stearns Theiss PhD

Ridiculed as "petticoat masonry," critics of the Order of the Eastern Star did not deter Rob Morris' goal to establish a Masonic organization that included women as members. As Rob Morris (1818-1888) came "into the light," he donned his Masonic apron and carried the ideals of Freemasonry through a despairing time of American history.

Demand the Impossible: Essays in History as Activism
Edited by Nathan Wuertenberg and William Horne

Demand the Impossible asks scholars what they can do to help solve present-day crises. The twelve essays in this volume draw inspiration from present-day activists. They examine the role of history in shaping ongoing debates over monuments, racism, clean energy, health care, poverty, and the Democratic Party.

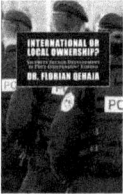

International or Local Ownership?: Security Sector Development in Post-Independent Kosovo
by Dr. Florian Qehaja

International or Local Ownership? contributes to the debate on the concept of local ownership in post-conflict settings, and discussions on international relations, peacebuilding, security and development studies.

The Bahai Movement: A Series of Nineteen Papers
by Charles Mason Remey

Charles Mason Remey (1874-1974) was the son of Admiral George Collier Remey and grew up in Washington DC. He studied to be an architect at Cornell (1893-1896) and the Ecole des Beaux Arts in Paris (1896-1903), where he learned about the Baha'i faith, and quickly adopted it.

Ongoing Issues in Georgian Policy and Public Administration
Edited by Bonnie Stabile and Nino Ghonghadze

Thriving democracy and representative government depend upon a well functioning civil service, rich civic life and economic success. Georgia has been considered a top performer among countries in South Eastern Europe seeking to establish themselves in the post-Soviet era.

Poverty in America: Urban and Rural Inequality and Deprivation in the 21st Century
Edited by Max J. Skidmore

Poverty in America too often goes unnoticed, and disregarded. This perhaps results from America's general level of prosperity along with a fairly widespread notion that conditions inevitably are better in the USA than elsewhere. Political rhetoric frequently enforces such an erroneous notion.

westphaliapress.org